Naftali Brawer was born in Boston and grew up in Montreal. He has served as a rabbi in the United States and is now the senior rabbi of the Borehamwood and Elstree Synagogue in North London. He has a PhD from University College London and writes a regular column in the *Jewish Chronicle*. Rabbi Brawer is an occasional broadcaster on the BBC and is also responsible for a variety of interfaith activities on behalf of the Chief Rabbinate of Great Britain. He and his Italian-born wife Dina have four sons.

Titles available in the Brief History series

A BRIEF GUIDE TO

JUDAISM

Theology, History and Practice

NAFTALI BRAWER

ROBINSON

RUNNING PRESS
PHILADELPHIA · LONDON

ROBINSON

First published in Great Britain in 2008 by Robinson

3 5 7 9 10 8 6 4 2

Copyright © Rabbi Dr Naftali Brawer, 2008

The moral right of the author has been asserted.

A CIP catalogue record for this book
is available from the British Library.

ISBN 978-1-84529-601-8

Robinson
An imprint of
Little, Brown Book Group
Carmelite House
50 Victoria Embankment
London EC4Y 0DZ

An Hachette UK Company

www.hachette.co.uk
www.littlebrown.co.uk

First Published in the United States in 2008 by Running Press Book Publishers
A member of the Perseus Books Group

Books published by Running Press are available at special discounts for bulk purchases
in the United States by corporations, institutions and other organizations. For more
information, please contact the Special Markets Department at the Perseus Books Group,
2300 Chestnut Street, Suite 200, Philadelphia, PA 19103, or call
(800) 810-4145, ext. 5000, or email special.markets@perseusbooks.com.

US Library of Congress number: 2007936641
US ISBN 978-0-7624-3389-6

10 9 8 7 6 5 4 3 2 1

Digit on the right indicates the number of this printing

Running Press Book Publishers
2300 Chestnut Street
Philadelphia, PA 19103-4371

Visit us on the web!
www.runningpress.com

Printed and bound in Great Britain by Clays Ltd, St Ives plc

Papers used by Robinson are from well-managed forests and other responsible sources

MIX
Paper from
responsible sources
FSC® C104740

To Dina

שלי ושלכם שלה הוא

All that is mine and yours is hers

(Talmud, Nedarim 50a)

CONTENTS

LIST OF ILLUSTRATIONS

A relief from the Arch of Titus, Rome. © *TopFoto* (1064479).

The Tomb of the Patriarchs, Hebron, Israel. © *Jon Arnold / JAI / Corbis* (42-18718942).

A Mikveh, or ritual bath, in the ruins of Masada, 2001. © *Hanan Isachar / Corbis* (HY002266).

Chief Army Chaplin Brigadier Rabbi Shlomo Goren after the Israeli Army capture of the Old City. Wailing Wall, Jerusalem. 7 June 1967. © *Topfoto* (1072687).

Jewish men in traditional dress. Wailing Wall, Jerusalem. © *Mary Evans Picture Library* (10102633).

A Jewish girl after lighting her first Shabbat candle. Yale University, New Haven, Connecticut. August 2008. © *Peter Hvizdak / the Image Works / Topfoto* (imw0153359).

A Jewish household celebrates the Passover. Oil on Canvas. © *Mary Evans Picture Library* (10030544).

The blowing of the Shofar. Woodcut. © *Topfoto* (0829223).

The Old New Synagogue. Prague, Czechoslovakia, 1933. © *Bettman / Corbis* (U221533ACME).

Sanctuary of the Shul Temple of Bal Harbor, Florida. April 1997. © *Dan Forer / Beateworks / Corbis* (42-18901806).

A Yeshivah, or Talmudic academy. Jerusalem, Israel. 12 August 1987. © *Alain Keler / Sygma / Corbis* (0000229688-050).

A young man celebrates his Bar Mitzvah, 2008. © *B Greenberg*.

A Jewish boy wrapping a Tefillin around his arm. Hebron, West Bank. 1995. © *David Turnley / Corbis* (TL030062).

The scrolls of the Torah, Torah cover and the Ten Commandments. Oil Painting, 1797. © *Musée de Cluny / HIP / TopFoto* (hip0006435).

Page from the Mishnah with Maimonides' commentary. Jerusalem, 1492. Printed by Joshua Soncino and Joseph Peso in Naples. © *Topfoto* (0829217).

ACKNOWLEDGEMENTS

First and foremost I want to thank the Almighty for blessing me with good health, a wonderful supportive family, inspiration and lots of patience; all the ingredients necessary to write a book.

In the human realm, my thanks must first go to Louise Greenberg, literary agent par excellence and close personal friend. Louise's belief in my ability and constant encouragement has been a great source of inspiration throughout the writing of this book.

Thanks to my editor, Leo Hollis, for his guidance, insight and critical eye.

Thanks to my parents for their unconditional love, concern and wisdom. I am especially grateful to my father who taught me all I know about Hasidic theology. Many of the metaphors in Part 1 are his ideas. I first heard them as a teenager and they have remained with me ever since.

I want to thank two very dear friends, who wish to remain anonymous, for the generous use of their summer home as my personal writer's retreat: I could never have finished this work without them.

Northwood United Synagogue, the community I have led for eleven years, deserves an honourable mention. Many of the ideas in this book were first tried out on them in the form of lectures, talks and sermons. They are an unusually intellectually engaging community, and through them I have refined my ideas and thoughts over time. I am particularly grateful for the time they afforded me to research and study over the years; this book is a culmination of that study and I hope they agree it was well worth it.

Special thanks go to my four children, Aryeh, Mendel, Asher and Yakir for ensuring that my life is anything but dull. I am particularly grateful to Asher for his assistance in compiling the glossary.

Last but not least, my deepest gratitude goes to my soul mate Dina, whose love is one of the great blessings of my life.

INTRODUCTION

I frequently meet people, Jews and non-Jews alike, who are interested in learning more about Judaism. Inevitably I am asked to refer them to a good book on the subject, and this is where it gets difficult. Judaism is complex and multi-faceted. It consists of a people with its own culture and history as well as a vast body of literature, legal, ethical and mystical. It professes a unique theology as well as prescribing a detailed and structured set of rituals. While there are numerous guides to Jewish practice, introductions to Jewish thought and brief histories of the Jewish people, there is no one book that brings all these strands together for the intelligent novice.

The problem is not only that one must read many books to fill the various gaps, but, more importantly, the reader is left without a clear picture of how these strands fuse together to form a whole, and so is left with a rather fragmented view of Judaism. This book attempts to present a guide to Judaism that encompasses all its major facets and brings them together in a clear narrative.

At the core of the book lies the idea that Judaism is the meeting point between heaven and earth. That is to say, that

Judaism is primarily concerned with bringing godliness into the material world, or, to put it slightly differently, Judaism is concerned with elevating the material world to a higher spiritual plane.

This is reflected in the paradoxical practice of Judaism. On one hand it calls on its adherents to transcend the material world through ritual and prayer. It also curtails physical pleasure by proscribing various foods and regulating a couple's sex life. Yet, on the other hand, Judaism positively celebrates the physical because so much of Jewish ritual and culture is connected to food, family and society. The Sabbath is a perfect example of this paradox. The day of rest is a time to disengage from the mundane world and to turn one's thoughts to a loftier plane. Yet the celebration of the Sabbath involves physical enjoyment as well, such as large meals with family and friends, sleeping later than usual and, for married couples, sexual intimacy.

Part 1 of this book contains six chapters dealing with key elements in Jewish theology. These elements are God, Torah, Mitzvot, man, the Jewish people, and the Land of Israel. While Judaism is an ancient, vast and complex faith, its most important ideas centre on these six themes. An appreciation of these themes and the role they play in the idea of bridging heaven and earth is crucial to understanding the history and practice of Judaism.

Part 2 focuses on Jewish history. It breaks 5,000 years of Jewish history into small manageable episodes, highlighting important events and the development of ideas. The primary concern here is with the intellectual history of the Jewish people, although the reader will also find sociological developments in this section. The result is more than just another sketch of Jewish history – there are many books that do just that. The aim here is rather to pick up on the theology in Part 1 and to demonstrate its influence on the development of Judaism and its expression in Jewish history.

Part 3 is a guide to Jewish practice and is itself broken down into three chapters. The first deals with day-to-day Jewish life; the second with the Jewish year cycle; and the third, the Jewish lifecycle. This section, describing the various rituals, festivals and ceremonies, follows on logically from Parts 1 and 2 and emphasizes how the theology, with which by now the reader is familiar, is put into practice.

The pages that follow set out my own view of the development of my people and my faith: it is a profoundly personal narrative. I am guided by my experience, education and upbringing. I am an Orthodox Jew and rabbi from a Hasidic background, and it is through this prism that I view Judaism.

Yet there is another part of me that writes as an outsider. Over the years I have been involved in various forms of interfaith work. In the course of this work I have been privileged to meet many outstanding world faith leaders. This has afforded me the rare opportunity to see my religion from the perspective of others who do not share my faith.

This book is my attempt to tell one of the world's oldest and most complex of narratives – the story of Judaism and the Jewish people.

PART I

Theology

Chapter 1

GOD

Such knowledge is too wonderful for me; it is high, I cannot
attain it.
Where shall I go from Your spirit? Where shall I flee from Your
presence?
If I ascend up to heaven, You are there! If I make my bed in
Sheol, behold, You are there!
If I take the wings of the morning, and dwell in the uttermost
parts of the sea,
Even there shall Your hand lead me, and Your right hand shall
hold me.   (Psalm 139)

If I understood Him I would be Him.

  (Judah ha-Levi; Spanish rabbi, philosopher and poet, twelfth century)

It is the ninth century BCE and you are a Jew living in the
ancient city of Jerusalem. Your home is situated on a rocky
ridge leading down to the Kidron valley and overlooking the
pool of Siloam, just south of Mount Moriah. You rise early and

gaze at the summit of the mount. There, silhouetted against an azure sky and bathed in sunlight, is the Jewish Temple, known as the Bet ha-Mikdash, built by King Solomon as God's temporal dwelling place. Although you do not attend the Temple on a daily basis you have visited on many occasions, most notably on Yom Kippur, the Day of Atonement and holiest day of the Jewish year. In your mind's eye you retrace your last visit to this special place. You follow the ridge along the valley bearing slightly east as you ascend Mount Moriah. You enter through the eastern gate into a wide open pavilion known as the Women's Court, the point beyond which only men are permitted to advance. At the far western side are fifteen wide steps leading to a set of imposing gates that open into a much narrower pavilion known as the Men's Court. This is as far as you, an Israelite, may go. Only descendants from the priestly caste, known as Kohanim, may proceed further into the Court of the Priests.

Right in the centre of this large court stands an enormous copper altar upon which animal sacrifices are offered up to God. On the other side of the altar stands an imposing edifice known as the *Heichal*, which dominates the entire Temple complex. Inside this structure is a room with a number of ritual articles. Directly across from the entrance stands a small altar made of pure gold. Unlike the copper altar outside, this one is used exclusively for the burning of incense. A little further up along the south wall stands a seven-branched golden candelabrum known as the *menorah*, symbolizing God's spiritual light. Directly across from the menorah on the northern wall stands a golden table displaying twelve fresh, warm loaves of bread, representing God's blessing of abundance. Straight ahead, spanning the entire width of the wall from north to south, hangs a curtain of elaborate embroidery. It separates the Heichal from the innermost sanctum known as the Holy of Holies.

Beyond this point no one may enter, with the exception of the High Priest once a year, on Yom Kippur. Inside this small chamber stands the Holy Ark of the Covenant, a wooden chest covered in pure gold containing the most sacred object in Judaism – the Torah. On top of the Ark, representing God's eternal presence, are two golden winged figurines known as the cherubim.

And here is the strange part. The dimensions of the Holy of Holies were 20 by 20 cubits. The dimensions of the Ark were 1½ by 2½ cubits. It would stand to reason that if one were to measure from each end of the Ark to the nearest wall it would measure 9¼ in one direction and 8¾ in the other direction. Yet, remarkably, this was not the case. The measurements from each end of the Ark to their nearest respective walls were exactly 10 cubits and yet the chamber was not 21½ by 22½ but exactly 20 by 20.

What makes this so difficult to comprehend is not its miraculous nature. It would have been miraculous had the Ark taken up no space at all. It could then be said that the Ark representing God's presence is transient. What makes this so enigmatic is that the Ark, representing God's presence, takes up space and no space at all, at the same time.

What does this mean? And what does it say about God?

In order to understand the Jewish idea of God we must work in stages. The following themes are the necessary building blocks in constructing the complex Jewish idea of God: monotheism, God as Creator, God as perfect, God as transcendent, the problem of transcendence, God and godliness, God's continual sustenance, faith, and God and man.

Monotheism

Monotheism is the bedrock upon which Judaism was founded. The first Jewish patriarch, Abraham (see pp. 89–90) rejected the polytheism so prevalent in the society in which he was brought up. Jewish tradition recounts how, as a child, Abraham began to question the credulity of polytheism by observing nature. It occurred to him that all aspects of nature had innate limitations. The sun set in the evening and the moon started fading in the morning. This led him to rationalize that neither the sun, moon nor stars (deities worshipped by the polytheists of his time) could be said to have supreme power. It also occurred to him that there was a unity and harmony in nature that could only be explained by a single force or power that stood outside nature and brought everything into existence. Abraham identified this power as the one and true God, and as he grew older he began to share his discovery with his family and an ever increasing circle of disciples. In so doing, he laid the foundations for the oldest monotheistic faith: Judaism.

The centrality to Judaism of belief in one God was later underscored in the first two of the Ten Commandments that were given to Moses on Mount Sinai (see p. 22): 'I am the Lord your God . . . Have no other gods before Me.'

Monotheism is not just about the belief in the singularity of God. It also insists that God is free of any human characteristic or limitation. While this may seem fairly obvious to us, it was not at all obvious to the ancient polytheists.

The polytheists not only attributed divine powers to more than one god, but they also attributed to the gods human notions and characteristics. It makes no difference whether they were Greek, Roman or Norse gods; they all seemed to have human characteristics. These gods got angry, jealous, disappointed, excited, happy and content, just as human beings. The only difference between the gods and human beings was that in the gods these human characteristics were greatly magnified. The idea that the gods could be anything other than magnified human beings was simply not contemplated. Monotheism, on the other hand, rejected these crude anthropomorphisms and introduced an entirely new concept, that of a transcendent God who is entirely above human conception and characterization. The idea of transcendence is rather more complicated than it first appears and it is something we will revisit a little further on.

God as Creator

As stated earlier, the first two of the Ten Commandments instruct Jews to believe in God. Some rabbinic commentators explained that this means to believe that God is the creator of heaven and earth. This seems a reasonable proposition, so reasonable in fact, that the sixteenth-century rabbinic scholar Don Isaac Abrabanel argued that it is not an article of faith but rather of empirical reasoning. The existence of the Creator can be logically deduced by observing nature.

God as perfect

It is because of this that Don Isaac Abrabanel suggested a deeper understanding of the commandment to believe in God: that is, to believe that God, whom we already *know* to exist, is perfect. What Abrabanel meant by this is that, unlike the rest of creation, which owes its existence to God, God owes his existence to nothing. In other words, everything in life exists *because* of something else, and if you go far enough up the chain of causality you find God as the first cause. God on the other hand, does not exist *because* of anything. He just is. He always has been and always will be.

However, there is an inherent weakness in Abrabanel's idea. Using his own logic it could be argued that the notion of God as a supreme being, who does not owe his existence to anything outside himself, is equally not a matter of faith but of pure reason. After all, if one can logically deduce that there is a god, what kind of god would He be if he owed His existence to anything but Himself?

God as transcendent

This led the Tzemach Tzedek, an early nineteenth-century Hasidic master, to propose an even deeper formulation. Jews, he argued, are commanded to believe that God is essentially so far above and beyond our limited capacities that he is incomprehensible. This leads us back to the idea of transcendence.

The idea of God as an incomprehensible deity has been a

mainstay within Judaism from the time of the Bible. The prophet Isaiah drives this point home when he says of God 'My thoughts are not your thoughts and My ways are not your ways.' The entire book of Job is a lesson on the futility of trying to comprehend God and his ways. Even Moses, the greatest prophet of all, sought to understand God's essence and was rebuffed when he was told by the Almighty, 'Behold you shall see My back but not My face.' The twelfth-century Spanish rabbi and poet Judah ha-Levi put it succinctly when he wrote, 'If I understood Him I would be Him.'

The problem of transcendence

There is an equally strong tradition in Judaism of God's nearness. The Psalmist says 'God is close to all those who call out to Him.' Furthermore, His hand can clearly be seen in Jewish history. In the book of Exodus He is a God who descended, as it were, to Egypt to redeem His people from bondage. He sustained them in the wilderness and brought them to the Promised Land. He is also, according to Jewish teaching, a God of justice who punishes the wicked and rewards the righteous. These are not the acts of a transcendent God far removed from mankind and creation, but rather of one intimately involved in the world He has created.

How does one reconcile this apparent contradiction?

There is another problem with transcendence: that it is by definition limited. It is limited in the sense that it *cannot* be limited.

Take a five-year-old student at his first day of school who learns that one plus one equals two. At the other end of the city, ensconced in his book-lined study, sits the world's leading theoretical mathematician absorbed in deep thought as he works on a mathematical problem that has been troubling him for years. Can there be any logical comparison between these two people in relation to mathematics? The answer would be an obvious 'no'. What's more, there is no way that the five-year-old can even begin to comprehend what the professor is thinking about. For all intents and purposes the professor inhabits an entirely different intellectual world from that in which the five-year-old finds himself. In this respect, one could say that the five-year-old is, intellectually, severely limited whereas the professor is, in relation to the child, intellectually unlimited.

But is this really the case? Suppose the child's teacher were to invite the professor to visit their class for the purpose of sharing with the children his thoughts on his mathematical problem. While he could no doubt stand in front of the class and *talk* about his problem he could not possibly *communicate* to them his problem and thought processes.

Despite his apparent genius, and to a large extent because of it, the professor is unable to put himself in the mindset of a five-year-old whose only mathematical training is one plus one equals two. While there is no doubting the intellectual superiority of the teacher, can it still be said that he is, in comparison to the five-year-old, intellectually unlimited? His limitations are obvious; he cannot communicate his ideas.

In a sense both the five-year-old and the teacher share something; they are both intellectually limited. The child is limited in the sense that he cannot break out of his five-year-old mind and enter the intellectual world of the professor. And the professor is limited in the sense that he cannot break out of his sophisticated professor mind and enter the simple mind of a five-year-old child. The child's mind is simply limited. The professor's mind is limited in the sense that he cannot limit his thoughts to those of a child.

Relating this back to God illustrates the problem of a transcendent Creator. If God is not of this world at all, is He any less limited than the professor who cannot communicate with children?

God and godliness

The solution to this problem according to the mystical tradition of kabbala (see pp. 134–6) is to see two dimensions in godliness. One dimension is far removed from all aspects of creation called *sovev kol almīn*, which translates as 'that which encompasses all worlds'. The image of something encompassing yet not penetrating or infiltrating does justice to the transcendent aspect of the Creator. There is another dimension called *memale kol almin*, which translates as 'that which fills or occupies all worlds'. This describes the aspect of godliness that is intimately involved in all aspects of creation.

The kabbalists are not saying that there are two Gods, one above and the other below. They are not even talking about God but rather *godliness*. The distinction is crucial. There is only one God: *memale* and *sovev* refer to *expressions* of God. One form of expression, *sovev*, is not limited or defined in terms of creation. The other form of expression, *memale*, is not limited in terms of transcendence. Going back to our example of the maths professor, it would be as if the professor could effortlessly flit back and forth between his hyper intellectual world and the simple mind of a five-year-old.

What emerges from this idea is that the Creator is both near and far; He both occupies and transcends creation and He does so at the same time. The eighteenth-century Hasidic master Rabbi Menachem Mendel of Kotsk put it succinctly: 'He who does not see God everywhere, sees Him nowhere.'

It was this subtle idea that was graphically illustrated in the dimensions of the Ark and the Holy of Holies at the beginning of this chapter.

The greatness of God is not His ability to create a brilliant sunset or a magnificent mountain range. For Jews, God's true greatness lies in his transcendent ability to leave his supernal realm in order to create and occupy our world, investing Himself in the creation of what from His perspective can only be an infinitesimal mountain so that we might take pleasure in our physical surroundings.

God's continual sustenance

What emerges from all this is that the God who sustains nature is the same God who inhabits the supernal realms. There is no hierarchy of deities, each with a specific sphere of influence, but rather one Creator to whom all creations, both physical and spiritual, owe their continued existence. I say *continued* existence because unlike a carpenter who builds a table and walks away from it, God constantly sustains His creation. The carpenter can walk away from his finished product safe in the knowledge that unless someone deliberately destroys his work, it will be there tomorrow. This is because the carpenter is not really the *creator* of the table. He merely assembled what were already the pre-existing materials that constitute the table and these materials exist independently of the carpenter's efforts. With God however, it is different, as he creates *ex nihilo*, from absolute nothingness. Were He to cease sustaining creation for even a moment all would revert back to nothingness. This is a difficult concept to grasp because it is almost impossible to find anything comparable in our experience, since by our very limited nature we are capable of creating something only out of something else. However, it may be possible to illustrate this with an example from our world of thought.

Imagine you are in your office having a daydream. In your daydream, you are a military general leading men into battle. The scene is vivid; planes roar overhead, shells explode all around and your men inch forward trying to take the high ground. Suddenly the phone rings; it's your secretary telling you that your next appointment is due. You are pulled back into the real world. For the next hour you are immersed in your client's concerns. You may or may not resume the day-dream once the client has left – that is not the point. The point is, what happened to that raging battle during the hour you spent with your client? Did your men press on without you? Were they successful? Were they repelled by the enemy? The answer obviously is that nothing happened. The entire world you created in your mind simply ceased to exist the moment the phone rang. This is because it had no independent existence outside your mind; it began and ended in your head.

Similarly, the universe has no independent existence outside God. 'You existed before the world was created; You exist after the world was created' is a phrase Jewish believers recite each day in morning prayers. Since the universe has no independent existence it depends on God's ceaseless sustenance for its endurance. This is reflected in another passage from the morning prayers in which the worshipper thanks God for his kindness of 'daily renewing His act of creation'.

The result of this is that for the believing Jew every aspect of creation bears testimony to the existence and closeness of the Creator. It is for this reason that many of the early Hasidic masters – who will be introduced in the second part of this book – would prefer to pray alone in forests or meadows rather than in crowded synagogues. Being alone with nature enabled them to contemplate and commune with the Creator better.

Some Hasidic masters found they were able to sense godliness in physical matter closer to home. The story is told about Rabbi Shalom DovBer of Lubavitch (1860–1920) who, when asked what his thoughts were during prayers on Yom Kippur, responded by saying that he contemplated the lectern at which he stood.

Faith

Judaism is often unfairly caricatured as a religion that puts practice before belief. It has been argued that so long as a Jew observes the ritual practices it doesn't much matter what he believes. This, of course, is portrayed in contrast to other faiths that place great importance on doctrinal belief. This is a gross distortion of the truth. Judaism places a high premium on ritual practice, yet the essence of practice is to draw the participant close to God. Ritual practice that does not take God into consideration is shallow, even empty.

This is not to say that every practising Jew finds it easy to believe in God. Doubts may arise in the minds of the most

devout Jews. Sometimes doubts are triggered by personal trag-
edies or by witnessing the needless suffering of others. Other
times one may just fall out of faith for no apparent reason. The
committed Jew does not allow such lapses of faith to interfere
with his daily practice of Judaism. He accepts the fact that such
lapses are inevitable and he even anticipates them. Yet he does
not suspend his practice of Judaism until such time as he is able
to regain his faith. To do this would be to admit defeat, a horrifying thought for a committed Jew. Instead he struggles and
wrestles with his doubts in the hope that he will discover a
deeper faith in God than he had previously. A believer in the
Jewish tradition is not characterized by his unquestioning and
constant faith in God, but rather by his unyielding desire to
believe in God even when such belief deserts him.

This idea is illustrated by a very touching Hasidic tale. A
hasid travelled many miles to visit his Rebbe. Upon entering
the Rebbe's study the Hasid broke down crying. 'What is the
matter, my son?' asked the Rebbe.

'Oh Rebbe,' sobbed the hasid, 'I don't know what to do
with myself, I've always been a pious and practising Jew but,
how can I say this? Lately I find myself doubting the existence
of God!'

The Rebbe looked at the miserable man standing before him
and asked, 'but tell me, son, does this lack of faith disturb you?'

'Disturb me!?' shouted the man. 'Of course it disturbs me, I
can't eat, I can't sleep, I can't relax, it's eating me up alive.'

'Well then,' said the Rebbe, 'so long as it disturbs you you've
nothing to worry about. Go home and please God you will
regain you faith. Only this time it will be deeper and stronger
than before.'

Faith is not a constant. It ebbs and flows, and so long as one
remains committed to pursuing it, it grows and develops. The
faith of a forty-year-old is not the same as the faith of a teenager; it is deeper, subtler, more sophisticated.

An eminent rabbi and philosopher recounted how as a
young man he was plagued by doubts about God's existence.

He confessed these doubts to his rabbi in the hope that he would help resolve them. The rabbi looked at his watch; it was time for afternoon prayers. 'Come,' he said to his student, 'let's pray then we'll talk.' The fact that the rabbi saw no inherent conflict in asking a doubter of God's existence to join him in prayer sharply illustrates the asymmetrical relationship between faith and practice.

God and man

No discussion of the Jewish view of God would be complete without reference to the innately Jewish practice of arguing with God. The Jewish tradition of arguing with God goes back to the biblical account of Abraham, who, after being informed of God's decision to wipe out the inhabitants of Sodom and Gomorrah, begins to argue on their behalf. 'Should the One who judges all beings not be just?' he rhetorically asks the Creator. Moses continued this tradition when he was informed by God that He would wipe out the rebellious Israelites as punishment for worshipping a golden calf. 'Why should the Egyptians say He redeemed his people from Egypt only to slaughter them in the desert?'

And as if this were not enough, Moses told God that if He could not find it in His heart to forgive His errant people then Moses did not want his name associated with the Torah. This tradition of argumentation with God continued throughout Jewish history, finding its most forceful proponent in the eighteenth century with Rabbi Levi Yitzchak of Bardichev who, as a rabbinical judge, was not above calling his Creator to account in a court of religious law.

Where does such irreverence come from? And how does one reconcile this irreverence to God with Judaism, the mother of all monotheistic faiths?

The answer has partly to do with the fact that God himself invited Abraham to challenge Him over His decision to destroy Sodom and Gomorrah. Why else would God inform Abraham of His plans? In the case of Moses, God, after informing Moses that He planned to wipe out the Israelites, added 'and now leave me', the implication being that if Moses refused to leave God he might convince Him to alter His decision. The fact that in Abraham's case God actually allowed Abraham to bargain with Him and in Moses' case He altered His decision as a result of Moses' challenge indicates that such challenges were not only permissible but in fact even desirable.

On the other hand, there are clear boundaries that neither man was willing to cross. Abraham pushed God only so far. In the end he was not successful. The cities of Sodom and Gomorrah were destroyed and Abraham accepted God's ultimate judgement. Moses was successful in saving his people from God's wrath, but he was not successful in his plea to be allowed to enter the Promised Land. As with Abraham, Moses, although deeply disappointed, accepted God's judgement without the slightest complaint.

The idea that emerges from these stories is that God is both a fatherly figure who invites his children to share their feelings with Him and yet also sovereign of the universe whose will must unquestioningly be obeyed. The multi-dimensional conception of God finds expression in one of the central high holiday prayers called *avinu malkenu*, which translates as 'our father our king'. Indeed, throughout Jewish prayer the Almighty is at times addressed in the lofty terms of sovereign and at other times in the familiar terms of a parent.

An outsider visiting a synagogue service for the first time will probably be struck by its relaxed atmosphere. This does not mean that Jewish worshippers are irreverent, only that they are relaxed in God's presence. This sense of ease is absorbed by osmosis from a young age when children learn through Jewish ritual that God is present at their dinner tables on Shabbat and festivals and in their bedrooms when they recite their prayers before going to sleep. Theirs is not the image of an angry bearded man in the sky but rather of a faceless benevolent power that is intimately involved in all aspects of their lives.

It is the two diametrically opposed dimensions of *avinu-malkenu*, father–king, that give rise to the creative tension enabling the Jew to argue and question God and yet at the same time to submit to His will. God invites us to raise questions about how He runs the world, but also warns us not to expect easy answers. Judaism is not just about raising questions, it is about learning to live with them.

Chapter 2

TORAH

I prefer Your Torah to thousands of gold and silver pieces
(Psalms 119:72)

I have invested My very Essence in writing (Talmud, Shabbat
105a)

The great second-century rabbinic sage Rabbi Akiva insisted
on teaching Torah in public to his many disciples despite the
fact that it had been outlawed by the Romans. When he was
confronted by a colleague who wondered why the rabbi was
willing to risk his life in this way, Rabbi Akiva responded with
the following parable.

There once was a hungry fox walking along the river bank.
He peered into the clear rushing waters and saw a school of
fish darting about.

'Why you are so agitated?' the fox asked.

'We are trying to avoid the fishermen's nets,' they replied.

'Ah,' said the hungry fox. 'Why not come up onto dry land

with me, that way you will be safe from the fishermen's nets.'

'And it is you whom they call the cleverest of animals!' replied the incredulous fish. 'If we remain in the river there is a chance we will get caught, but until then at least we are alive. If however we were to abandon the river for dry land we will certainly die, for the water is the very source of our life.'

'It is the same with me,' said Rabbi Akiva. 'I know that sooner or later the Roman authorities will catch up with me. But in the meantime the Jewish people are in need of Torah. It is their very life. To deny them this, would be to condemn our people to certain spiritual death.'

Anyone vaguely familiar with Judaism knows that at its heart is the Torah – but what exactly is the Torah? On one level one could say that the Torah is the Humash, the five books of Moses beginning with the story of creation in Genesis and ending with the passing of Moses in Deuteronomy. These are, after all, the five books that appear in the Torah scroll.

On another level one could say that the Torah is the entire Hebrew Bible, known as the Tanakh, incorporating twenty-four individual books, not just the Humash but also the Hebrew prophets and scripture. On yet another level one could say that the Torah includes all the interpretations of the Tanakh as understood by rabbis and scholars throughout the ages. This is the most comprehensive definition of the Torah since it incorporates the Talmud, Midrash and Jewish legal works as well as mystical literature. While each of these definitions is accurate in specific contexts, for the purpose of this chapter I adopt the most comprehensive definition, that the Torah includes all biblical and rabbinic literature.

What is Jewish scripture?

The most important part of Jewish scripture is the Humash, the five books of Moses. Jews believe that these five books (Genesis, Exodus, Leviticus, Numbers and Deuteronomy) are the word of God as dictated to Moses. It is these five books that make up the content of the Torah scroll, which is the most sacred object in Judaism. So sacred is the Torah scroll that if it were to fall to the ground the congregation would be obliged to fast as a mark of deep distress. Since the Humash is treated as the very word of God it is subjected to the most detailed and scrutinizing analysis. Sentence structures, seemingly superfluous words and repetitive phrases are all imbued with deep and often multiple hidden meanings.

The next most important parts of Jewish scripture are the books of the prophets, the books of Joshua, Judges, Samuel, Kings, Isaiah, Jeremiah and Ezekiel. Also included are the twelve minor prophets (so called, not because of the quality of their spiritual stature, but because of their minor quantitative output): they are Hosea, Joel, Amos, Obadiah, Jonah, Micah, Nahum, Habakkuk, Zephaniah, Haggai, Zachariah and Malachi.

Following on from the prophetic writings is a third section of scripture. This section includes the books of Psalms, Proverbs, Job, Song of Songs, Ruth, Lamentations, Ecclesiastes, Esther, Daniel, Ezra, Nehemiah and Chronicles. This section is also treated with great reverence. Together these three

Acronyms, known in Hebrew as *Roshei teivot*, meaning 'the heads of words', are common in rabbinic literature. It seems that the use of acronymns originated long before the advent of the printing press, when Jewish scholars would transcribe their ideas on the margins of the manuscripts they studied. In order to make maximum use of the limited space available they resorted to using acronyms instead of writing out full words. The practice also extends to the names of great rabbinic scholars. For example, Maimonides' full Hebrew name was Rabbi Moshe Ben Maimon, yet he is best known amongst the Jewish scholarly community by his acronym RaMBaM. The same is true for Rabbi Shlomo Itzhaki, known simply as Rashi. There are literally thousands of acronyms throughout rabbinic literature. Some of them recur frequently and so they are well known. Others are more difficult to unravel. There are special dictionaries for this purpose. One such dictionary has almost two hundred pages of closely typed acronyms and their meanings.

sections, referred to collectively by the acronym TaNaKH (taken from their Hebrew titles Torah Nevi'im and Ketuvim), form what is known as the written Torah.

The oral Torah

The written Torah is so named because, according to Jewish belief, the Almighty instructed that it be transcribed. Another part of Jewish scripture is called the oral Torah because it was, at least initially, not intended to be transcribed but rather transmitted orally. The oral Torah, which began to be transcribed in the first century, is vast and continues to expand to this day.

The oral Torah is essentially everything that is not TaNaKH, that is, all the traditions that have been passed down throughout the ages that clarify the written Torah and plumb its depth for meaning. A classic example of the demarcation between the two is the mitzvah of laying *tefillin*, small black leather boxes containing passages of scripture strapped to a worshipper's arm and around the head. The Bible instructs every Jewish male to bind the word of God on his arm and between his eyes. That is it. Without an oral Torah we would know very little about what the tefillin ought to look like or how we should bind them. It is also unclear from the Bible how often we should perform this mitzvah. Do we do it by day or by night? It is the oral Torah that fills in these gaps by telling us to insert the passages of the *shema* inside black leather boxes and to wrap them on one's weaker arm seven times each morning.

What is interesting about the oral Torah is that it sometimes appears to contradict the plain meaning of the written Torah. For example, regarding tefillin, the written Torah says to bind them as a sign on your hand and as a marker between your eyes. The oral law explains that 'hand' does not mean 'hand' but 'arm', and in fact the tefillin must be placed on the upper arm across from one's heart. Similarly, 'between the eyes' does not mean literally so but rather on the edge of one's head, just above the hairline, on the spot between the two eyes. To take another example, the written Torah states that 'You shall have no fire in all your dwellings on the Shabbat.' This seems straightforward enough and the reader could be forgiven for believing that what is being proscribed is any form of illumination in the home on Shabbat. The oral Torah, however, explains that what is meant by the verse is that one must not *create* fire on Shabbat but one may certainly *benefit* from fire that has been created beforehand.

Where did the oral Torah come from? The answer is that it came from Sinai, just as did the written Torah. The Bible tells us that Moses spent forty days and nights on Mount Sinai. Forty days and nights is a long time. It is certainly longer than he would have required to absorb the written Torah; rather, it was both the written and oral Torah that God taught Moses during that period.

Both from a theological as well as a legal perspective, the two Torahs are essentially one and have always been so treated by the rabbis. It was their job to disseminate the oral Torah as well as to apply its principles to emerging cases and scenarios. However, until the time the Mishnah was redacted it was forbidden to record in writing any of the oral Torah.

This placed a huge demand on the aspiring scholar, who required not just sharp analytical abilities but also a remarkable memory. Those who proved equal to the task eventually became rabbis in their own right, who then passed the tradition on to their disciples. By the time of the second century CE it was becoming exceedingly difficult for the young scholars to keep up. It was then decided that unless decisive action was taken there was a real chance that the Torah would be forgotten altogether. Thus began the enormous project of formulating, collecting and redacting the Mishnah so that it could be put into written form. This task was completed by Rabbi Yehudah ha-Nasi towards the end of the second century.

Another Talmudic opinion sees the relationship between tradition and innovation as slightly more complex, and illustrates this with the following story.

While Moses is on Mount Sinai studying the Torah with

Tradition and innovation in the oral Torah
One of the challenges facing the rabbis was the extent to which
the scholar could innovate by applying established principles to
new cases and yet remain true to the original tradition. In other
words, if the Talmudic rabbis debate an issue of Jewish law, and
in the course of their argument they discover novel truths or
establish new applications, could this be considered the same
Torah God gave to Moses on Sinai? One view is that it is. This
opinion holds that whatever novel idea any Torah scholar pro-
duces, it had already been taught to Moses on Sinai. In fact it is
precisely because this thought was already in the ether, so to
speak, that the contemporary scholar was able to formulate it.

God his eyes are drawn to the unique lettering of the Torah.
Some of the letters appear to have little crowns on them, and so
he asks God about this. 'Oh that,' says God, 'that is for the
great Jewish scholar Rabbi Akiva who will be born many years
from now. He will derive many laws from these crownlets
through his penetrating analysis.' 'I'd love to meet him.' says
Moses. God sends Moses into the future and he finds himself
sitting in the back row at one of Rabbi Akiva's public discourses. The fact that he is sitting in the back is significant, for
the front rows were reserved for the most able students. Try as
he may, Moses cannot follow the lecture. It is too innovative,
he is not familiar with the material and he cannot follow the
analysis. He suddenly feels faint. 'How is this possible, that I
the recipient of the Torah from God himself cannot follow this
Torah lecture?' he wonders to himself. Then a student in the
front row raises a question. It is a good question, one that challenges the basis of the entire discussion. Rabbi Akiva immediately defends it by saying, 'This, my students is a law that was
given to Moses on Sinai. It is a sacred principle and it must be
accepted.' Moses hears this and immediately feels better.

The point of the story is that Rabbi Akiva's analysis and
methodology are indeed novel, so much so that Moses cannot
follow the discussion. However, ultimately the discussion
must come back to the hard established principles that Moses

was taught by God on Sinai. So long as the creative scholar is rooted firmly in those principles the outcome of his creativity can rightly be called the Torah of Moses.

The Talmud

The Mishnah is characteristically concise, and it was used by scholars of subsequent generations as a departure point into a deeper discussion. Eventually scholars subjected the Mishnah to intense analysis, giving rise to a much broader and deeper body of Jewish law known as the Talmud. There are actually two Talmuds, one Palestinian, the other Babylonian. The first was completed in Palestine in about the fifth century, the second in Babylonia in about the sixth century. Of the two Talmuds it is the Babylonian that is most widely used and commented on. This is also the larger of the two. If one were to study a double folio page of it a day it would take just over seven years to complete. It is the basis upon which all subsequent Jewish law was developed and it is to this day, besides TaNaKH, the most important work in Jewish religious literature. In fact, when one refers to the Talmud without specifying which one, it is taken for granted that the Babylonian one is meant.

One of the characteristics of the Talmud is its argumentative style. This is because Jewish law emerged from vigorous debates amongst scholars. Argumentation is inculcated in the young Talmudist from an early age. One is taught to question everything and to marshal sources in the defence of one's opinion. One of the things that so excited me as a child when I was first introduced to the Talmud was the fact that you could openly challenge the teacher. In fact, my teacher would be disappointed if we just took in whatever he said without raising a challenge.

Although the Talmud is full of debate and all opinions are equally considered, in the final analysis Jewish law is decided through the application of quantifiable principles, one of which is that the law is decided in favour of the majority. A dissenting scholar is fully entitled to retain his own opinion and even teach it to others, provided that it remains purely academic. As far as the practical application of the law, he is bound by the majority opinion of his colleagues.

In illustrating this point the Talmud tells a story of an argument between the second-century Rabbi Elazar and his colleagues over whether or not a particular oven was kosher. Rabbi Elazar claimed it was; yet despite his best efforts to persuade his colleagues to his point of view, they were convinced otherwise. Seeing that his logic failed to move them he tried other methods. 'If the law is in accordance with my opinion,' he declared, 'then may the carob tree outside this study hall spring a distance of four hundred cubits.' Behold, the carob tree sprang the distance, but his colleagues were not convinced. 'If the law is in accordance with my opinion,' he continued, 'then may the water in the aqueduct outside reverse its direction.' The water reversed its direction, but still his colleagues would not agree. 'May the walls of this building collapse if the law is in accordance with me!' he cried. The walls began to cave in; still his colleagues were adamant. Finally, in his desperation, Rabbi Elazar called on heaven to testify that the law is in accordance with his opinion; a voice then boomed out, 'The law follows the view of Rabbi Elazar.' At this Rabbi Joshua jumped to his feet and said, 'This does not impress us at all! The Torah is not in heaven, it is here on earth and Jewish law is decided accordingly!' The Talmud then imagines God, who is observing the proceedings with great interest, breaking out into a smile and saying, 'My children have triumphed over me, My children have triumphed over me.'

There are several messages in this fantastic story. First, it illustrates the rigorous process that decides Jewish law. No one is above the process, and appeals to supernatural phenomena, while impressive, are insubstantial in the context of reaching a legal decision. Secondly, it illustrates how God gave the Torah to man to develop and interpret His will. God desires that we make the Torah our own by investing our energy and intelligence in order to make sense of it. Appealing to heaven over a difficult case is to deny this truth and to admit moral and intellectual failure.

The oral Torah is not exclusively about the development of Jewish law. It also contains a vast amount of homiletic material. This subsection of the oral law, known as Midrash, is comprised of rich and colourful tales, not to be taken literally but as metaphors conveying profound ethical and spiritual wisdom. It takes much training and sensitivity to be able to understand Midrash. To the uninitiated they can appear little more than fairy tales, but that is only because one takes the story at face value while failing to grasp the essential wisdom it can impart.

In addition to the legal and homiletic aspects of the oral Torah there is yet a third subsection, known as kabbala. We will discuss kabbala and its development in greater detail in Part 2. Briefly however, kabbala is the mystical dimension of the Torah. It is concerned with the spiritual and the celestial. Kabbala is not for everyone. Traditionally only the most accomplished biblical and Talmudic scholars were initiated into this realm of study. Kabbala, which means 'received tradition', was taught in private by a master to his disciple, who in turn would faithfully 'receive' this mystical teaching.

The purpose of the Torah

At first glance it would appear that the purpose of the Torah is to serve as a guide for the Jewish faith. It offers instruction on every aspect of a Jew's life, legal, ethical and spiritual. Jews are encouraged to spend every spare moment studying the Torah and mastery of Torah is, and always has been, the highest achievement in Jewish society. But there is a deeper aspect to Torah study that goes beyond the need to know how to live: it is for the purpose of connecting with the Almighty.

Before elaborating on this point, I must explain that not all aspects of the Torah have practical ramifications for daily life. Beginners being taught the Talmud are surprised at how highly theoretical and impractical so much of the Talmud can be. It is true that it is the basis for all Jewish law but that does not mean that one can easily detect the practical law in the Talmud itself. Much of the Talmud is devoted to theoretical analysis, and beginners find this aspect of it difficult to comprehend. What is the point of spending an hour analysing a case that is so theoretical that it is nearly impossible for it actually to happen?

The simple answer is that those asking this question are not familiar with legal analysis. The job of legal thinkers is to test the limits of any given law. It is only by seeing how far a logical argument can lead that one can begin to define legal principles and boundaries. There is an interesting parallel here with Islamic law, much of which is highly theoretical. The point there is the same; it is only through testing each argument to its end that one can formulate legal principles.

With the Torah there is an added dimension: through its study one connects in a profound way with the Creator. Torah study is not just a practical exercise to accumulate useful knowledge, nor is it an intellectual exercise alone. While it certainly combines both of these, its prime purpose is essentially much loftier than either. Torah study is primarily a religious experience. If you were to ask a theoretical Talmudist what purpose he achieves by spending all his waking hours poring over a text without much practical relevance, he will answer you that he is fulfilling the *mitzvah* of Torah study and in so doing he connects with God.

In order to understand this concept let us take a step back for a moment to examine one of Maimonides' principles of faith. Maimonides (1138–1204), who is discussed at greater length in the second part of this book, formulated thirteen principles of faith that in his opinion every believing Jew must affirm. The history and nature of this entire formulation is not relevant to our discussion here. What is relevant is his ninth principle, which states that the Torah is immutable. In Maimonides' own words, the Torah:

Will not be abrogated and that no other law will come from before God. Nothing is to be added to it nor taken away from it, neither in the written or oral law, as it is said *Thou shalt not add to it nor diminish it.*

The reason for the formulation of this principle would have been obvious to Maimonides' contemporaries, although it is less so to us. Maimonides formulated this principle in the twelfth century, when both Christianity and Islam were putting forth the argument that God had annulled his covenant with the Jewish people and that the Torah was supplanted by either Christianity or Islam. Maimonides' ninth principle rejects this claim outright.

As an aside, twenty-first-century Jews can also be confronted with the idea that their faith has been updated. At an interfaith meeting I attended between rabbis and imams, over lunch a Sufi imam leaned over and said to me, 'You know, all our differences are superficial. Essentially we share the same faith. It's kind of like you have Windows 98 and we have Windows 2000.' He seemed so impressed with this idea that I could not point out that comparative religious theology was slightly more complicated than that.

Maimonides supports his ninth principle by citing in his great Jewish legal code several proof texts from the Bible. In his philosophical work, *Guide for the Perplexed*, he reinforces this principle from a rational basis: the Torah, as the word of God, must be, *de facto*, perfect. Something that is perfect, Maimonides concludes, is never susceptible to change. But while all rabbinical scholars agree that the Torah will not be changed by God in practice, not all agree with Maimonides that it is not possible for the Torah to be changed even in theory.

Joseph Albo, a leading fifteenth-century rabbi and philosopher, argued that the Torah can in fact be changed at least in theory provided that two criteria are met. First, that the change is directed by a prophet greater than Moses, and second, that the collective Jewish experience that verifies that prophecy be greater than the one that verified the prophecy of Moses, namely, God descending on Mount Sinai with the Ten Commandments.

Besides the fact that it is highly unlikely that God would choose to outperform his Sinai manifestation, the Torah itself states that Moses would remain the greatest prophet that ever lived. Albo knew this, and that is why from a practical point of view he is in agreement with Maimonides.

But there is an obvious problem with Maimonides' principle. The Torah has manifestly changed over time. Adam and Noah, pious though they may have been, were not commanded by God to circumcise themselves. This commandment first appears in relation to Abraham. Similarly, in Abraham's time there was no prohibition on eating the sciatic nerve of an animal; this is not banned until Jacob's time. How then can Maimonides say that the Torah never changes? A solution to this problem is that Maimonides is referring to the Torah as it was given on Sinai. The various ritual practices of the patriarchs that predate Sinai are not included in his formulation.

Another problem with Maimonides is his insistence on including this idea amongst the other twelve principles of faith. Putting aside the external pressures of Islam and Christianity, what does the immutability of the Torah have to do with faith in God? Why can't a Jew believe that the Torah is susceptible to change and still hold firm in his belief in God?

A simple answer would be that if the Torah could change we might lose confidence in its timeless message. On what basis should one be troubled to observe the kosher dietary laws or the restrictive Sabbath law if there is a possibility they are no longer relevant? Perhaps these laws were meant to apply only to a certain time and place such as the land of ancient Israel in biblical times. What confidence could a practising Jew have that he was not wasting his time by observing the detailed laws of the Torah? This may be reason enough for Maimonides to include the belief in the immutability of the Torah amongst the principles of faith, for without it one's entire religious practice could be undermined.

A deeper answer lies in the difference between Maimonides and Albo. Whereas practically they both agree that the Torah *will not* change, Albo, at least in theory, admits that it *can* change, while Maimonides denies even the *possibility* of change. What Maimonides is hinting at here is a radical idea with far-reaching consequences for our understanding of the theology of Torah. He is implying that even God himself cannot change the Torah.

What does this mean? How can one suggest that God himself, the giver of the Torah, cannot, if he so chooses, change the Torah?

Hasidic thought explains that the reason is that God Himself cannot change and the Torah is an expression of God's essence. The Talmud states that the acronym for the first word of the Ten Commandments, the Hebrew word *Anochi*, meaning 'I', stands for *ana nafshi ketavit yehavit* – I have invested My very essence in writing (the Torah).

This takes us back to the beginning of our discussion regarding the religious significance of Torah study. The Torah does not exist to achieve a functional purpose but rather it exists because God exists.

Take medicine, for example. The science of medicine exists for one purpose, to treat or prevent illness. Since its purpose involves affecting something extraneous to itself, it is susceptible to change. Only a fool would suggest using a nineteenth-century cure to treat illness in the twenty-first century. Medicine adapts and responds to the needs of the hour, that is its sole purpose and function.

Another example is educational philosophy. While publicly humiliating errant pupils might have been considered a cutting-edge disciplinary tactic in the nineteenth century, it is known today to be not only cruel but also counterproductive. To my knowledge, no reputable educationalist is suggesting we bring back caning in schools. This is because educational philosophy exists to serve a practical purpose to educate children effectively. As society and its norms change, so too must educational philosophy. The same is true for most sciences and disciplines, which no one would dream of terming immutable.

The Torah on the other hand is different, since it does not exist to serve a secondary utilitarian purpose. It exists because it is an expression of God and God exists, simply because He exists.

It should be stated, however, that the Torah does serve a utilitarian purpose as well. The Talmudic rabbis were emphatic that the Torah improves society through its values and ethics. One cannot deny this. The point is that the Torah was not designed with this purpose in mind; the improvement of society is merely a beneficial, albeit crucial, by-product of the Torah.

The Torah, then, was not created for the world, but rather it is the world that was created for the Torah so that it might find expression. Take, for example, the law stated in the Talmud that if two people appear before a rabbinical court holding on to a garment, each claming to have found it first, the law is they must divide the garment between them. The conventional wisdom is that this law of the Torah was designed to deal with the eventuality of two people each claiming to have found a cloak. It presupposes that since the world is filled with people and cloaks the two are bound to come together in the situation just described. In order for there to be some sense of order and justice in the world the Torah addresses this problem by laying down this ruling.

However, based on everything we said earlier, precisely the opposite applies. God pre-exists the world and so too does His intrinsic will – the Torah. It was God's will that if two men should argue over a cloak in this particular manner they divide it. This results in the creation of a world in which such a scenario might play itself out in order for the Torah to be expressed. It is the same with every other aspect of the Torah. The reason the Torah perfects and harmonizes society is because society was created with the view of its being ordered according to the ethics and principles of Torah.

Hasidic thought distinguishes two types of desire. One is called *penimiyut ha-ratzon*, meaning 'primary desire'. The other is called *hitzoniyut ha-ratzon*, meaning 'secondary desire'. The distinction between the two is readily discernable in human beings. We have many desires, such as the desires to eat, sleep and earn money. Yet for most of us, none of these desires can be classed as a primary desire. The proof is that if there were a way of living without the need to eat sleep or earn money we would find little pleasure in pursuing these otherwise tedious activities. The only reason we engage in these activities is because they feed our primary desire, which is to stay alive. It is primary because it does not exist to serve any other purpose than itself. We may all search for meaning in life; but our desire to live is primal and deeply ingrained. So whereas secondary desires are susceptible to change, primary desires, being part of our essential self, are permanent.

Applying this notion to God helps us clarify the relationship between the Torah and creation. The Torah is part of God's essence; it is his primary desire. Creation is also a result of the Creator's desire. After all, he desired to create the universe. However, His desire to create the universe is a secondary one. His only interest in it is its ability to reflect Torah values.

A Hasidic reading of Maimonides suggests the reason he may have been so adamant that the immutability of the Torah be counted amongst the principles of faith. By categorically stating that the Torah can never change, he drives home the point that the Torah is bound up with the essence and will of God and that it is the basis upon which the need for creation arises.

Having explained that the Torah is the essence and will of the Creator we are left with a slight difficulty. One would imagine that the Creator's mind would be preoccupied by matters slightly more elevated than the struggle over a cloak, or for that matter any of the other laws in the Torah that address the mundane. Are we really to believe that two men struggling with a cloak is the extent of the essence and will of the Creator? The answer is that two men struggling with a cloak do preoccupy the mind of the Creator but not quite in the way we think.

Take, for example, a couple returning home from a night at the opera. When they get home their four-year-old, who should have been asleep hours ago, comes bounding down the stairs to greet them. 'Where have you been?' she wants to know. 'Well, we were at the opera,' answers Dad. 'What is an opera?' she persists. 'Ah, the opera', he replies, 'is where one hears the sweetest singing in the world.' What Dad has done is unintentionally to use a metaphor to describe the pleasure of listening to singing. The problem is that his daughter, who has clearly never been to an opera, has no way of understanding the metaphor. Her limited frame of reference simply does not extend that far. For her, the term 'sweet' conjures up images of good things to eat. And so as she walks back up to her room she is likely to think that Mum and Dad heard someone sing – boring – but then ate some sweets – exciting.

The next day Mum's uncle comes to dinner. He is an eminent philosopher and has just spent the last two days closeted in his study contemplating a particularly difficult philosophical problem. Earlier that day he had a breakthrough and now, at dinner, he is in exceptionally high spirits. Dad, who is a dentist, cannot understand the pleasure to be had from solving an abstruse philosophical problem after almost forty-eight hours of contemplation. 'What can I say?' asks the eminent philosopher. 'It is the sweetest pleasure I have ever known.' Here it is the philosopher who inadvertently uses a metaphor in the hope that his nephew will understand how he feels. But he is no closer to the mark than Dad was the previous evening when trying to explain his feelings about the opera to his little girl. The problem is the same. Dad's frame of reference simply does not extend that far. He is a cultured and intelligent man, but he is no intellectual. He is unable to equate sweet with the world of ideas and so, like his daughter, he is left baffled thinking that his uncle's pleasure is somehow similar to what he experiences when he listens to opera.

Here we have three people each using the same phrase to describe a sensation: yet, while the phrase is the same, the sensation it describes is so radically different in each of their worlds as to be unrecognizable to the others.

Bearing this in mind, the image of two physical men struggling over a physical cloak is the lowest manifestation of the Torah. It is what we are able to understand. This does not preclude loftier manifestations of the same idea. Accusing God of being preoccupied with a mundane Torah is no different from accusing the philosopher of spending his time in pursuit of a packet of sweets.

There is, however, a problem. We have managed to show how the Creator's Torah is far removed from our comprehension and our world. The question this then raises is if the Torah as we have it bears no resemblance to the Torah of the Creator, what is the point in engaging with it? Are we doomed to spend our lives believing that our infantile conceptions of the Torah are in any way an honest reflection of what the Torah really is? How are we any different from the little girl for whom the term sweetness does not extend beyond the edible?

The answer is that, despite her ignorance, the little girl grasps in her mind the very metaphor that her great-uncle makes use of. The fact that she is unable to comprehend it to the fullest extent does not diminish the fact that she contains in her mind the same metaphor as her uncle.

There are two ways of communicating difficult concepts to those who lack the maturity or intelligence to grasp them. One way is by leaving out complicated material and sticking only to the bare facts. The downside of this method is that as the student develops he must return to the teacher to discover what the teacher had previously left out. Another method is to teach by metaphor. The point of metaphor is that nothing is left out, only concealed. As the student develops he will be able to uncover the wisdom within the metaphor. Furthermore, despite the student's ignorance it could never be said that he does not grasp in his mind, albeit concealed in metaphor, the entirety of his teacher's wisdom.

The Torah is like metaphor. The fact that we will never even come close to penetrating its deepest meaning does not make engagement with it on our level meaningless. The student of the Torah holds in his mind the will of the Creator in its totality. The fact that one is unable to appreciate its full extent does not in any way diminish its awesome significance.

It is for this reason that the Torah is often, throughout scripture, likened to water.

Water falls from above to below, but, unlike light, it is not diminished as it travels the distance. The very same water that was above falls below. The water itself has not changed at all; it arrives in its entirety. The Torah is the same; despite the immense journey it makes from God's will to our physical world it retains its essence. The Torah one studies below is essentially the same Torah as that above.

What happens to the student when he studies the Torah is that he connects with the very will and wisdom of God. This intellectual connection is more profound than any physical connection one can conceive. When one connects with something physically; say another individual through an embrace, the two remain essentially separate entities. They may be holding each other, but they have not entered into the other's being or essence. The intellectual connection achieved through Torah study on the other hand enables the student to enter into its very essence. When one is engrossed in a Torah thought it means precisely that; one is engrossed in the world of the Torah. One's mind completely is encompassed by the Torah. This is perhaps why the Talmud is often referred to in rabbinic literature as the *yam shel Talmud*, the sea of the Talmud. Any student who has plunged into the complexity of a Talmudic argument will agree that the image of swimming in a vast ocean of ideas is an apt one. Yet, in addition to the Torah's encompassing the student's mind, there is a later stage when the student's mind encompasses the Torah. This is achieved when he has thoroughly understood the idea so that it can be said that he grasps the idea. As mentioned earlier, there is no parallel in the physical world to the unity one can achieve with ideas. When those ideas are the will and wisdom of God the student is united with his Creator.

The theoretical Talmudist, who spends his days absorbed in an abstract thought, will tell you that his time is extremely well spent because he is absorbing the essence and will of God. 'But what does it have to do with the real world?' you may ask. 'The question is, what does the real world have to do with the Torah?' he might reply, with a twinkle in his eye.

Chapter 3

MITZVOT

The Holy One, blessed be He, wished to refine His people; He therefore gave them an abundance of Torah and mitzvot (Mishnah, Makkot 3:16)

The scene is graphically described in the Bible: Abraham at the age of ninety-nine has just undergone circumcision, yet despite his pain he is anxiously waiting in the doorway of his tent to offer hospitality to passers-by. The heat is excessive, but God had deliberately unsheathed the sun that day in order that Abraham would not be bothered. Instead of appreciating the solitude, Abraham is distressed. He desperately wants to fulfil the mitzvah of offering hospitality to guests and he eagerly scans the horizon for a cloud of dust that would indicate the arrival of a traveller. God Himself appears to Abraham to offer him comfort, but Abraham's mind is still on the elusive travellers. Finally, God takes pity on Abraham and sends him three angels in the guise of men. No sooner does Abraham spot them on the horizon than he leaps up, makes a hurried apology to God and runs off to greet the strangers. Any sensitive reader will immediately pause at this point in the story, perplexed. How is it that Abraham walked out on God in order to greet mere mortals? If it was the mitzvah of hospitality that he was seeking, how could he abandon the Commander of the mitzvah in the process?

Abraham's act of walking out on God is one of the most audacious acts in all of biblical literature; and it leaves us with a profound message about the meaning of mitzvot. The message is that one draws closest to God by doing His will. Abraham did not abandon God. By showing hospitality to strangers he fulfilled God's will and, in that sense, he drew closer to God than he had been just moments before in His very presence.

Before we go on it is important to clarify what exactly is a mitzvah. The term mitzvah is often associated with a type of act, namely, a good deed. Hence the term often crops up in the following sentences: 'Would you do me a mitzvah and help me carry my groceries to the car?' Or, 'You should really try to befriend that new kid in your class, it's a real mitzvah.' Sometimes the term can be laden with guilt, as in 'Our babysitter just cancelled and we have no one to look after our kids for our mini-break to Paris, could they stay with you? I know it's last minute and all but we are desperate and it would be a really really big mitzvah.' In a similar sense, after doing someone a favour, people might say 'I've done my mitzvah for the day.'

While there is no doubt that all these are accurate examples of mitzvot, helping another in need is only one small part of the totality of mitzvot, which are essentially divine commands. There are a number of ways to categorize mitzvot. One way is to distinguish between positive mitzvot – *mitzvot asei* – and negative mitzvot – *mitzvot lo ta-asei*. Positive mitzvot are those that command action, such as giving charity, fixing a *mezuzah* to one's doorpost and honouring one's parents. Negative mitzvot are those that involve a prohibition, such as not eating pork, not stealing and not telling a lie.

Another way is to divide them between those that involve our relationship with other people – these are called *ben adam le-havero* (man to man), such as our examples above – and mitzvot that involve our relationship with God, called *ben adam le-makom* (man to God). Examples of the latter would be prayer, the observance of Shabbat and kosher dietary laws. Both categories are equally significant and a *shomer mitzvot*, meaning 'one who observes the mitzvot', must be committed to both categories equally. This point is illustrated in God's choice of the Ten Commandments: half of them are God-related and half are people-related.

Another way of breaking down the mitzvot is to divide them into the categories of *eydot*, *mishpatim* and *hukkim*.

Eydot are mitzvot that attest to significant events in Jewish history. The festival of Passover, for example, falls into this category as it commemorates the Jewish people's exodus from Egypt. So, too, does the festival of Sukkot, in which Jews commemorate their ancestors' sojourn through the desert on the way to the Promised Land. Observance of Shabbat also falls into this category as it testifies that God created the world in six days and rested on the seventh.

Mishpatim are the vast body of mitzvot that appeal to human reason. Amongst these are the mitzvot of business ethics, hospitality, charity and social justice.

Finally, hukkim are the mitzvot that defy human understanding. These include the intricate laws of ritual purity and impurity, prohibition against mixing wool and linen and the kosher dietary laws.

Yet another way of categorizing mitzvot is to distinguish between those which are biblical-based (*de-orayta*) and those that are rabbinic in origin (*de-rabbanan*). All the mitzvot mentioned above are explicitly found in the Bible and therefore fall into the *de-orayta* category. Examples of mitzvot in the *de-rabbanan* category are the festivals of Purim and Hanukkah, both of which commemorate events that occurred many years after the biblical period. There are also aspects of *de-rabbanan* which are grafted onto pre-existing *de-orayta* mitzvot. For example, the Bible prohibits construction on Shabbat. The rabbis eventually added the prohibition against swimming on the Shabbat lest this leads one to construct a raft. Therefore, if one were to build a raft they would be in violation of a *de-orayta*; if they only went swimming, they would be in violation of a *de-rabbanan*. This is only one example of many. There is hardly a *de-orayta* mitzvah today that does not have elements of *de-rabbanan* associated with it.

Generally speaking, violation of *de-orayta* carries a more severe penalty than violation of *de-rabbanan*. On the other hand, alert to the fact that *de-rabbanan* is perceived as a less authoritative category, the rabbis sought to reinforce it by regarding its violation as more severe than that of a *de-orayta*.

The concept of *de-rabbanan* is a difficult one, both from a legal and a theological point of view. If the definition of a mitzvah is a divine command, how can the rabbis add to the body of mitzvot years after it had been given by God? The Talmudic rabbis wrestled with this problem and concluded that their authority to create new mitzvot is enshrined in the Torah itself, where God exhorts the people to follow the words of the rabbis.

For the sake of clarity I should point out that no rabbi today has the authority to add any mitzvot. Indeed, even in the past, rabbinical legislation was more concerned with the clarification and categorization of pre-existing mitzvot than adding new ones.

One final categorization of mitzvot is important, the distinction between time-bound mitzvot (*zeman grama*) and mitzvot that are not time-bound (*eyn ha-zeman grama*). This distinction is important in relation to the difference in obligation of mitzvot between men and women. While women may, if they choose, observe most of the mitzvot, their obligations are significantly less then that of men. The general rule is that women are bound by all the negative commandments; that is, they must adhere to all the Torah's prohibitions. Yet when it

comes to positive commandments, they are obliged to observe
only those that do not have a time element connected to their
performance. The reason behind this distinction is that Judaism
considers the woman's primary role to be a mother and educa-
tor to her children. Any mitzvah that interferes with this role is
considered insignificant by comparison. So, for example, the
mitzvot of praying three times a day or of donning tefillin each
morning are not applicable to women. As with any rule, there
are of course numerous exceptions. Women are obliged to
observe the Shabbat, hear the sounding of the *shofar* (ram's
horn) on Rosh Hashanah and listen to the reading of the
megilah on the festival of Purim, despite the fact that all these
are examples of time-bound mitzvot. The reasons for these
exceptions are detailed and not something we need to explore
in a basic introduction to mitzvot.

As to the actual number of mitzvot, the general consensus is
that in total there are 613: 248 positive and 365 negative. Yet
there is some disagreement as to how this number is achieved.
Before you react with amazement at the sheer size of the
mitzvot let me say that the number 613 can be deceptive. Of
this total, less than half are applicable today. This is because
many deal with laws that relate to the Temple service, the
priesthood and ancient Israel.

The number 613 is deceptive in another way as well, as it
relates only to the actual mitzvot but does not take account of
the myriad laws associated with any given mitzvah. A case in
point would be the mitzvah of Shabbat, which constitutes two
of the 613 mitzvot; namely, a positive commandment to
observe the Shabbat and a negative commandment against vio-
lating the Shabbat. Yet there are hundreds, if not thousands, of
laws that determine the nature of this observance or violation.
Similarly, the mitzvah of giving charity bears with it numerous
laws that define the nature of this mitzvah.

Mitzvot and the Jewish life

The result of these numerous mitzvot and laws is that they impact on every aspect of a Jew's life. This gives rise to the well-worn adage that Judaism is not so much a religion as a lifestyle. Part 3 of this book lays out in detail what the average day of an observant Jew looks like. Suffice it to say here that there is really not a waking moment in which some mitzvah does not call for his attention. And it is not just the sheer quantity of mitzvot that makes the practice of Judaism more of a lifestyle than a religion; it is the range of the nature of the mitzvot themselves.

The demands of Judaism on its practitioners extend to the recital of blessings and prayers for every conceivable occasion; before eating, after eating, upon witnessing a rainbow, beholding the ocean, hearing a thunderclap – and the list goes on. Kosher dietary laws greatly impact on a Jew's social life. Mitzvot even extend to the boardroom, as an entire section of Jewish law deals with business ethics. Mitzvot also determine how a Jew dresses; women must dress modestly and men must cover their heads at all times and wear a special four-cornered fringed garment called *tzitzit*.

The interesting thing about all this is that a Jewish child is introduced to Judaism a long time before he or she ever sets foot in a synagogue or religious school. Judaism is learned to a large extent by osmosis as the child absorbs it through the experience of a Jewish home. This is why the Jewish home is the most central of Judaism's institutions and why, as mentioned earlier, women are freed from time-bound mitzvot in order to devote their full attention and resources to bringing up the next generation of Jews. Jewish commitment should not be determined by synagogue attendance, although, admittedly, committed Jews regularly attend synagogue. It should rather be determined by what goes on at home. If one contrasts the quantity of mitzvot capable of being performed in synagogue with those capable of performance at home and at work, the latter will far outnumber the former.

This is one of the common difficulties encountered by prospective converts to Judaism. Anyone who seriously contem-
plates adopting the Jewish faith must be well read enough to
know just what it entails. The problem, encountered often, is
that there is only so much one can glean from books. Judaism
is a living faith, and, while books are its backbone, they cannot
fully portray what Jewish living is all about. To overcome this
handicap prospective converts are often invited to live with a
Jewish family, at least for a while, so as to gain some first-hand
experience about what being Jewish really entails.

The sheer volume of mitzvot also presents a challenge to the
observant Jew. Although to an outsider this might sound
strange, the challenge is not in keeping up with the practice.
For someone born into religious practice it comes easily, almost
as second nature. I often tell people who ask what it feels like
to wear a *kippah* all day on my head, that I don't really know.
Since I was a little boy I have always worn a kippah – it is
normal for me. The feeling of a kippah on my head is the only
feeling I know. The only time I am aware of it is when it falls
off. Similarly, I instinctively remember to pray the afternoon
prayer each day even when I am in an atmosphere that does not
necessarily bring prayer to mind. Likewise, I have never lusted
after pork or shellfish, as I have no idea what they might taste
like. I admit to being curious from time to time, but I don't
think I am in danger of my curiosity getting the better of me.

As for a religious boy's desire for pork, I recall the time
when my friend came rushing into the dining hall at our rabbinical school with a small jar firmly clasped in his hand. 'You'll
never believe what I've got!' he shouted. Everyone crowded
around. 'What do you have?' we demanded. 'I've got a jar of
kosher bacon bits.' We must have looked horrified, so he
explained: 'look, it's not real bacon, it's made out of soya but
it's supposed to taste like real bacon. It's a brand new product
and my brother just sent it to me from New York.' He mag-
nanimously poured a little mound of bacon bits into each of
our outstretched hands. Not without some trepidation we

began to munch on them. I can no longer recall what they tasted like nor do I remember whether or not we were particularly impressed at the time. The thought occurred to me later though, that the manufacturer was a genius. It didn't matter what those wretched soya bits tasted like, we would always think that we experienced the illicit pleasure of tasting bacon since we couldn't compare it to the real thing.

On the whole keeping the mitzvot is relatively easy for those brought up that way. This, you may think, is a good thing, and in certain respects it is. But it can be too easy. This is not to say that Judaism must be difficult, but, rather, that when things come naturally one loses appreciation for them. I was aware of this problem from an early age as my parents were both brought up in non-religious households. They rediscovered their faith in their early twenties, shortly before I was born, and ensured that I, and later my siblings, would be brought up in the type of religious environment that they missed out on. My parents, particularly my father, had difficulty understanding my lackadaisical attitude towards mitzvot. It was not that I violated them, only I was very relaxed about them. My father on the other hand, having discovered mitzvot at a mature age, and having made a conscious decision to live a life of observance, took every mitzvah seriously. They really mattered to him. What he could not understand, nor could I at the time, is why they mattered less to me. Later I learned that this can be the price one pays for absorbing Judaism with one's mother's milk.

That is not to say that one ought simply to accept this as a fait acompli. A religious Jew must strive to infuse his ritual with meaning and not allow it to become routine. This is one of the things the Hasidic movement sought to address, as discussed in the second part of this book. Hasidism railed against what it perceived to be a dry superficial adherence to mitzvot without any real appreciation of its inner dimensions.

The meaning of mitzvot

One of the most interesting rabbinical debates is about the nature of the meaning of mitzvot. This debate is not just about what this might be, but also about whether one can ascribe any meaning to mitzvot at all.

The debate, conducted over centuries, begins in the Talmud where two sages debate the significance of the biblical prohibition against taking the garment of a widow as surety for a loan. Rabbi Yehudah rules that this prohibition applies to any widow, rich or poor whereas Rabbi Shimon rules that the prohibition applies only to taking the garment of a poor widow. The basis of the argument, as the Talmud makes clear, is that Rabbi Yehudah does not ascribe a reason to the prohibition. The Torah states that it is prohibited, and that is sufficient. Since the Torah itself makes no distinction between a rich or poor widow there is no reason we should. Rabbi Shimon on the other hand does ascribe a reason to the prohibition. In his opinion, the reason one cannot take the garment of a widow is based on another prohibition recorded elsewhere in the Torah. This prohibition states that if one takes the garment of a poor debtor, in this case a man, as surety for his loan he must return the garment to the debtor each night so that he may cover himself with it as a blanket, since he has no other garment other than the one he is wearing. Although in the case of the widow there is no indication that she is poor, Rabbi Shimon decides that this must be the case and the prohibition against taking her garment as surety is that, in keeping with the law just cited, he will have to return it to her each night. Imagine what the neighbours would say about this single woman who each night is visited by a strange gentleman.

The difference between Rabbis Yehudah and Shimon is not only in the way they apply the mitzvah but, more fundamentally, in how they understand the nature of the mitzvah itself. For Rabbi Shimon the mitzvot may be rationalized; it is only a question of discovering the true rationale. Rabbi Yehudah, on the other hand, rejects outright the notion of rationalizing mitzvot. In his mind they are to be adhered to exclusively as divine commands and any rationalization is to ignore their lofty source.

This debate continues elsewhere in the Talmud, where it is taken up by another two rabbis of a later generation, Rabbi Yose bar Avin and Rabbi Yose bar Zevida. Their argument centres on an interesting law relating to what is considered suitable language for the one leading prayers. As a brief historical background to this law, in the time of the Talmud there were no prayer books and the liturgy was not yet fixed. Each congregation would appoint a leader to recite prayers aloud on behalf of the entire congregation. The leader would follow a basic skeleton laid down by the rabbis, but it was up to each individual prayer leader to flesh it out in the way he saw fit. In fact, prayer leaders were chosen not so much for their pleasant voices but because they had a way with words. The text upon which our debate centres discusses certain phrases or references that are considered unacceptable for the leader to use in prayer. Should he use such phrases the law decrees he is to be silenced. One of these prohibited phrases is 'God is so merciful that His mercy extends even to the bird's nest.' This is a reference to the biblical command that should you wish to take fledglings or eggs out of a bird's nest you must first drive away the mother bird before taking the fledglings or the eggs. What the fictional prayer leader is clearly trying to do with this reference is extol the merciful qualities of God who is, apparently, so concerned about all of His creatures that he does not want even a mother bird to experience the pain of seeing her fledglings or eggs being taken from her.

What is wrong with a moving reference like that? On this, these rabbis offer their opinions. One says the reason is that by singling out the bird there is an implication that not all creatures are equal, or at least that God's mercy does not extend to all creatures equally. This prayer, then, may evoke the opposite of the reader's intention, leaving his listeners with the uncomfortable feeling that God's mercy is not equally available to all.

The other opinion is that by linking the mitzvah of driving away the mother bird to God's compassion the reader has ascribed a rationale to the mitzvah and this is to undermine the very nature of mitzvot. In the words of the Talmud: 'He is ascribing compassion to the Creator's mitzvot whereas in reality they are simply decrees.'

The debate continued through to the Middle Ages and on to the modern period. Maimonides, the supreme rationalist, admits that there are mitzvot in the *hukkim* category that defy human understanding and can only be approached as one would approach the decrees of a king, that is, with total submission. Yet he suggests that wherever it is possible to apply reasoning to mitzvot one ought to do so, and this he attempts at great length in his *Guide for the Perplexed*. He explicitly rejects the view that all mitzvot transcend rationale, and goes so far as to say that most of the mitzvot are for the purpose of character development. Rashi (Rabbi Solomon ben Isaac, 1040–1105: see pp. 120–1), on the other hand, takes the view that one should not seek to rationalize mitzvot. Mitzvot in his view were placed on the Jewish people as a mark of their submission to the Almighty.

The difference between Maimonides and Rashi is rooted in two very different traditions. Maimonides, born in Cordoba, was deeply influenced by the philosophical enquiry so prevalent in the Iberian Peninsula in the twelfth century. It was only natural for him to try to reconcile mitzvot with human logic. Rashi, on the other hand, was a product of northern France's pietistic tradition. His was not a world of philosophy but of spiritual devotion and submission of the intellect to God.

The rise of Hasidism in the eighteenth century brought an entirely new dimension to this debate. Until this point the debate had centred around whether or not one could ascribe *empirical* value to mitzvot; that is, to what extent we can understand mitzvot as having a practical effect on our lives. Maimonides for example, believed that mitzvot led to character refinement, while Rashi believed that mitzvot have no empirical value and that their value is in submission to God's will. What Hasidism injected into the debate is the question of *mystical* value; to what extent we can understand mitzvot as having an effect not on our physical world or lives but on the spiritual realm.

By introducing the mystical, Hasidism manages, in a sense, to embrace both views. It takes a very hard line about the rationalization of mitzvot. Hasidism teaches that one must perform mitzvot for the sole purpose of fulfilling the Creator's wish. It is generally understood that one ought to fulfil the *hukkim* of the Torah with the same appreciation as one approaches the mishpatim. Hasidism turns this notion on its head and says that a Hasid must perform the rational mishpatim with the same blind devotion he demonstrates when observing the hukkim. Yet, despite its insistence that one does not look for the meaning of mitzvot in this world, Hasidism ascribes significant meaning to mitzvot in a spiritual context.

The mystical meaning of mitzvot exists on numerous levels. On one level, which links us back to our discussion in the previous chapter on Torah, each mitzvah is an opportunity to connect with the Creator in a profound way. The mitzvot of the Torah are the will of the Creator and by observing them one is, in the words of the Tanya, an early Hasidic work, embracing God. In the opening story of this chapter, although it appears that Abraham is walking away from God, he is in fact drawing closer. This is because what he initially experienced was only a *revelation* of God. By observing God's will Abraham connected with God's *essence*. The Hasidic masters point to the Hebrew spelling of the word mitzvah and draw our attention to its similarity to the Hebrew word *tzavta*, which means to bind or connect. This, they say, illustrates the inner purpose of each mitzvah, which is to bond and connect with the infinite Creator.

On another level, mitzvot serve to channel spiritual energy from the spiritual to the physical. This conceptually complex mystical idea, known as *yichudim*, sees the spiritual lifeforce of the universe flowing through various conduits. The alliance and position of these conduits affects the nature and direction of the flow of this energy. The observance of mitzvot serves as what can crudely be described as levers that effect the positioning of the conduits and, in turn, the flow of spiritual energy. Although most Hasidim are familiar with this concept in general terms, a deep understanding of its workings is limited to bona fide kabbalists.

Finally, mitzvot serve as a means to bring godliness into the physical world, which, according to the Midrash, is the entire purpose of creation. God created the world so that He might manifest Himself in it and this is achieved through the observance of His mitzvot. The reason ritual objects are deemed holy is because through performing a mitzvah with them they become imbued with a sense of godliness. It is not just the ritual objects that become imbued with godliness but the entire surroundings of a mitzvah. That is why a synagogue building retains its holiness even when services are not taking place. Even a home in which mitzvot are observed becomes imbued with a sense of sanctity.

One of the most extreme, approaches to the meaning of mitzvot was posited by the late Israeli professor Yeshayahu Leibowitz (1903–94). Leibowitz was of the opinion that not only is it wrong to ascribe any rationale to mitzvot but that the practice of mitzvot does not lead the practitioner any closer to God. In his own words:

> Performance of the mitzvot is man's path to God, an infinite path, the end of which is never attained and is, in effect, unattainable. A man is bound to know that this path never terminates. One follows it without advancing beyond the point of departure.
>
> The aim of proximity to God is unattainable. What then, is the substance and import of the mitzvot? It is man's *striving* to attain the religious goal.

In Leibowitz's view, any attempt to ground the mitzvot in

human needs runs the risk of utilizing them for personal benefit and therefore compromising their expressions of worship of God solely for the sake of worshipping God. Whilst one can understand this stance, it is difficult to see how it leads to any spiritual, not to mention uplifting experience of mitzvot.

Contrast Leibowitz's unattainable path to God with the approach of a Hasid. The Hasid does not delve into the meaning of mitzvot in order to discover their empirical benefits. He observes them because that is what God commands. Yet he is also keenly aware of the significance and sheer power of these acts. He knows, though he does not understand how, that through the observance of mitzvot he brings God into his life and into his world. Nothing for him could be more significant.

Chapter 4

MAN

When I look at your heavens, the work of your fingers, the
moon and the stars, which you have established;
What is man, that you are mindful of him? And the son of man,
that you visit him?
For you have made him a little lower than the angels, and have
crowned him with glory and honour.   (Psalms 8: 4–6)

Growing up in Montreal in the 1970s I encountered many
Holocaust survivors in our community. They were, on the
whole, very stoic figures who were determined to put their
horrifying past behind them and to try to create a new life for
themselves and their families. Unlike today, where there is a
proliferation of Holocaust information, in those days very few
survivors were willing to discuss their ordeals. It was no secret
that they spent time in the death camps; it was obvious from
the tattoos on their arms. But they could not be persuaded to
talk about what exactly happened in those death camps.

One of these survivors was a Hungarian whose entire family
perished at Auschwitz. He was only seventeen years old at the

time and somehow managed to emerge from that living hell. He once told a story about his time in Auschwitz that will remain with me for ever. It was in dark December and he was out in the freezing rain harvesting sugar beets for the Nazis. He described the excruciating experience in vivid detail; the gnawing hunger, the threadbare pyjamas soaked through by the driving rain, body lice swarming about and the near total exhaustion. Despite the fact that they were literally starving – their only nourishment was a bowl of watery soup – they dared not eat any of the sugar beets they harvested. Those who were caught eating a sugar beet were shot on the spot. Day after day this torment ensued until late one afternoon the young man threw caution to the wind. When the guards were not looking he began to slip sugar beets into his pyjamas. Each time the guards looked the other way he slipped in another sugar beet. By the end of the day he had far more sugar beets than he could eat. He somehow managed to slip his arms out of his pyjama sleeves and tie knots at the bottom of each sleeve. He then filled the sleeves with his sugar beets. Miraculously, he slipped back to his barrack undetected by huddling close to the other inmates.

Later that night, when the lights were out, he unloaded his precious cargo and began to make the rounds through the barracks offering beets to his fellow inmates. Amongst those he revived that night was a childhood friend from Hungary who was close to death's door. Years went by and the young man somehow managed to get to Montreal. Despite his desire to forget all that happened in the camps he could not help himself wondering what had happened to his childhood friend to whom he fed sugar beets that night in Auschwitz. Then one day he discovered that his friend did survive the camps. They communicated and set a date for a reunion. The two men finally met and embraced; unable to let go of each other, tears streamed down their cheeks, tears of joy for finding each other mingled with tears of sorrow for all that they lost. It was then that the friend declared that the only reason he was alive at that moment was because of his friend's kindness: 'Had you not come then, I would surely have died of hunger.'

What superhuman qualities this man had! Courage, altruism, kindness, faith. I often wondered whether, if I was in that position, I would even have the courage to steal a beet for myself. I doubt very much that I would risk my life to save others, many of whom would be strangers. Here in my own neighbourhood lived a true hero, someone so full of love and concern for other human beings that he risked his own life to help others. It amazed me that such goodness and kindness could survive in the hell that was Auschwitz. What compounded my amazement is that inches away from this most elevated of human beings, slipping beets into his pyjamas to sustain others, stood the most depraved of human beings who would snuff out his life without a second thought, if only he knew what he was doing.

What is a human being? Can the sugar beet saviour and the Nazi death camp guard both belong to the same species? If one is human, then the other must be an aberration. Which one, then, is the aberration? Is the human an animal or an angel?

Many would say that the Nazi death camp guard is the aberration; that he is so depraved as to no longer be considered human. While this categorization may appeal to us on an emotional level – it is after all very disturbing to believe we have anything in common with such evil – it nonetheless poses problems on a philosophical level.

Free choice
To suggest that the Nazi is somehow not human is to exonerate him from his evil actions. One of the distinguishing features of a human being is his ability to make choices in life. Animals do not have this ability. They may *appear* to make choices, but essentially their actions are determined not by choice but by instinct. In the world of Disney and children's books, soft cuddly sheep are always good and hungry wolfs are always bad. In reality, the sheep is not good and the wolf is not bad.

They are neither, for the terms good and bad can apply only to one who has the ability to reflect before acting and to choose one path or another. Animals lack this capacity, and so the terms good and bad are not applicable. Animals are neither good nor bad; they simply are whatever they are.

Jews believe that man, on the other hand, is the only creature that possesses critical abilities. In this sense the rabbis felt that man resembles his Creator. A phrase in Genesis, regarding Adam and Eve eating from the tree of Knowledge, reads: 'Your eyes shall be opened, and you shall be as gods, knowing good and evil.' This godlike gift bears with it great privileges as well as heavy responsibilities. The privileges are obvious: man has the ability to exert his influence on nature in a way that no other creature can. In acknowledgement of this ability God explicitly instructs Adam and Eve to 'Be fruitful, and multiply, and replenish the earth, and subdue it; and have dominion over the fish of the sea, and over the birds of the air, and over every living thing that moves upon the earth.' On the other hand, man is responsible for his actions. The Talmud goes so far as to state that a man is responsible for every one of his actions whether he is awake or even asleep.

This sense of responsibility is a direct result of man's free choice. If man's actions were determined by anything other than his free unrestricted choice there would be no concept of good or bad since he would be no different from an animal. Consequently, there would be no concept of reward or punishment. Someone who is instinctively good deserves no reward and equally one who is instinctively bad deserves no punishment. That is why Jewish law absolves the mentally handicapped from responsibility for their actions. As they are unable to exercise free critical choice, they cannot be held responsible should they cause harm or damage to someone else.

Maimonides is adamant that every healthy individual possesses the ability of free critical choice. That is not to say that everyone finds it easy to make the right choices. People are

born or nurtured with various tendencies, some of which can
be very difficult to overcome. But difficulty is not the same as
lacking choice. Take, for example, people who are naturally
prone to temper tantrums. It would be foolish to deny that
such people have difficulty controlling their temper, yet, it
would equally be wrong to say that they cannot do so. When
provoked they have total freedom to choose how to respond.
They can take the easy option and lose their temper or they can
struggle to control it.

Here is an example. A Hasid complains to his Rebbe that he
is plagued by negative thoughts, which he just cannot drive out
of his mind. The Rebbe says he cannot help him and instead
refers him to a colleague in a far-away town. The Hasid, eager
to rid his mind of the troubling thoughts, sets out on the long
and arduous journey. It is mid-winter and by the time he
arrives at his destination, late at night, he is desperately cold
and hungry. As he approaches the Rebbe's house he sees a
warm light spilling out of the window onto the fresh snow
below. 'Ah,' the Hasid thinks to himself, 'Thank God he is still
awake. I'd really welcome a nice hot nourishing meal.' He
knocks on the door and waits for the Rebbe to answer; but
there is no response. He tries again, and still no response. He
walks away from the door and peers into the lit window. Sure
enough, there is the Rebbe deeply engrossed in a Talmudic
tome with a steaming glass of tea at his side. The man pounds
on the window but the Rebbe is oblivious to his presence.
After several more futile attempts at getting his attention the
man huddles up on the doorstep with nothing but a thin coat
to shield him against the biting cold and the howling wind. The
next thing he knows it is morning. The sun is shining and there
is the Rebbe standing over him urging him to come inside.
Once inside, he is given warm dry clothes, hot drinks and
plenty of food; the Rebbe could not have been more attentive.
The man, unable to contain his curiosity any longer, says, 'Tell
me Rebbe, is it really possible that you did not hear me banging
on your door and calling to you last night?'

'No, of course not,' says the Rebbe. 'With the racket you were making, the whole town must have heard you. I simply wanted to impart a profound message to you, and that is that a man is the master of his own house. He alone chooses whom to admit and whom to exclude. He is capable of resisting any external pressure that bears on his ability to exert free choice.' This was a painful lesson for the poor Hasid, but probably cured him of his persistent negative thoughts.

Maimonides had no patience for those who claimed their behaviour was simply unavoidable. In Maimonides' day, as today, people often shirked responsibility for their actions, blaming them on matters beyond their control, nurture, nature or even the stars. According to Maimonides, this is not just nonsense but also denies a fundamental truth, that God imbued man with the critical ability to make free choices. However, in asserting that man's ability to choose is totally free, Maimonides runs up against an age-old philosophical problem – the conflict between free choice and God's omniscience. If we believe that God is all knowing and that past, present and future are all open to Him, then by definition He must know in advance what people will do. It may appear to you that you have a choice of whether you are going to walk to work or take the bus; yet, whatever you choose has already been predestined, since God knows which choice you are going to make. This may not sound particularly troubling if the only choices we are talking about are how to get to work. But what about choices that have life-altering consequences? Does a murderer really have a choice not to pull the trigger and to walk away from his potential victim, leaving him unharmed? If he pulls the trigger, God already knew he was going to pull it, so what choice did he really have? If, on the other hand, he suddenly experiences a pang of regret or fear and instead of pulling the trigger drops the gun and offers his terrified and bewildered victim a ride home, can he really be credited with this immense turnaround? Not if it was predetermined by God. The problem Maimonides has is that God's omniscience appears to make a mockery of the notion of free choice.

This problem did not originate with Maimonides; many moral philosophers have wrestled with it before and since. One possible solution is that one must distinguish between God *knowing* something is going to happen and God *making* it happen. God's knowledge of an action does not necessarily have to influence that action. The action is a result of man's free choice and before he commits to the act he can choose either way. As God transcends time and space He is aware of what the person's choice will be. Foreknowledge of an act is not the same as influencing it.

There is a flip side to all this: while man has total choice over his behaviour he does not have any choice as to his tendencies. Whether it be through nature or nurture, genetics or social conditioning, we each have plenty of negative tendencies lurking beneath the surface. Some tendencies are little more than irritating, such as arrogance or laziness. Others can be darker and more disturbing, such as cruelty or the desire to dominate. Unfortunately, we have no control over these deep-seated desires or tendencies; they are part of our make-up and we carry them with us throughout life. The challenge of being a decent and moral human being is not to eliminate these tendencies altogether, which in any case is near impossible, but to overcome them through disciplined behaviour and correct choices. Judaism does not consider it sinful to have a greedy nature, but it is sinful to act greedily. Similarly, it is not a sin to feel lust, but it is sinful to act on it in an immoral way. For something to be considered a sin it must, by definition, be expressed in one of three ways: thought, speech or action. Anything that is not expressed in these ways is simply human nature, ugly and unpalatable though it may be. Ultimately we have no control over it, nor are we expected to. We are, however, expected to control our behaviour whether it is our actions, our speech or even our thoughts. What is meant by thoughts is not the instinctive thought that pops into one's mind – this is part of human nature and beyond one's control

– what is meant is to *entertain* the thought. To use a crude but effective example: the Torah prohibits one to lust after one's neighbour's wife. If you are a healthy man and your neighbour's wife is an attractive woman it is only natural that it might occur to you that she is attractive. This initial thought is nothing more than an impulse and as such it cannot be considered sinful. What is sinful is to dwell on the thought. Here a choice has to be made: to engage in an erotic daydream or to push the thought out of one's mind. Judaism believes that one has the power to push the thought away; otherwise it would be unfair for the Torah to consider it sinful.

One of the earliest Hasidic works; the Tanya, written by the Hasidic master Rabbi Shneur Zalman of Liadi (see pp. 153–4) in the late eighteenth century, deals with this very issue. He describes in great detail the inner world of man and his struggles and asserts that it is possible to control all our thoughts, speech and actions. In fact, not only is it possible, he argues, but this is what God expects of man. The hero of his book he calls the *benuni*, a person who has trained himself to such a degree that he never commits a sin. However, deep inside the *benuni* seethes with negative impulses and ugly tendencies. He struggles, nothing comes easily to him, he is not righteous by nature but by choice and by dint of hard work. He behaves compassionately, although deep inside he is cruel. He is charitable, despite the fact that he is naturally selfish; he has time for everyone, despite the fact that instinctively he is impatient. Even after a lifetime of struggle he knows that deep down inside he has changed not one iota; but that is not what matters. It is not what he is inside, but rather how he lived his life that matters. God deals each of us a hand of cards in life. You cannot choose which cards you're given, nor can you be blamed for holding a rotten hand. You are judged by how you play that hand, and that is entirely up to you.

I recall visiting a member of my congregation who had just lost her father. She showed me his photograph and began to tell me about his life, which had been fraught with difficulties.

He lacked parental love, financial stability, role models. His childhood, to put it mildly, was a real mess. What she said most impressed her about her father is how responsible, moral and upright he turned out to be, while he could easily have gravitated to a life of petty crime, and he could have justified this by pointing to his own dismal childhood. Many people do just that, but he did not. He brought up a beautiful family and became a respected businessman, and he contributed to society. Her story illustrates the power of a human being to make positive choices in the face of extreme negative pressure.

The soul

But where does this power come from? For Jews the answer is the soul. The soul is the little bit of godliness that we possess. We read in the first chapter of Genesis how God created the world through speech: 'Let there be light', 'Let there be a firmament in the heavens', and so on. When it comes to the creation of Adam something unique happens: God breaths into him 'and He blew into his nostrils the breath of life'. That breath of life is the soul. The reason it is imparted through breath as opposed to speech is because breath is more intimate than speech. The image of God breathing into the first man is a potent one. It demonstrates that while the rest of creation occurred through a diminished expression of God, the soul of man is an undiminished expression of the Creator Himself.

The purpose of the soul is to refine the body and, by extension, the world around it. But the soul does not have an easy time since it has to contend with another soul, known as the animal soul. The animal soul is so called because it is the part of man that is animalistic. It is from the animal soul that all the negative traits, tendencies and appetites come. This is the background of the personal struggle I described earlier. On the one hand is the divine soul with its agenda to elevate the body spiritually. On the other hand is the animal soul with its own agenda to enjoy life to the utmost. More often than not these two agendas clash, and when they do man must use his intelligence to make the right choices.

Returning

The idea of a divine soul is central to the Jewish understanding of man, not only in the sense just described but also because it means that, at his core, man is pure and good. The body is temporary, as is the animal soul; the godly soul is eternal and, in that sense, the essence of who we really are. This idea plays itself out in relation to sin and repentance. From a Jewish perspective no sin can ever blacken the soul. The soul may be denied expression by a particular sinful host but the soul itself, as an expression of God, remains untainted by sin. This is the basis for the Jewish idea of *teshuva*, which is erroneously translated as repentance when it is actually something else entirely. A Jew does not repent; he does teshuva, which means he returns.

The idea of return can be understood in two ways. One is that man returns to God. Through his sins he becomes distant from his Father in Heaven and through regret and a resolve to change he returns to God. A second understanding of the meaning of teshuva is that the sinner returns to himself; to his pure essence and the core of his being – in other words, to his soul. This is because, at his core, a person is good and pure. There are many unsavoury and animalistic aspects to our personalities but those aspects are superficial in relation to our core soul, which is divine.

The Talmud introduces us to one of its most enigmatic characters, Elisha ben Avuya. Elisha started out as a budding rabbinical scholar who could count amongst his colleagues the famous Rabbi Akiva and amongst his disciples the famous Rabbi Meir.

While the Talmud is not entirely clear about how it happened, and there are various accounts, it is clear that at some point Elisha lost his faith – and lost it in spectacular fashion. It was not enough for him to slink away from organized Jewish life; he had to turn his heresy into a spectacle. He became a

Rabbi Akiva

Akiva ben Joseph was born into a common family and lived the
early part of his life as an illiterate shepherd, until he met and fell
in love with his master's beautiful and intelligent daughter,
Rachel. Rachel detected great potential in Akiva and, braving the
wrath of her father, married him. Disowned by Rachel's father
the couple lived in dire poverty. Despite the financial hardship
Rachel convinced Akiva to go to the great rabbinical academies
to study the Torah. This he did and gradually blossomed into a
great scholar. He stayed away for years and when he returned
home he was accompanied by many of his own students. When
he introduced his wife to his students he said to them 'all that is
mine and yours is hers.' Akiva is one of the most important rabbinical sages of the second century.

Rabbi Meir

Rabbi Meir is the author of many of the anonymous Mishnahs.
While he is one of the most famous rabbinical sages of the second
century he is equally famous for being married to Beruriya, the
daughter of a leading scholar and an outstanding scholar in her
own right. Beruriya features in Talmudic stories as a ferociously
bright, deeply insightful woman who did not suffer fools gladly.

high-profile heretic and caused his former colleagues no end of
heartache as a result. At this point the Talmud stops referring
to him by his real name and begins to call him Acher, which
means 'another one', as if to suggest that he is no longer the
man once known and respected. Acher had a particularly
complex relationship with his former disciple Rabbi Meir, who
despite his master's obvious rejection of the faith still continued to refer to him as his rabbi. It appears that for all Acher's
bravado, or perhaps because of it, he was not content with his
life and secretly harboured hope of finding some form of rec-
onciliation with his abandoned faith; but somehow he could
never bring himself to do so. The Talmud relates how he
appeared to Rabbi Meir on the holy Shabbat whilst riding a
horse, a clear rabbinical violation. Rabbi Meir, who was

respected in his town as a great rabbi, went out to greet his former master. The Talmud describes how Acher continued to ride his horse whilst Rabbi Meir walked alongside him on foot, urging his master to return to the faith. As they approached the outskirts of town Acher remarked to Rabbi Meir that to go any further would be a violation of Shabbat (one cannot leave a city's limits on Shabbat) and that Rabbi Meir should return. 'Rabbi,' said Rabbi Meir, 'you return with me.' Acher declined and went on his way. Rabbi Meir for his part never stopped hoping that one day his master would return and resume his old identity. Alas, this was not to be.

This tragic story is important because it demonstrates the power of teshuva. Though, in fact, Acher never returns, Rabbi Meir believed that he could. His request of Acher to return with him is not a request to return to the town from which they departed but to Acher's own core self. This faith in the power of teshuva even for as high a profile heretic as Acher is not misplaced. Acher ignored the call; but what is clear from the Talmud is that, had he chosen to heed it, he would have found his way back.

There is another story, much more contemporary, illustrating the Jewish view that a soul can never be tainted and that it retains its purity always. In the 1960s the Lubavitcher Rebbe, a great Hasidic master, sent one of his Hasidim to some far-flung place in the hope of discovering lost Jewish souls. The Hasid assumed this mission with vigour and after some time returned to report his finding to the Rebbe. He had indeed located a few Jews and he was appalled at their lack of basic Jewish literacy. He had begun to instruct them and after a while found that he had succeeded in returning them to their faith. Searching for an apt metaphor he described his work as that of a ritual scribe who fixes faded letters on a Holy Torah scroll, the faded letters being the lost souls. The Rebbe looked up in astonishment:

'faded letters, you say? They are not faded letters. They are like the holy letters of the Ten Commandments etched in stone.

Letters engraved in stone never fade. At worst they get covered in dust. All that is required is for someone to come along and blow the dust away and there you will see the holy letters in all their majesty and glory.'

Man is a strange hybrid, between something lower than an animal and more elevated than an angel. He is unlike either in that he possesses the divine gift of free choice whereas animals and even angels do not. Of all of creation he alone can choose his destiny. He is capable of the most unspeakable cruelty as well as the loftiest and most noble acts. Either way, it is he and he alone who bears responsibility for his actions. It is not the easiest existence; indeed the rabbis said, 'how much easier would it have been had we never been born.' Yet it is a most challenging and rewarding existence. It is also the most uplifting as we alone live with the knowledge that deep inside us dwells a spark of God.

Chapter 5

THE JEWISH PEOPLE

And you shall be to me a kingdom of priests, and a holy nation
(Exodus 19:6)

A gentleman in Caracas, Venezuela, called Hayyim, had a
remarkable story to tell. He once lived on the island of Curaçao
in the Caribbean. Although the island boasts the oldest synagogue in continuous use in the western hemisphere, by the
time he lived there the Jewish community had dwindled. The
Lubavitcher Rebbe mentioned in the previous chapter saw it as
his responsibility to reach out to Jews wherever they might be.
To this end, in the 1960s he established what could only be
described as a spiritual peace corps. The corps sent young rabbinical students to the most far-flung Jewish communities for
several weeks each summer. Their goal was to identify and
connect with Jews, however far removed they might be from
Jewish life and practice. One summer, a couple of boys arrived
in Curaçao. They were greeted by Hayyim, who over the

course of their stay became increasingly interested in learning more about his heritage and faith. After they left, Hayyim wrote a long letter to the Lubavitcher Rebbe in which he praised the work of the students and thanked the Rebbe for his interest and concern for the Jews of Curaçao. When it came to signing the letter, instead of using his name, for some reason he signed as 'a little Jew from Curaçao'. It was not long before the Rebbe replied: 'How can you call yourself a little Jew? There is no such thing as a little Jew. Each Jew belongs to a glorious heritage stretching back to Abraham, Isaac and Jacob. No. you are not a small Jew, you are a great Jew.'

An imposed faith

What does it mean to be a Jew? Well, one really does not have much choice in the matter; one is simply born into Judaism. That is to say, anyone born to a Jewish mother is de facto Jewish. In the same way as you have no say over your genetic make-up, you have no say over your spiritual make-up. There is some element of choice involved for those not born Jewish who choose to convert to the faith, but these are rather a small minority.

This idea of a faith that is imposed from above is given expression in the timing of the circumcision ceremony. Circumcision is the most fundamental sign of one's Jewishness. It is the sign of the covenant of Abraham and therefore it is at the core of Jewish identity. Yet the strange thing about circumcision is that it occurs when the baby is only eight days old. Perhaps from a medical point of view this makes good sense; indeed, infants recover relatively quickly from what is a minor operation, whereas adults undergoing circumcision take longer to heal. From a religious point of view, however, it makes no sense at all. How can this most important of personal religious milestones pass without the baby's knowledge of what it means? It would make more sense to wait until the child is of an age, when he can appreciate what he is about to undertake, and make a conscious decision to submit to the covenant of his ancestors. The reason Jews do not wait until the child matures is because the covenant of Abraham is not something one chooses. It is God who does the choosing.

It is not just circumcision that highlights the idea of an imposed faith. This idea plays itself out in a fascinating and terrifying Midrash concerning the giving of the Torah. The Midrash relates that when God gave the Torah to the Jewish people he lifted Mount Sinai high above their heads and declared: 'If you accept my Torah then all will be well, if you refuse, I will crush you under this mountain and it shall become your grave.' Startling as the image may be, the idea of God forcing his people to accept his Torah underscores the point that the Jew has no real choice in the matter of his Jewishness.

This Midrash seems to conflict with the biblical description of the giving of the Torah, where, upon being offered it, the Jewish people collectively responded *na'ase ve-nishma*, 'we will do and we will hear'. This apparently indicates that an offer was made and that the Jewish people made a conscious decision to accept it. Yet upon closer inspection the phrase 'we will do and we will hear' actually indicates the opposite. If they were making an informed choice they would have said 'we will hear and we will do'. The implication of the latter is that after first hearing or learning about the Torah they would then decide to do or observe it. By phrasing it the other way around they are actually saying they will accept the Torah regardless of its content; they will accept their status as God's people irrespective of what that might entail. Only after making this assertion do they turn to the matter of content and say 'and now let us hear'.

An unconditional relationship

Why is the idea of an imposed faith so central to Judaism? The answer is that it is not so much an imposed faith as a faith that at its core transcends rationale. The relationship between God and the Jewish people is so deeply rooted and unconditional that it transcends, indeed at times defies, all forms of understanding.

It is hard to find a parallel for such an unconditional relationship in our own lives. The best example I can offer is the relationship between a parent and child. With all other relationships there are elements of self-interest and the relationship ultimately hinges on the mutual fulfilment of those interests. Although we may not wish to admit it, our friendships are not unconditional. They are based on various benefits that we derive from them. We do not freely choose our friends; we choose them because they bring into the relationship certain things that we want. That is not to say that we are interested only in making friends with people who will benefit us in a crude material sense. This is manifestly untrue. People can invest in long-term friendships that bring neither party any tangible benefit: there are plenty of other intangible benefits such as alleviation of loneliness, a sense of mutual understanding, good humour and emotional support. This does not mean that we go about choosing our friends in a blatantly calculating way. We may not even be fully conscious of why it is that we are attracted to certain people. But if we dig deeply enough and we are honest with ourselves, every friendship can be reduced to some logical or psychological benefit. The proof is that many friendships do not stand the test of time. We grow older, wiser, our priorities change, our perspectives in life change and suddenly we find that we have little or nothing in common with those we once considered our closest friends.

Friendship is not the only relationship that is based on mutual benefit: marriage is too. Again, this is not to say that we choose to fall in love only with someone who will ensure that we live comfortably – although this is not unheard of – but that we instinctively fall in love with one whose qualities we appreciate. This appreciation of another's qualities is itself a benefit, and so long as the qualities and one's appreciation of them endure, so too will the marriage. But there is no guarantee of that happening. Marriages, as we know all too well, have ways of breaking down. Sometimes it is because the two parties were unsuited to each other from the very start; at other times, it is the result of no longer appreciating the other's qualities, perhaps because your priorities have changed.

A parent–child relationship, on the other hand, is based on pure, unconditional love. I should hastily add that the unconditional love is in the parent–child direction, not necessarily the other way around. The Talmud makes the sharp and bitter observation that while parents' devotion is to their child, their child's devotion is to his own children. Be that as it may, a parent feels unconditional love for a child. If we are lucky we reap pleasure and joy from our children. But that is not why we love them. Even those parents who are unfortunate enough not to have any pleasure or benefit from their children will not deny that they love them profoundly. To take an extreme example: the mother of a serial killer will, despite her feelings of anguish, guilt and failure, always love the child whom she carried in her womb and brought into this world. Is this logical? Of course not. It is a profound love that transcends all logical or rational explanation.

Similarly, the relationship between God and the Jewish people is one that is founded on something much more profound than anything that can be explained logically. The Jewish people, not unlike a difficult child, have caused their Father in Heaven no end of heartache over the years, either through rebelliousness or apathy. Occasionally in the Bible the Almighty, like an exasperated parent, threatens to wipe them out, but in the end he never does. Sometimes he thinks of exchanging them for another people, but such thoughts are fleeting: 'I simply cannot exchange them for any other people,' says the Talmud.

Unlike the parent–child relationship of our world, in which it is primarily the parent who loves unconditionally, in the parent–child relationship between God and the Jewish people, this love is reciprocated by the child.

This is the idea behind the circumcision at eight days old as well as the phrase 'we will do' and 'we will hear'. Both these examples demonstrate the Jews' willingness to bond with God on a level that transcends logical understanding or appreciation.

This is also the idea behind one of the most central biblical texts, the binding of Isaac, known as the *akeda*. In this terrifying tale Abraham is asked by God to offer his son Isaac as a sacrifice. Abraham unstintingly obeys God's command and goes so far as to raise a knife to his son's neck, at which point God interferes and tells Abraham that the whole thing was just a test of Abraham's faith and commitment.

What is interesting about this story is that not only did God's command defy logic – after all, what God would demand a human sacrifice? – but it contradicted an earlier promise because in an earlier passage God promises Abraham that through Isaac he will build a great nation. This was Abraham's greatest hope and dream, that his children would carry on his holy work. Suddenly he is asked to sacrifice not just his child, but his entire future and everything he believed in and hoped for. Yet he overcomes whatever doubts he may have had and sets out to fulfil the command of God. This idea, called *mesirat nefseh* (self sacrifice) in Hebrew, is what Abraham demonstrated at the akeda. By sacrificing Isaac Abraham would not only have lost his precious son, which for a parent is worse than the loss of one's own life, but also ensured the end of his dreams and all the promises that God had made to him concerning Isaac. Sacrificing Isaac was the most irrational thing Abraham could do, not just as a parent but as one who hoped that his life's purpose; the spread of monotheism would carry on through his child. Nonetheless, Abraham demonstrated his selfless commitment to God by obeying His command. Why? If asked, Abraham himself would not be able explain. Ultimately it is because the bond he had with God was not rooted in self-interest, material or spiritual. It was so pure and profound that it was able to withstand the most intense external pressure. We read the story of the akeda each morning in prayer so as to remind ourselves of the supra-rational bond we have with the Creator.

A supra-rational love

Judaism believes that each Jew possesses, deep inside, a super-rational love for God. This love is often depicted in Hasidic literature in Yiddish as *der pintele yid*, the quintessence of the Jew. For most, it lies dormant because it is not tested. However, at times of extreme spiritual stress it has the power to emerge in remarkable ways. Jewish history, as we will see in the next section of this book, is particularly blood-soaked. Jews were often confronted with the terrible choice between abandoning their faith or paying with their lives. Many Jews chose the latter rather than disconnect from the God of Israel. What is remarkable about these martyrs, or *kedoshim* (holy ones) as they are called in Hebrew, is that for the most part they were simple folk. They were certainly not well versed in Jewish theology and, if asked, they probably would have found it difficult to put into words just what their faith meant to them. Yet, when presented with the stark choice of either betraying their faith or protecting life and limb, they found that for some inexplicable reason they could not betray their faith. Were they fools? In a sense they were, if the definition of a fool is someone who defies logic – for that matter, so is the mother who continues to love her child despite his deep flaws. Both share an unconditional connection to the one they love that stands above all reason. Hasidic thought has a term for a Jew's irrational love for God: *shtut de-kedusha* (holy folly). A glance through Jewish history demonstrates that while we are, in the words of the Bible, 'a wise and intelligent people', we are equally capable of behaving in a most irrational manner when it comes to maintaining our bond with the God of Israel.

Corporate responsibility

This idea of a super-rational bond between God and the Jewish people also extends to the relationship Jewish people share with each other. One of the key ideas underpinning Jewish peoplehood is the notion of *areyvut*. In a legal sense areyvut means a guarantor, as in one who guarantees a loan for another and has thus taken responsibility on behalf of the other. In the context of the Jewish people it means that each Jew bears responsibility for the other. We are one people and the concerns of another Jew, even if a stranger, are to be considered as if they are one's own. Areyvut also lends itself to another meaning, blended or mixed together. This reinforces the previous definition that Jews do not see themselves as separate entities but rather as part of one larger entity, that of *klal yisrael*, 'the totality of the people of Israel'.

The idea of areyvut is closely connected to the mitzvah of *ahavat yisrael*, which is to love one's fellow Jew as one loves ones self. The idea is that as Jews bear a deep bond that unifies them, the distinction between self and other becomes, or at least should become, immaterial.

This is obviously easier in theory than in practice. However, Rabbi Shneur Zalman of Liadi explains that it is all a matter of perspective, internal or external. Externally we are all different people. We may share the same faith and even similar genetic make-up; yet we are clearly not all the same. Externally Jews are no different from anyone else. Some are inspiring, others are boring and yet others irritating. If one is only able to perceive the externals it is very difficult to put *ahavat yisrael* into practice. There will be people one feels instinctively drawn to and others whom one is instinctively repulsed by. If one is able to get beneath these externals the perspective changes. The same *pintele yid* that is essentially bound to God is also bound to all other Jews. What makes Jews one people is not race or genetics but something profoundly spiritual, the *pintele yid*. If one is able to conceive of each Jew possessing this essence, then the external differences become irrelevant and all that matters is that Jews are, on a spiritual level, intimately bound together as one.

Another way of conceptualizing this unity is to think of the distinction between imposed unity and organic unity. Imposed unity, like conditional love, brings various people together for a common benefit. An example of imposed unity is New York

City. The eight million or so inhabitants of that great city do not have anything intrinsically in common with each other. What they share is that they all reside in New York City in order to reap the collective social, cultural and economic benefits a great metropolis has to offer.

Organic unity, on the other hand, is where the disparate elements of a whole are intrinsically and intimately linked. Take, for example, an apple tree. The tree possesses many disparate elements, roots, a trunk, bark, leaves and fruit. Yet these elements are not anything apart from the apple tree. They are different, but they are unified in an organic way, so that when one looks at all elements together one does not see roots, bark, branches and leaves, but rather an apple tree.

The spiritual unity of the Jewish people is an organic whole. What one sees if one is able to look beneath the externals is a single people with the same spiritual history and destiny.

It is important to point out, however, that organic unity does not preclude diversity. Anyone vaguely familiar with the Jewish people knows that we are a most fractious and argumentative people. Judaism makes no attempt at homogeneity. The rich diversity of Judaism in its personalities, philosophies and ideas is its greatest strength. The concept of areyvut sees the Jewish people very much like the apple tree whose disparate parts are ultimately all part of a single whole.

The idea of areyvut also finds expression in the area of Jewish law. A well-known Jewish legal principle states that one may perform a mitzvah on behalf of another. So, for example, on Rosh Hashanah, the Jewish New Year, one designated individual will sound the shofar on behalf of the entire congregation. He will recite the blessings, the congregation will respond amen and he will then sound the shofar on everyone's behalf.

But there is a caveat; the person performing the mitzvah on behalf of the other must share the same level of obligation as the one for whom he is performing the mitzvah. For instance, since a boy under the age of thirteen does not share the same responsibility as one over the age of thirteen, the under-thirteen cannot fulfil the mitzvah on behalf of someone over that age. Similarly, as mentioned earlier, a woman does not share the same obligation as a man, thus in certain mitzvot where her obligation is weaker, she cannot fulfil them on behalf of a man.

Despite this caveat, if someone has already fulfilled the mitzvah, say of shofar, and another has not yet fulfilled their obligation, the person who has already fulfilled his obligation can perform the mitzvah *again* on behalf of the other. This appears inconsistent with the ruling that they must both share equal responsibility. How can it be said that one who has already fulfilled his obligation bears the same responsibility as one who has not yet fulfilled his obligation?

The answer is areyvut. Since all Jews are responsible for each other, the person who has already fulfilled the mitzvah has not entirely fulfilled his obligation. He may have fulfilled his obligation in the sense that he performed the mitzvah but he is still responsible for his fellow who has yet to do so. It is as though he has not yet discharged his own obligation, and so he is allowed to perform the mitzvah on behalf of the other.

On a lighter note, Jews tend to recognize others as Jews even if they have never met. It is difficult to explain how, but one just knows. American Jews tend to be very upfront about it. If they meet someone on holiday or while travelling whom they think might be Jewish they will come out with it directly and ask if the person is Jewish. Brits on the other hand are either more reticent or polite, depending on how you see it. They will engage in an elaborate game of dropping names, places and phrases that to a Jew are laden with meaning in the hope that their interlocutor will be the first to drop her guard and confess to being MOT (a Member of the Tribe). The discussion will go something like this. 'Oh, hello, nice to meet you, where are you from?' 'We're from London.' (Not a lot of information to go on there, so you press on.) 'London, really? Whereabouts?' 'Edgware'. (An intensely Jewish neighbourhood, good chance they are Jewish, but it's best to be certain.) 'Edgware, really?

You know we vacationed in Eilat last year.' (This is tanta-mount to declaring one's Jewishness, but the other side is playing it cautious.) 'Eilat, hmm, interesting. We went to New York and had the most amazing salt beef at this little deli on the Lower East Side.' (They've pushed out the boat as far as it will go, it's now or never, so you take the plunge, and in a voice disguised by a cough you mumble) 'You MOT?' 'Yeah,' replies the other visibly relaxed. The game is up, and before the hour is over you will have discovered that not only are you distantly related but that you used the same caterer for your children's bar mitzvahs and that your mothers attended the same Jewish youth club in the 1950s.

Conversion

Judaism is not a proselytizing faith. That is to say it does not seek converts from other faiths. It is content in the knowledge that all ethical monotheists are beloved by God and will gain a place in heaven in the afterlife. Not only that, but they are capable of drawing near to God and experiencing true spiritu-ality. In one of the most moving passages in Jewish legal litera-ture, Maimonides writes about the ability of all peoples to draw near to God and experience His presence: 'Any person from any nation of the world who is moved to dedicate his life to God . . . he is considered holy of the holies and God will be his portion for ever.'

The only souls Judaism is concerned with saving are Jewish souls. It is the Jew who must be faithful to Judaism, not the gentile. This laidback, at times even suspicious, attitude to con-version is partly responsible for the relatively small size of the Jewish people today. This, of course, must be coupled with the effects of generations of persecution and assimilation. Yet, despite Judaism's small numbers, there is no sense that it must grow by converting others to its ranks.

This is not to say that Judaism rejects converts. On the con-trary, some of the most esteemed rabbis in Jewish history were either themselves converts or they descended from converts.

But Judaism believes that the desire to become Jewish must stem from within the convert himself and not be imposed from without. This is consistent with the doctrine of the *pintele yid*. External factors cannot implant within a prospective convert a Jewish quintessence. This is something that must well up from deep within. Indeed, while some rabbis believe that the convert attains this Jewish essence only after converting, others, notably Rabbi Hayyim Yosef David Azulai (an eighteenth-century rabbi), believe that despite being born to another faith the Jewish essence was always there. Indeed, it is precisely this essence that motivated the individual to join the ranks of the Jewish people in the first place.

In keeping with the two key elements of being Jewish – an unquestionable bond with the God of Israel and His Torah and an unswerving loyalty to the totality of the Jewish people – a prospective convert is expected to demonstrate his commitment to these two areas before being accepted as a member of the Jewish people. In addition he will be required, as mentioned in the chapter on mitzvot, not just to accumulate sufficient Jewish knowledge but also to absorb the unique atmosphere of Jewish life.

Once a rabbinical court has taken a decision to admit a prospective convert into the Jewish people the convert will be required to immerse in a *mikveh*, a ritual pool of water, signifying rebirth. If the convert is a male he must undergo circumcision as well. Finally, as a sign of spiritual rebirth, the convert is asked to choose a Jewish name.

Chosenness

Another central idea connected to the Jewish people is the idea of chosenness. This idea is given expression in the Torah where Moses says to his people, 'For you are a holy people to the Lord your God; the Lord your God has chosen you to be a special people to himself, above all peoples that are upon the face of the earth.' The idea of chosenness is often misinterpreted and misunderstood, leading to resentment and, worse, animosity amongst those of other faiths. What the Torah means by chosen is not that Jews are necessarily better than anyone else but rather that they have been chosen to fulfil a unique mission in God's world. This is to be an example of the highest spiritual and ethical behaviour through adherence to the Torah and mitzvot. While this makes the Jewish people special it also implies that they are to be held to higher standards. The fact that Judaism does not seek to dominate others or draw them away from their faiths is an indication that it does not see itself as superior, just different. Judaism is not an exclusive club, since converts are welcome. It is, however, a very demanding club, and as such is clearly not for everyone.

What is interesting is that the idea of choseness applies within Judaism itself. Jews are divided into three ranks: *kohanim*, *leviyim* and *yisraelim*.

The kohanim are the descendants of Aaron, the high priest. In Temple times they would have conducted the Temple services and rites. Today, as there is no Temple, this crucial element is missing. Nonetheless, the kohanim do have certain privileges and responsibilities that other Jews do not have. Amongst these is the right to be called up first, before anyone else, to read the Torah. Leviyim are the descendants of the tribe of Levi, who also functioned in the Temple, if to a lesser degree than the kohanim. Leviyim today do not bear any responsibilities, although they retain the privilege of being called up second to read from the Torah. Finally, at the bottom, are the rest of us, yisraelim, good ordinary Jews without any particular privileges or responsibilities other than keeping the Torah and observing the mitzvot. As with the chosenness of the Jewish people, the chosenness of kohanim and leviyim denotes particular responsibilities as opposed to an affirmation that the *kohain* is intrinsically better than the *levi* and that the *levi* is intrinsically better than the *yisrael*. In fact, the Talmud states that a Torah scholar who has the misfortune of being born a bastard is to be shown greater honour than a kohain who is an ignoramus. This demonstrates that a person's true rank is not something that they are born with but rather the result of what they achieve through their own dedication and hard work.

Holiness

This chapter on the nature of the Jewish people would not be complete without a discussion about the concept of holiness. The Jewish people are explicitly commanded to be holy. The Bible says: 'You shall be to me a kingdom of priests and a holy nation' (Exodus 19:6). It also says: 'You shall be holy, for I, the Lord your God am holy' (Leviticus 19:2). What is the nature of this holiness? What does it mean for a human being to be holy?

As with many Jewish ideas, the notion of holiness has various interpretations. The great Jewish scholar Rashi, writing in the eleventh century, interprets this holiness as abstinence from sensual or physical pleasures such as food and sex. Rashi was not advocating a monastic lifestyle: the Torah itself encourages marriage and the celebration of festivals through food and drink. What Rashi means is that one should seriously curtail such activities and limit them to those times when they are absolutely necessary.

Nahmonides, a thirteenth-century scholar, takes a different approach. He believes that the idea of holiness means that one must be as concerned with the spirit of the law as with the letter of the law. He says that one could technically follow the law to the letter and yet still behave in a coarse, sordid fashion. For example, one could follow kosher dietary laws to the letter, recite all the appropriate blessings before and after eating and yet eat like a glutton. The idea of holiness directs the person to a more refined and elevated existence which is, in effect, the essence of Judaism.

Maimonides strongly disagrees with Rashi's notion that holiness is achieved through abstinence and the denial of physical pleasures. Such abstinence is not natural, nor expected, argues Maimonides, quoting the verse from Ecclesiastes: 'So do not overdo goodness and do not act the wise man to excess, or you may be dumfounded'. Instead, Maimonides believes in the concept of achieving holiness through elevating, not denying, the physical. To return to our example of food and sex, Maimonides would argue that provided the purpose behind eating or making love is positive, then that elevates the physical act and turns it into something holy. Therefore if one eats kosher food in order to honour the Shabbat or in order to maintain one's health in order better to serve God, the mundane act of eating becomes elevated to a level of holiness. Similarly, if one has intercourse with one's wife in the context of love and mutual respect, then that too becomes a holy act. This notion of balance in Maimonides' thought is consistent with his views relating to medical health. In addition to being a rabbi and philosopher, he was also a physician. His medical advice on maintaining good health is to live a life of balance and moderation. It appears that his prescription for physical health and well-being also leads to spiritual health and well-being.

The early rabbinical writings of the Talmud are divided on the nature of physical pleasure. Avot de-Rabi Natan (28:5) takes a dim view of physical pleasure:

> Anyone who denies pleasure in this world will receive pleasures in the next world, and conversely, he who partakes of physical pleasures in this world will be denied pleasures in the next.

Yet, on the other hand, the Jerusalem Talmud (Kiddushin 48b) seems to endorse the value of physical pleasures, provided that they are permitted by the Torah:

> A person will have to answer in heaven for all permitted things he could have partaken of in this world but did not.

Both these conflicting views are authentic Jewish perspectives and have found expression at various points in Jewish history.

From the twelfth to the fourteenth centuries, Judaism in Germany was influenced by a strong pietistic strain that subscribed to the view that physical pleasures should be avoided in order to attain holiness. In sharp contrast to this, the Hasidic movement of the eighteenth century taught that holiness can be achieved through embracing and elevating the physical.

The driving force behind this positive view of physical pleasures is the mystical doctrine of 'raising the sparks'. This doctrine, which we will revisit in greater detail in the second part of this book, first emerged from the mystical circles of Safed in the sixteenth century. Simply put, the doctrine posits that there are divine sparks of holiness embedded in all aspects of physicality. These sparks are essentially trapped, and the purpose of life for a Jew is to release them back to their source through the performance of mitzvot. What this means in a practical sense is that when a Jew makes a blessing over a cup of wine on a Friday night, for example, he releases the holy sparks trapped in the wine back to their source. The same is true for any mitzvah involving a physical dimension, which, as stated earlier, most mitzvot do. Hasidism is not frightened of physical pleasures, provided they are permitted. Instead, it sees them as untapped opportunities to release holy sparks, which in turn shed holiness on the one performing the mitzvah.

It is not just particular mitzvot that lead to the raising of the sparks but even broader activities guided by the Torah and mitzvot, such as ethical business practices that also serve to raise the sparks of holiness. This is illustrated by a story of a very wealthy Hasid who was adding up his end-of-year profits. When he got to the total, instead of putting down the monetary sum he wrote 'sakh ha-kol; eiyn od milvado' (sum total: there is nought but Him). His colleague was not impressed. 'What do you mean by this?' he asked. 'I too know that when all is said and done there is nought but Him, but right now we are in the midst of business and in this material world real figures matter.' 'Try to understand,' replied the Hasid. 'When I pray, it is not uncommon for thoughts about my business to interfere with my concentration on God. So why is it so terrible if thoughts about God interfere with my concentration on business?'

While Maimonides would not necessarily agree with the

Kabbalistic doctrine of the 'raising of sparks' he does share a core idea, that physical pleasure is in itself not necessarily an obstacle to holiness. On the contrary, at times it can be the conduit to achieving holiness. It is the question of timing, circumstances and purpose that can make all the difference.

Chapter 6

THE LAND OF ISRAEL

A land which the Lord your God cares for; the eyes of the Lord your God are always upon it, from the beginning of the year to the end of the year.   (Deuteronomy 11:12)

Ten measures of beauty descended to the world: nine were taken by Jerusalem and one by the rest of the world.
(Talmud, Kiddushin 49b)

The Land of Israel holds a special place in the heart of Judaism. The bond between the people of Israel and the Land of Israel was established when God made what has become known as the ancestral covenant with Abraham, described in the Book of Genesis. After a troubling vision in which Abraham beholds the suffering of his descendants throughout history, God makes him the following promise: 'To your seed have I given this land, from the river of Egypt to the great river, the river Euphrates.' This promise is the background to the rest of the Hebrew Bible. The exodus from Egypt and the wandering in the desert was a prelude to the most important act, the conquest and settlement of the Promised Land. The books of Judges, Prophets and Scripture are all preoccupied with either sustaining the Jewish presence in the Holy Land or, after being exiled from it, its eventual return.

Godliness in the Land of Israel

What is also obvious from the Hebrew Bible and from subsequent Jewish teachings is that the Land of Israel is holy; that it was chosen by God as the place in which he would manifest his glory; and that this holiness remains for all time. What does it mean for a land to be holy? How can something as physical as a patch of earth be considered sacred?

By now you may have guessed at the answer. Based on our earlier discussion in Chapter 1 about God transcending all limitations, both spiritual and physical, the notion of God choosing a finite place on earth to manifest himself is not so strange after all. Furthermore, we have just finished discussing how godliness is manifest in the physical through the Torah and mitzvot. Similarly then, God chose the Land of Israel as the locus of his manifestation in this physical world. This does not mean that the Creator is absent from the rest of the world. On the contrary, 'there is no place free of his presence', as the mystical text, the Zohar states (see p. 136). What it means is that while God's presence is elsewhere hidden, in the Holy Land it is revealed.

This sense of God's revelation was nowhere more visible than in Jerusalem and particularly in the ancient Temple there. In describing Solomon's Temple the Bible says that its windows were *shekufim atumim*. The Talmud interprets this to mean that as they were set in extremely thick walls, the windows tapered towards the inside. The reason for this unusual arrangement is that the Temple did not require light from the outside; the Temple was the source of spiritual light, and its purpose was to beam that spiritual light out into the wider world.

So taken were the Talmudic rabbis with the notion that the Land of Israel is imbued with a spiritual quality that they

declared that the very atmosphere of the Holy Land illumi-
nates one's intelligence.

Some 2,000 years later a similar sentiment was expressed by
the Hasidic leader Rabbi Menachem Mendel of Vitebsk. Rabbi
Menachem Mendel left his native Russia for the Land of Israel
in the late eighteenth century, settling in Tiberias. After several
months he wrote to his followers in Russia saying that, despite
his joy at being in the Holy Land, he was finding it difficult to
sleep. 'The night air', he wrote, 'is pure and I constantly hear
voices calling on me to repent.'

Exile and redemption

Intimately connected to the idea of the holiness of the Land of
Israel and God's presence there are the twin concepts of exile
and redemption. As we will see in the second part of this book,
there were two Temples in Jerusalem. The first was built during
Solomon's reign during the ninth century BCE and destroyed
by the Babylonians in the fifth century BCE. The second was
built in the fourth century BCE and destroyed by the Romans
in the first century CE. Jewish tradition has it that the destruction of both Temples, separated by almost half a millennium,
occurred on the ninth of the Hebrew month of Av. Both
destructions were followed by a period of exile. The first exile
was relatively short, as the return to Israel and the rebuilding
of the second Temple commenced within a century. The latter
exile lasted much longer – indeed, continues to last. Despite the
foundation of the modern State of Israel, the spiritual notion of
exile is still present. This will be discussed at greater length in
the second part of this book. Suffice it to say at this point that
the experience of exile will only be terminated when the
messiah arrives and rebuilds a third Temple in Jerusalem.

There are a number of theological problems with the destruction of Jerusalem and the subsequent exile of the Jewish people
from the land. The first is the question of what happened to
God's presence in the Holy Land, particularly in Jerusalem,
after the city had been destroyed and the Jewish people driven

out. Did it remain a Holy Land? Or did God's presence depart? If His presence departed, where can it be found today? Another problem relates to the status of the Jewish people in exile. Are they still God's people? Or has God broken his covenant with them? Finally, is there any deeper purpose to the exile beyond mere punishment for sins?

The rabbis seemed to be of two minds about the locus of the divine presence, known as the *shekhinah*, after the destruction of the Temple. On one hand they agree that the shekhinah followed the Jewish people into exile and so she too (the shekhinah is always referred to in the feminine) is in exile. This is a beautiful and comforting concept for a people who have lost their connection, at least in a physical sense, with the Holy Land. The notion that the shekhinah follows them into exile and that they are still God's people is a powerful one that helped to sustain the Jewish people through a long, dark and bitter exile. On the other hand, the rabbis believed that something of the shekhinah never really left the Temple precinct, Jerusalem, or, for that matter the Holy Land. Despite the physical destruction, the spiritual quality of the Land of Israel remains intact and it retains its intrinsic sanctity. Nonetheless, the manifestation of the shekhinah is not as obvious as it was during Temple times and remains to a certain extent concealed. These two ideas are not necessarily contradictory. God is unlimited and therefore notions of time and space do not apply. The shekhinah is not limited to one place or another. It can be both in Jerusalem as well as in exile with her people.

As far as the status of the Jewish people in exile, the Hebrew prophets are clear: Jews remain God's people despite their sins and expulsion. What is more, God promises that he will return his people to their land and rebuild the Temple.

The purpose of exile

What then is the purpose of exile? On a very simple level it is punishment for abandoning God, his Torah and mitzvot. In both periods leading up to the Temple's destruction the Jewish people had turned from God. Despite warnings from the prophets and later the rabbis, they failed to rectify their behaviour. The result, although tragic, was inevitable. God's people had ceased to act as a holy people and therefore they forfeited their right to live in a holy land.

On a mystical level, the nature of exile has an entirely different dimension: to raise the sparks of holiness so as to elevate and sanctify the world. From this perspective exile is not so much a punishment as a mission, painful and difficult though it may be. The mission to raise the sparks is something we discussed in the previous chapter. Behind it is the notion that godliness is hidden everywhere and it is the Jew's mission to discover it. The earliest mission involving the raising of the sparks occurred in the Holy Land. This was relatively easy, as holiness was not difficult to detect there. The difficult, but most significant, part of the mission is to detect the sparks of holiness outside the Holy Land, in places where one would not think holiness could reside. The 2,000-year Roman exile, as it is called, ensured that the Jewish people, and through them the Torah, would spread to the farthest reaches of the globe. The mission is not to convert others to the Jewish faith, but rather for Judaism to illuminate the world in a moral and spiritual sense. Once this task is complete the redemption, not just of the Jewish people but indeed of all mankind, is complete. This perfection and spiritual harmonization of the world will be manifest in the return of the shekhinah to Jerusalem and the third Temple.

There is a curious incident recorded in the Talmud about the period of the Babylonian destruction of the Temple. The holiest article in the Temple was the Ark of the Covenant, containing the tablets of stone that Moses brought down from Mount Sinai. The Ark itself was a large chest covered in gold with a golden lid. On top of the lid stood two winged creatures, called cherubim. One had the face of a male, the other the face of a female. The Talmud relates that when the Jewish people did the will of God the two cherubim faced each other, symbolizing the love between God and His people. However, when the Jewish people were sinful the cherubim (miraculously) swivelled away from each other. The Talmud records that when the enemy entered the Temple to destroy it they discovered the Ark with the cherubim facing each other. They brought it out for their compatriots to see and they ridiculed it, believing it was childish.

What is fascinating about this passage is that it describes the events on the day of the Temple's destruction, clearly not a time of love between God and his errant people. Yet the cherubim indicate otherwise by facing each other. Hasidic thought links this enigmatic text with the mystical idea of exile. Indeed, on the surface the destruction appears to be a rupture between God and his people. Yet beneath the surface something else entirely is unfolding. God loves his people and yet despite the suffering He knows they will endure, He sends them into exile to achieve a holy purpose.

The destruction then can be viewed in terms of demolishing a house in order to build an even greater one in its place. To an outsider the demolition of what appears to be an otherwise fine home seems dreadful. Yet, to the one who anticipates its superior replacement, the loss of the old house is of little concern. It is similar to the destruction of the Temple and the subsequent exile. From the perspective of the Jew in exile it is a tragedy. From the perspective of God, it is nothing but a temporary experience leading on to something far greater than anyone could imagine.

There have been some great men who, despite the suffering of exile, have been able to imagine redemption in the most vibrant colours. These were the great Jewish leaders throughout the generations who have managed to keep the spark of hope burning in the hearts of their people. One such leader, named Rabbi Akiva, lived in the immediate aftermath of the destruction of the second Temple. The Talmud relates how on one occasion his colleagues, with whom he was walking, witnessed a fox darting out of the ruins of the Temple. They began to cry, yet Rabbi Akiva just laughed. 'Why do you laugh?' they asked in disbelief. 'Why do you cry?' he retorted. 'We cry because we have just seen the fulfilment of the prophecy of Micah that the Temple will be destroyed and Jerusalem will become heaps of ruins.' 'This is precisely why I laugh,' replied Rabbi Akiva. 'Since the prophecy of Micah has been fulfilled I know that it is only a matter of time before the prophecy of Zachariah will be fulfilled as well. For Zachariah said, "There shall yet be old men and women in the squares of Jerusalem . . . and the squares of the city shall be crowded with boys and girls playing in the squares."'

This current exile has lasted for almost 2,000 years. During all that time Jews never stopped hoping and praying for the final redemption and the return to the Promised Land. Three times a day we face Jerusalem in prayer. References to the redemption and the restoration of the Holy Land are abundantly scattered throughout Jewish daily prayers. When we have suffered a loss we are comforted with the phrase, 'May the Almighty comfort you amongst the mourners for Zion and Jerusalem.' Each year on the ninth of the Hebrew month of Av Jews fast and mourn the destruction of the Temple and Jerusalem. Even at weddings, the most joyous moment in life, the groom traditionally breaks a glass underfoot to remind the assembled that no joy is complete without the redemption.

Exile has also exposed the Jews to a much wider world and, equally, exposed the wider world to the Jews. The consequences of this have not always been pleasant or fruitful, particularly for the Jews; yet Jews continue to pursue their mission of *tikkun 'olam*, repairing God's world and inspiring others to do likewise.

Has the world become more enlightened in the past 2,000 years? In some ways it has, in others it has become only darker. Do Jews despair? No, that has never been the Jewish way. Jews hope and trust in a brighter tomorrow. They are also alert to a most important truth, that the night is darkest just before dawn.

PART 2

History

Chapter 7

THE BIBLICAL FOUNDATION

Remember the days of old, consider the years of many generations; ask your father, and he will show you; your elders, and
they will tell you.   (Deuteronomy 32:7)

1813–1506 BCE – the patriarchs

Although there is no hard archaeological proof to back up the
early stories of the Bible, these stories are included here as part
of Jewish history in the sense that they make up a significant
part of the Jewish narrative. It is not really possible to understand Jewish history without considering the biblical accounts.
For a believing Jew, these are a matter of fact, and they impact
significantly on the way he understands not just his early
history but all subsequent history as well.

Jewish history begins with Abraham, the first monotheist
and the father of the Jewish people. As recorded in the Bible,
Abraham emerged from the polytheistic pagan society of
ancient Mesopotamia and gradually came to the realization
that there was one God who created heaven and earth. While

the biblical account is somewhat sparse concerning the details
of Abraham's childhood and conversion, it relates that at some
point he had his first religious experience, when God spoke to
him and instructed him to abandon his birthplace of Ur and to
journey to the land of Canaan.

Despite God's promise that the move would benefit
Abraham, initially he and his wife Sarah suffered many setbacks and disappointments, not least Sarah's inability to conceive a child. Despite these trials Abraham never lost faith in
God, and God continued to reveal himself to Abraham. In
these subsequent revelations Abraham was promised that
Sarah would give birth to a son, Isaac, that eventually Abraham's
descendants would be more numerous than the stars in the
sky, and that they would inherit the land of Canaan. One of
the most difficult trials Abraham encountered was the 'binding
of Isaac', or akeda.

The Bible relates how Abraham was commanded by God to
offer his precious son Isaac as a human sacrifice. The narrative
describes Abraham's unquestioning devotion to God's will
and how he came to within inches of actually committing this
deed. At the last moment God dramatically intervened and
spared Isaac's life. The story throws up profound theological
questions, and there are countless approaches to understanding the meaning of this harrowing psychological drama. On
the most basic level it is about the ultimate test of faith and how
Abraham was willing to surrender to God that which was
more precious than his own life, his son's life. The story has
had profound meaning for Jews throughout history.

The second of the Jewish patriarchs is Isaac. Unlike his
extrovert father, Isaac appeared introverted, intensely so. Yet
he too experienced God's revelation and in his own way continued his father's project of spreading monotheism. He is followed by his son Jacob, the third and final patriarch. Of all the
patriarchs Jacob had the most difficult life. He is hounded,
pursued, and deceived by enemies all around, his beloved wife
Rachel dies in childbirth and he is separated from his favourite

son, Joseph. Despite all of his struggles he is the most prolific of the patriarchs, fathering twelve sons who in turn become the fathers of the twelve tribes of Israel. It is in recognition of Jacob's struggles, spiritual and physical, internal and external, that he is given a new name: Israel. Israel is derived from the same root as the Hebrew word for *struggle* or *strive*, indicating that Jacob and indeed his descendants would struggle and eventually prevail. It is from this point on that the Jewish people are referred to in the Bible as the children of Israel, reflecting both their connection with Jacob as well as hinting at their destiny.

1506–1313 BCE – Egypt: bondage and redemption

All was not well with Jacob's sons. His second youngest and favourite son, Joseph, provoked his brothers by sharing with them his grandiose dreams of rising to power at their expense. As a result he was sold into slavery by his brothers. Joseph ended up in Egypt, where, because of his talents and charisma, he was eventually raised to the level of viceroy of Egypt. In time Jacob and his family, driven by famine in the land of Canaan, joined Joseph in Egypt. Although the children of Israel initially settled as free men, over time they were pressed into slavery by the Egyptians. Thus began one of the most important chapters in the formation of the Jewish people. There are constant references to this period throughout the Bible, reflecting at least two reasons for this harsh fate. First, it was so that this fledgling people would witness the awesome power of God who would redeem them from bondage and lead them to His service as a free people in the Promised Land. Secondly, if the Jewish people were going to serve as the ethical inspiration for mankind, it was important for them to experience first hand the humiliations and deprivations of slavery. Time and again when the Bible calls on the Jewish people to feed the hungry, clothe the naked and welcome the stranger it goes on to remind them that they too were once hungry and naked and exploited as slaves in Egypt. Eventually God redeemed his people through the agency of Moses.

Moses, the greatest leader and teacher of the Jewish people, was an extremely reluctant leader. The Bible recounts how in order to save her baby from Pharaoh's officers, who at the time were drowning any Israelite baby they could find, Moses' mother hid him in a basket on the Nile. As fate would have it, the basket was discovered by Pharaoh's daughter, who, despite knowing that this was an Israelite child, adopted the crying baby as her own. Moses was eventually made aware of his Israelite origins and he remained in two worlds. On the one hand he was a prince of Egypt with all the privileges and freedoms associated with that position. Yet, on the other hand, he was an Israelite at heart, who felt deeply for the plight of his brethren. One day Moses saw an Egyptian taskmaster striking a helpless Israelite slave and leapt to his rescue, killing the Egyptian taskmaster in the process. Pharaoh was enraged by this and Moses was forced to flee to Midyan. Here he married a local girl and tried to lose himself in shepherding his father-in-law's flocks of sheep.

There is a legend that Moses was an exceptionally caring shepherd and that on one occasion he followed a lone lost sheep for days in order to return it to the flock. It was then that God knew he had found the leader for his people. The Bible recounts how God appeared before Moses in a burning bush and instructed him to lead His people out of slavery. Although full of self-doubt, Moses reluctantly agreed. He was eventually joined by his elder brother, Aaron, and together they approached Pharaoh to demand that he set the Israelites free. Pharaoh refused and God unleashed, through Moses, ten plagues which devastated Egypt. Pharaoh finally realized what he was up against and so grudgingly let the Israelites leave.

1313–1273 BCE – giving of the Torah, wandering in the desert

The singular most important event in the history of the Jewish people occurred shortly after their redemption from Egypt. This was the giving of the Torah at Mount Sinai. Then the

Jewish people could basically be described as a large extended family or tribe. It was the giving of the Torah, God's law, that forged them into a nation. The Jewish people are bound to each other neither by race nor nationality but by the Torah. In fact any non-Jew who desires to tie his fate to the Jewish people and to live by the Torah is accepted as a convert and is treated no differently from any born Jew.

Seven weeks after the exodus from Egypt Moses ascended Mount Sinai to receive the Torah. After God spoke the Ten Commandments, Moses remained on the mount for forty days and nights to learn the deepest secrets of the Torah from the Almighty himself. There is a fascinating and deeply insightful Midrash that takes us behind the scenes as Moses reached the summit of the mount, which in the Midrash is the portal to heaven. As Moses entered heaven the angels were in an uproar. Never before had a man of flesh and blood reached this high. 'What is man born of a woman doing here?' the angels asked the Almighty. 'To take the Torah back down to earth,' the Almighty replied. 'What right does man have to the holy Torah?' demanded the angels, 'By right it should remain here with us in heaven.' 'Moses,' said the Almighty, 'respond to their challenge.' Moses addressed the angels: 'Holy angels,' he began 'what is written in the Torah? *Thou shalt not steal.* Tell me, do you angels have possessions so that it would be possible to steal? What else is written in the Torah? *Thou shalt not covet.* Do you angels have possessions to covet? Furthermore, it is written in the Torah, *Honour your father and mother*: do then angels have parents whom they might honour? No. The Torah was not written for angels, it was written for human beings, with all their shortcomings, imperfections and frailties. I am taking the Torah down to earth where it belongs.' Moses' argument was so compelling that not only did it silence the angels but they also sent him on his way with many gifts.

Unfortunately, while this spiritual drama was unfolding before Moses in the celestial realms, his people back on earth had other things to consider. By a simple miscalculation they believed that Moses' forty-day sojourn had come to a close; yet there was no sign of their leader. Certain elements in the camp began to panic, afraid that something terrible had happened to Moses and that they would now be left leaderless in the desert. The Bible recounts how, due to their lack of faith, they fashioned a statue of a calf out of molten gold and proceeded to worship it as a replacement for God and his Torah. Moses, blissfully unaware of what his people had got up to, was suddenly jarred into action by God who told him to descend the mount rapidly with the Ten Commandments etched in tablets of stone. On his approach Moses beheld the sight of the Israelites dancing around the enormous idol and in a moment of rage he hurled the stone tablets to the ground, where they shattered.

Moses reprimanded the people and then, in his characteristic way, he interceded on their behalf before God. God pardoned them and Moses ascended once again and returned with a new set of tablets.

It was assumed from the very beginning that shortly after receiving the Torah the Jewish people would make their way into the Promised Land. However, not everything went to plan. As they approached the land of Canaan the Israelites began to doubt their ability to conquer the land and, with Moses' consent, they sent twelve spies on a forty-day reconnaissance mission. The spies chosen were leaders in their own right, representing each of the twelve tribes of Israel. The mission was a disaster. So awesome did the inhabitants of the land appear to the spies that they resolved it would be impossible to conquer the land. Ten of them returned with such negative reports that they managed to frighten the people off the whole project. With this overwhelmingly defeatist attitude prevailing, the objections of Joshua and Caleb, the two spies who thought the conquest possible, were drowned out by the crowd. God then decreed that they would have to wander in the dessert for forty years and die out before a new generation, born free, without the shackles of a slave mentality, would enter and conquer the Promised Land.

A Hasidic interpretation of this story explains that the reluctance of the Israelites to conquer Canaan was not fear of physical defeat but rather of spiritual defeat. The desert was a spiritual haven. They were isolated, they had limited possessions and it was an ideal place for the contemplation and worship of God. The land of Canaan, they knew, would be different. After engaging in many heavy battles they would have to begin the demanding task of building a national home with its complex infrastructure. They were afraid of what such demands would make on their spiritual state of being. It is like feeling relaxed and happy on holiday and knowing even as you enjoy yourself that the feeling will not last much beyond your first day back at work. Although the Israelites were concerned about spiritual matters they were deeply mistaken to believe that contemplative life in the desert was the reason God brought them out of Egypt and gave them the Torah. In line with Moses' response to the angels, the Torah was meant for the real world. A Jew comes closest to God not in isolation from the demanding reality of the world but rather by engaging with it and shaping it in accordance with the Torah.

During this forty-year period of wandering God instructed the Jewish people to build a tabernacle to serve as His dwelling place on earth. Moses' brother, Aaron, was designated high priest, and together with his children he conducted the various rituals and services. The tabernacle was a makeshift structure which the Israelites took with them on their travels. The first permanent structure would eventually be built on Mount Moriah in Jerusalem in the year 826.

1273–879 BCE: the conquest of Israel; reign of the judges

Moses and his generation passed away in the desert and a new generation entered the Promised Land under the leadership of Joshua. Thus began a long period of conquest and settling the land. One of the themes that emerges during this period of history is the Israelites' relative lack of security and stability in their new land. It took years for them to conquer the land, and even when they finally did so they were regularly threatened by their aggressive neighbours, the Philistines to the west and the Moabites to the east. Another theme that recurs during this period is that the Jewish people were not consistent in their commitment to God and his Torah. There were stretches of time in which they strayed, which were, without fail, followed by persecution and domination by Israel's neighbours. The persecutions led to a national mood of repentance; and when the persecutions ceased there was relative peace and calm for a brief time until, once again, religious commitment waned and the pattern started all over again.

After Joshua's passing, the Israelites were led by various leaders called judges. Some of these judges, such as Deborah (1107), the first female leader, were of exalted spiritual character. Others like Yiftach (982) were little more than war lords. One of the most fascinating and yet tragic of these judges was Samson (951), who, due to his supernatural strength derived from his uncut hair, struck fear into the hearts of the Philistines. Unfortunately, Samson also had a great weakness for women and in the end he was betrayed by Delilah, a woman he loved, who cut his hair and had him delivered to his enemies.

The period of the judges is not a particularly glorious one. But the fact that the Bible is open about this says something important about its view of history. The Bible never tries to whitewash history. It tells it as it was. What emerges from the Books of Judges and, later, of Kings and Prophets, is a rich depiction of a real world with real people, warts and all. Even the most venerated characters such as Kings David and Solomon do not emerge unscathed by the Bible's criticism. This does not diminish them in the reader's eyes. On the contrary, one sees how, as real people, they struggled to make the right choices in life. Even when they fail, sometimes spectacularly, one cannot help but admire, if not identify with, their struggle.

879–797 BCE – Saul, David, Solomon: the United Kingdom

The period of judges gave way to the first Jewish monarchy. The prophet Samuel was the bridge between the judges and the monarchs. He was the last of the judges and by far the most gifted and spiritual one. Samuel's birth was a miracle; and in recognition of this his mother, Hannah, dedicated her son to God from the age of three. Samuel grew up under the watchful eye of Eli, the high priest, and soon surpassed him as God's spokesman to the people. It was during Samuel's tenure that the people began demanding a monarch who would unite and represent them. Samuel was deeply distressed by this request since he believed that God alone should reign over the Jewish people.

The fact that they dared to ask for a king of flesh and blood was a slight to God's honour. In one of the most dramatic speeches in the entire Bible, the elderly prophet Samuel berates the people for spurning God and demanding a human king. In the hope of dampening their enthusiasm he sets out in brutal detail the powers of a such a king. 'The king', says Samuel, 'will press your sons into his army, he will take your daughters to do menial labour in his palaces, and he will expropriate your property.' Strange as it seems to the modern reader, the people ignored his warnings and continued to press for a king. Samuel begrudgingly accepted the people's will and turned to God for guidance to choose the appropriate candidate. God's choice for the first king of his people was a young man, Saul, son of Kish of the tribe of Benjamin. Saul was as surprised as anyone else and very reluctantly agreed to assume the position. On the surface it is easy to see why Saul was chosen. He was physically imposing – the Bible recounts that he stood head and shoulders over any other man, and this meant a great deal in the ancient world. He also appeared, at least at the beginning of his reign, to be of a gentle disposition. Saul, however, had one flaw that is fatal in any leader and certainly in a king, and that is he liked to be popular. This eventually led to his downfall.

At first Saul was successful. He united the people and waged successful wars against their enemies. However, he soon came up against what appeared to be an insurmountable challenge in the guise of a giant Philistine named Goliath. The Philistines had massed on Israel's border but instead of engaging the Israelite army directly they challenged the Israelites to present one man who would be able to fight Goliath hand to hand. If the Israelite fighter won then the Philistines would retreat. If Goliath won they would overrun Israel. Goliath was so unnaturally large that there was not a man in all Israel who would agree to fight him. In his desperation, King Saul offered the hand of his daughter Michal to anyone courageous enough to take up the challenge. The challenge was accepted by a most unlikely candidate, a young shepherd boy named David, son of Yishai. In what is one of the best-known stories of the Bible, David cunningly slayed Goliath with a stone from his slingshot but not before crying out to his incredulous adversary: 'You come to fight with armour and weapons, but I come to fight with the help of God.' David became a national hero overnight and, as promised, was given Michal's hand in marriage.

The happy story should have ended there, but it didn't. At first Saul was only too happy to listen to the crowds proclaim his young son-in-law a hero; but his initial joy soon gave way to jealousy and suspicion. How soon would it be before the people exchanged him for this youthful figure? His dark thoughts gave way to erratic behaviour when, one night as David was playing the harp for the king, Saul threw his spear at him and missed. Thus began a dark and painful chapter in the lives of both men, with David on the run and the tormented Saul hot in pursuit. On more than one occasion David tried to reach out to his tormented father-in-law to convince him of his loyalty. These overtures calmed Saul temporarily, only to give rise to greater fury and suspicion in the long term.

David was not Saul's only problem. His fate was cast years earlier, when he very publicly disobeyed God. The occasion involved a battle against the army of Agag, King of Amalek.

The Amalekites were the sworn enemies of the Israelites. In fact, it was the Amalek nation that first attacked the Israelites generations earlier during their sojourn in the desert. Saul was instructed by God through the prophet Samuel not to leave a soul alive and to destroy the Amalekites and everything belonging to them, including their cattle. After a victorious battle his soldiers expressed their disappointment at the loss of the spoils of war. In the hope of remaining popular with his men Saul made the fateful mistake of not destroying the spoils as Samuel had instructed him. When Samuel heard of this he reprimanded Saul in the harshest of terms. 'You might think of yourself as insignificant,' he told the errant king, 'but you are a leader of God's people.' The punishment for disobeying God would be that he would lose his kingdom to another. There is little doubt that this curse played on Saul's mind as he watched David grow in popularity.

Saul's eventual demise came at the hand of his old adversaries, the Philistines. Always in the background, they once again massed their troops against Saul's armies. The king decided to lead his men into battle, and there on the heights of Gilboa he was slain.

David, during his time as a fugitive, garnered enough support and men to be taken seriously as a contender for the throne, and so after Saul's death David was declared King of Israel. Ascending to the throne did not make David's life any easier; in fact in many ways it only made it more difficult. While David is regarded as the greatest King of Israel, nothing came easily to him and he struggled throughout his life. He was constantly fighting Israel's enemies. He had to face down numerous rebellions, twice from his own sons. His family life was complex and he did not seem to have much joy from his children; one was killed and another raped. The one thing that brought him comfort was composing hymns; the Book of Psalms is attributed to him. The Talmud imagines King David rising at midnight to the sound of the wind blowing through his harp and sitting up until daybreak composing his beautiful psalms. It is said that in the Book of Psalms one can find every human emotion possible, from desperation and fear to intense joy and love. This is because the principal composer of the psalms, King David, himself experienced all these emotions. There is hardly an occasion, whether joyful or sad, that could not be expressed by a psalm.

David was the first to be in a position to build God's Temple on Mount Moriah in Jerusalem. From the time of Joshua's conquest the Israelites had not established a permanent Temple in Israel. This is essentially because they did not have control of Jerusalem, which had been a Jebusite stronghold until David's conquest. They did, however, erect a makeshift tabernacle at Shilo, which, although it remained there for some considerable time, was never meant to be the permanent resting place of God. It was only after David had secured his throne and his borders that he turned his mind to building God's house. Yet, for all David's passion and excitement for the project, God would not allow him to go ahead with it. God acknowledged David's sincerity and commitment but explained to him that as a man of war with blood on his hands he could not erect the house of God, which was to be a house of peace. That task, explained God, would fall to David's son, the next King of Israel, who thanks to David's lifetime of struggle would never have to wage war or struggle himself. That king would be Solomon.

Solomon was only twelve years old when his father died, and he almost did not make it on to the throne. Adoniya, Solomon's half-brother, had long harboured the desire to succeed his father David. Seeing that David, now elderly and ill, had still not appointed a successor, he drew around himself many leading military and political figures including David's loyal general, Yoav, and fixed a time and place for his coronation ceremony. The prophet Nathan heard about the plot and swiftly enlisted the help of BatSheva, Solomon's mother. Together they informed David of the rebellion and urged him to take control of the situation by declaring young Solomon his successor. David heeded their call and in his last act of power appointed Solomon his successor. Word of this got out and the rebellion quickly fell apart. Shortly thereafter David passed away, but not before instructing Solomon to be true to God and his Torah.

Shortly after Solomon ascended to the throne God appeared to him in a dream, offering to grant any wish the young monarch might have. Solomon knew exactly what he wanted and asked God to grant him unparalleled wisdom so that he might rule his people justly. So begins the reign of the wisest king who ever lived. One of the better-known stories in the Bible recounts how shortly after this dream Solomon had the opportunity to demonstrate his wisdom. Two distraught women clutching a baby appeared before the young king, each one claiming that she was rightful mother and that the other was lying. Solomon's courtiers are baffled by the case since both women seem equally distraught and it is by no means apparent who is telling the truth and who is lying. The young king requests that a sword be brought. 'What are you doing?' asks one of the mothers through her tears. 'It's very simple,' explains Solomon, 'since no one can be certain who is the true mother, it is only fair and equitable that we cut the baby in half for you both to share.' 'Yes, that's a great idea,' cries the other woman. 'That way we both have something.' 'No, wait!' shouts the first. 'Give him to my rival but whatever you do please do not kill him!' The king then sheathes the sword, saying: 'You are the rightful mother. Only a true mother would sooner endure the pain of giving up her child than to see any harm befall him.'

This story and other similar ones gradually made their way around the region, and neighbouring rulers in awe of the young king sent tribute to Jerusalem. Eventually news travelled as far as distant Sheba, and the queen of that land made the long journey to Jerusalem to meet the king herself. One of the most fruitful relationships Solomon made was with Hiram, King of Tyre. So awed was Hiram by Solomon that when it came time for Solomon to build the Temple it was Hiram who assisted him by contributing both lumber and thousands of labourers from his own country.

Like his father, Solomon was a poet. At least three biblical works are attributed to him, Ecclesiastes, Proverbs and Song of Songs. It is said that the passionate Song of Songs was written in his youth, the wise and insightful Proverbs in his middle age and the searing and cynical Ecclesiastes in old age.

The Talmudic rabbis looked upon Solomon's reign as the apex of Israel's glory; secure in its borders, prosperous, respected by its neighbours and, crucially, devoted to the service of God in His Temple in Jerusalem. As with most things in life, it was too good to last. Unfortunately, Solomon's son and successor, Rechavam, had neither his grandfather's courage nor his father's wisdom; but that belongs to our next chapter.

797–423 BCE – the Divided Kingdom

Rechavam was young, impatient and arrogant. One of his first acts as monarch was to get rid of his father's counsellors, who had advised the inexperienced king to rule with a soft touch in order to gain the people's trust and love. Instead, he followed the advice of his young friends, who urged him to rule with an iron fist so as to earn the people's fear and respect. The result of this miscalculation was that the northern tribes (that is all the tribes except Judah and Benjamin in the south) rebelled against his rule and appointed their own king, Jeroboam ben Nevat. Initially, at least, the break was somewhat tempered by the fact that the northern tribes made regular pilgrimage to the Temple in Jerusalem, the seat of the southern kingdom. After a few years Jeroboam, concerned that he might lose power, put a stop to this and banned any travel to the southern kingdom. As for the pilgrims, he erected two giant golden calves as idols for the people to worship instead.

A word about idol worship in the Divided Kingdom is necessary here. It might strike the reader as odd that the monotheistic Israelites should turn so quickly from God and be tempted with idolatry. It might also strike the reader that Jeroboam's choice of idol, a golden calf, conjuring up images of a similar idol in the desert all those years ago, is particularly perverse. Idolatry was indeed rife during this period, and while it is difficult to enter into the mind of anyone who would choose to worship a statue of gold, we must accept that not all idolaters were fools. There must have been something overwhelmingly attractive that they found difficult to resist.

Perhaps one way of looking at it is to see idolatry as a means of exerting control over one's life. Everyone likes to feel in control of their destiny. Whether we obsessively follow the weather forecasts or the stock market we display that same human need to exert some level of control in our otherwise unpredictable lives. It is a rare person who has sufficient faith in God not to be troubled by the uncertainties of life. Similarly, the ancient idolaters believed that through the worship of particular deities they could pacify or stimulate otherwise unpredictable phenomena such as rainfall or fertility. The idolatrous urge is the same as it always has been; only contemporary man has found more sophisticated idols to worship than his predecessors.

The rest of this period can be described as a litany of battles and rivalries between the two kingdoms and between the Divided Kingdoms and their external enemies, Egypt and, later, Assyria. The familiar repeat patterns we saw during the period of the judges plays itself out here again. The Israelites turn their back on God, God in turn abandons them to their enemies, the Israelites realize the error of their ways and repent only to start the whole process all over again. Towards the end of this period the pattern seems to accelerate into a downward spiral where idolatry and corruption are predominant and moments of clarity and repentance are few and far between.

Then, into this dismal period of Jewish history, enter some of the most inspired spiritual leaders that ever lived. These were the prophets sent by God to rebuke His people and urge them to repent. No prophet willingly chose his role. They were chosen by God and reluctantly pressed into His service. They came from all walks of life: Isaiah was an aristocrat, Jeremiah, a priest, Amos a tender of sycamore trees. What they all had in common was an unswerving commitment to the truth and to speak God's words to rich and poor without fear. This was no easy task. Some prophets, such as Elijah, openly defied the king by exposing his corrupt and idolatrous practices. So unwelcome was this exposure that Elijah had to flee for his life. Others, like Jeremiah, were called on by God to give political messages that were not pleasant to hear. In Jeremiah's case it was to submit to the yoke of Babylon, when conventional wisdom was to forge an alliance with Egypt. All the prophets decried what they saw as the exploitation of the poor and weak by the rich and strong. Understandably, none of these messages were popular with those in power and it took courageous men to speak them. The beauty and majesty of the prophets' ethical messages ring true to this day. One can read passages in Isaiah and think he is addressing a greedy multinational company, a corrupt African dictator or a dishonest politician.

Not all the prophecies were doom and gloom. Isaiah describes a brilliant future at the end of days, Jeremiah offers some of the most comforting passages in all of scripture and Ezekiel, a prophet of exile, urges his people not to abandon hope. Like their harsher messages, these too have a deep resonance and meaning for our troubled world today.

Through a series of political blunders and bad alliances the northern kingdom was invaded by the Assyrians. This eventually led to the exile of all ten tribes from the Land of Israel. Since they never resurfaced they are referred to as the ten *lost* tribes. Theories abound as to what became of them. It seems most likely that they assimilated into whatever cultures they had been exiled to and they ceased to be identified as Israelites. Of course, every now and then someone will claim to have discovered one of the lost tribes. Not long ago it was said that a Native American Indian tribe in New Mexico was thought to have been one of the lost tribes because they kindle lights on Friday afternoon as Jews do before the Sabbath. Unfortunately for those who made the discovery, Sabbath candles were introduced as a Jewish practice during the Mishnaic period, some five hundred years after the ten tribes were driven into exile. An interesting by-product of the Assyrian exile of the Israelite (northern) kingdom, though it is unlikely that anyone noticed it at the time, is that from that point onwards the people of Israel would be referred to as Jews, a name originating from the Judaean (southern) Kingdom.

423–349 BCE – destruction of the Temple, Babylonian exile

More than a century had passed since the Assyrian exile of the northern tribes. The great power now looming on the horizon was that of Babylonia. Despite the prophet Jeremiah's call to submit to this great kingdom the Judaean kings believed they could repel its advance. In the end it was as the prophet had foreseen: Nebuchadnezzar, King of Babylonia, unleashed his armies on Jerusalem, razed the Temple, drove thousands into exile and laid all of Judaea to waste.

And yet despite all this, it was not the end of the Jewish people – far from it. In a certain respect it was just the beginning. It was the first time that the Jews were exiled to live under the dominion of another nation, and the challenges inherent in this predicament helped to strengthen and define the Jewish people.

One of the first challenges was how to balance loyalty to the host nation against Jewish nationalism and the hope of one day returning to their land. Jeremiah makes it very clear that although his people must hope and pray for their return to Jerusalem they must make the most of their exile; they must not become a fifth column, warns Jeremiah. They should be loyal citizens and contribute to the betterment of society. In Jeremiah's famous words: 'Seek the peace of the nation to which you have been exiled and pray for her prosperity for in her peace you shall find peace.' This idea, first expressed by

Jeremiah, would eventually give rise to a far-reaching Jewish ethic called *darkei shalom*, literally meaning 'ways of peace'. It calls on Jews to play a full role in the wider society and to work alongside their gentile neighbours to create an atmosphere of peace and goodwill amongst all people.

It is important to note that Jeremiah was not advocating total assimilation into Babylonian society and culture. It was crucial for the Jewish people to remember that while Babylon was now their home, it was only their second home. And while they bore responsibility to contribute to the welfare of their host nation, their highest responsibility was to serve God. This point would be emphasized by two great Diaspora Jewish leaders, Daniel in Babylonia and Mordechai in Persia, whom we will discuss shortly. While the Babylonians were fearsome warriors they were also benign hosts. The Jews rapidly made themselves at home in their new land and even prospered. So successful were they in integrating into Babylonian society that Daniel, a leading scholar and prophet, was chosen by King Nebuchadnezzar to serve amongst his advisors. This of course did not please the older Babylonian advisors at court, and Daniel was slandered before the king and accused of disloyalty. His crime? He had been found praying to God in his room, facing the direction of Jerusalem. At Nebuchadnezzar's orders Daniel was thrown into a lions' den, but remained unscathed by the ferocious beasts. Nebuchadnezzar quickly came to the realization that this was a holy man who served the all-powerful God of Israel. Daniel was henceforth permitted to follow his conscience in religious matters.

The Daniel story is important in that it counterbalances Jeremiah's call for good citizenship. It teaches that there is an important difference between civic and religious matters. A Jew is bound to observe and respect the law of the land, but only insofar as it does not interfere with his religious beliefs. Daniel knew that he lived in a pagan society and that by worshipping the God of Israel he was breaking the law. But it was a price he was willing to pay, since the alternative was unacceptable. Daniel is one of the few figures in the Bible to engage in civil disobedience in matters of conscience. His message is an important one and it must have resonated with the people of his time as they tried to balance their dual identity as Jews and as Babylonians.

Empires come and go, and before long the great Babylonian Empire gave way to an even greater power, the Persians, under Darius I. After Darius' death his successor, Cyrus, gave the Jews permission to return to Jerusalem and rebuild the Temple. Over 40,000 Jews returned, but the vast majority remained behind. Exile had become comfortable for them and they were not keen on uprooting their families and starting life all over again in what had become a desolate land. While this may strike the reader as quite remarkable, there is a parallel today. The State of Israel has been in existence since 1948 and any Jew who desires to immigrate is offered full citizenship. Yet the vast majority of Jews continue to live in the Diaspora. Some argue that it is almost sinful to remain in the Diaspora when living in Israel is such a real possibility. Others argue that this judgement is unfair and that it is perfectly acceptable for Jews to live wherever they choose and it is important for them to work and contribute to wider society. It is a heated argument, which has been going on since the time of Cyrus; and it appears to be no closer to resolution after all these years.

Unfortunately, after only one year, Cyrus, under pressure from the Samaritans living in Israel, halted the construction of the Temple. Building was resumed one generation later under the reign of Darius II when the first exile, known as the Babylonian exile, had come to a close.

It was during the period of the Babylonian exile that the story of Purim occurred. After the death of Cyrus, Ahasuerus (Xerxes) became ruler of the Persian Empire. According to the Book of Esther, Ahasuerus had an evil advisor named Haman, who plotted to annihilate all the Jews in the empire. In a complex plot Ahasuerus marries Esther, a Jewish girl, who conceals her religious identity from her husband. The plot thickens and then comes to a dramatic close when at the last possible moment Esther reveals her true identity to the king. Haman is killed, the decree is overruled and Haman is replaced by Esther's uncle Mordechai, a venerated Jewish sage.

As with Daniel, Mordechai stands out as the loyal Jew throughout. While others are keen to assimilate, Mordechai remains committed to God and serves as the people's moral conscience throughout the story. It is a fascinating tale and in a sense a commentary on exile where the Jew often assumes a dual identity, where things are never quite as they seem and life is precarious. Although God's name is not mentioned once in the entire book, it is evident that it is He alone who turns the plot; an important and comforting thought for the Jew in exile.

349 BCE–CE 70 – the Second Temple period

The Temple was rebuilt under the guidance of Ezra, a leading Jewish sage who led a contingent of Jews back to Jerusalem. He was later joined by another sage, Nehemyah, and together they raised the standard of Jewish observance, which had slipped considerably during the years of exile.

The Persian Empire gave way to the Greek Empire, and the Land of Israel was conquered by the armies of Alexander the Great. Rabbinic attitudes were positive towards Alexander. There is even a Jewish legend that tells of Alexander riding to Jerusalem, where he is stopped in his tracks by Simon the High Priest wearing his priestly vestments. Alexander dismounts in respect and tells his entourage that it is the image of this very priest that appears to him in his dreams before each battle, promising him victory.

The legend goes on to tell how Alexander entered Jerusalem in peace and how he requested that a statue of himself be erected in the Holy Temple. The rabbis did not want to offend Alexander, but, equally, to erect a statue of a human being in God's Temple was out of the question. So in a diplomatic stroke of genius they offered in exchange for the statue that every Jewish baby boy born that year be named Alexander in the emperor's honour. Alexander liked the idea and the rabbis kept their promise. However one judges the historical accuracy of this story, one thing is true beyond any doubt: that Alexander is a Jewish name. In fact, it has been a Jewish name for so long that it even has a Yiddish diminutive – the name Sender, a popular Yiddish name, is short for Alexander.

After Alexander's death his empire was divided up amongst his generals, giving rise to the Ptolemaic dynasty in Egypt and the Seleucid dynasty in Syria. Both fought over the Land of Israel, which lay in between the two countries. In the year 198 BCE the Seleucid Antiochus III forced Israel from the Ptolemys and turned it into a Syrian province. At first this did not make much difference to the Jews living in Israel, but eventually, under the reign of Antiochus IV, life became exceedingly difficult. The difficulties began when Antiochus unleashed a zealous Hellenization campaign. The purpose was to force the Jews to abandon Jewish culture and adopt Greek culture instead. Ironically, under the relatively benign rule of his predecessors the Jews had themselves begun to adopt aspects of Greek culture, just as their grandparents had shown an interest in Babylonian culture. But Antiochus' campaign succeeded in backing the Jews into a corner by forcing the issue. He was not satisfied with the grafting of Greek culture on to Jewish society: he wanted the Jews to abandon their religion entirely. When his initial overtures were rejected he took strong measures by outlawing the study of the Torah and the observance of various mitzvot, including observance of the Shabbat, circumcision and kosher dietary practices. Ultimately he overran the Temple, pillaging its precious gold vessels and offering a swine on the holy altar. This enraged many Jews, who felt humiliated and threatened, and in one of the most spectacular military episodes in Jewish history, the Maccabees came into being.

The Maccabees (the term is the Hebrew acronym for 'who is like you oh Lord amongst the mighty') were led by a priestly family called the Hasmoneans. Over the course of twenty years they fought a successful campaign and drove off the mighty Seleucids. This, as will be explained in Part 3, gave rise to the festival of Hanukkah. A Hasidic reading of this story sees Antiochus' opposition not to the Torah or mitzvot per se but to the irrational or supra-rational aspects of the Torah and mitzvot. It was not the laws of honouring one's parents, feeding the poor or celebrating Passover as a national redemption festival that disturbed him. Nor was it the various moral and ethical prohibitions against murder and theft. What troubled Antiochus was mitzvot of purely spiritual significance such as Shabbat and circumcision. He refused to believe in the notion that something spiritual could transcend man's own understanding; and it was that aspect of Judaism that he sought to eradicate.

As a pagan himself, Antiochus would have worshipped numerous pagan deities, a practice which appears to us entirely irrational. The Greek gods were in essence fashioned in the image of man, only on a much grander scale. The Greeks imbued their gods with human characteristics and limitations. The notion of a totally transcendent and omnipotent God who calls on man to observe his commands despite their apparent lack of rationale did not match mainstream Greek perceptions. It was precisely this notion that Antiochus despised in the Jews and it was precisely this point of principle and faith that the Maccabees fought so hard against. Whether or not this reading is an accurate reflection of Antiochus' true feelings at the time, it does shed light on the distinctiveness of Jewish life and practice. For the believing Jew not everything in Judaism has to make sense. He will scrupulously practise the mitzvah of eating kosher even though there is no compelling scientific basis for this practice. He does it because it is the will of God and in so doing he connects his finite self with the infinite Creator.

Although the Maccabees were hailed as heroes for having routed the Seleucid Greeks, it was not long before they drew resentment. This is because in the absence of any ruling power they filled the role of de facto Kings of Israel. This was particularly distasteful to the rabbis, who felt that, as the priestly

Hasmoneans were from the priestly caste they had no right to usurp the throne, which was designated for the Davidic dynasty from the tribe of Judah.

Eventually Israel fell under the power of Rome. Rome ruled a vast empire and to facilitate effective governance made use of client kings. These kings, while able to exercise relative power within their kingdoms, were ultimately answerable to Rome. One of the greatest client kings in Israel during this period was Herod, known as Herod the Great. Herod, a non-Jew from the Edomite people in the south of Israel, was as ambitious and ruthless as he was mad. Despite murdering scores of people, including his own family members, he is credited with entirely rebuilding the Temple in Jerusalem. Acknowledging his debt to Rome, he placed an enormous golden eagle (the symbol of Rome) at its entrance. The famous western wall (or Wailing Wall as it is sometimes called) that still stands in Jerusalem is the last remnant of this once magnificent Temple.

Life was not pleasant under Roman rule, and brought a rebellious spirit. The Romans, paranoid about rebellion, took even harsher measures to prevent uprisings happening. So began a vicious circle of rebellion and harsh reprisals that steadily worsened.

The problem amongst the Jews was the lack of unity. Various rebel groups competed with each other. In addition, the elder and wiser rabbis argued against rebellion altogether. They understood too well the power of Rome and realized that any rebellion would be short-lived and would bring in its wake further Roman reprisals. Their advice was to submit to the power of Rome and sit it out. So long as they were able to maintain their religious life there was no point in upsetting their masters. Unfortunately, the rebels would not listen to reason. In the end they provoked Rome to a showdown that could only have one result: the mighty General Vespasian was called on to destroy the rebellion. Having made headway in the north of Israel, Vespasian was then replaced by Titus, who ultimately destroyed the Temple and drove the Jews into exile.

So began the longest of exiles, the Roman exile as it has become known. It would be another 2,000 years before the Jews would return to their land as a sovereign nation in 1948, with the foundation of the State of Israel. Although, from a religious point of view, the State of Israel is only the beginning of the end of exile, the definitive end of the Roman exile will occur only when the messiah comes and the third Temple is rebuilt in Jerusalem.

Whereas Judaism makes no attempt to know the mind of God – and it would be facile to explain the cause of every catastrophe – the Talmudic rabbis attributed the destruction of both Temples to specific sins committed by the Jews. The sins that brought about the destruction of the first Temple by the Babylonians are said to be bloodshed, idolatry and adultery. The sin that caused the destruction of the second Temple by the Romans was simply baseless hatred amongst people. This last comment can be understood in a very practical sense. The Jews lost to the Romans because of their infighting and factions. Had they united under the leadership of the sages and submitted to Roman domination, the Romans would presumably never have bothered with them. Yet the comment can also be understood on a deeper level. Respect for one's fellow is the basis of any decent society. Once that fails society loses its purpose and simply disintegrates.

The Talmud also recounts that in the aftermath of the destruction and exile there were voices in the Jewish community that advocated a complete withdrawal from life and its pleasures. They called for a ban on drinking wine, eating meat and even on marrying and bringing up families. In essence they were prepared to die out, mourning their great loss. The overwhelming majority of rabbis rejected this defeatist attitude. While they would mourn their loss intensively on the anniversary of the Temple's destruction (on the ninth of the Hebrew month of Av) and would keep it in the forefront of their minds always, they still believed in the future. They argued for life to resume as normal, for Jews to take pleasure in God's world and, crucially, to marry and bring up families. It is largely because of the optimism and courage of these rabbis that the Jewish people physically survived throughout the long and dark exile.

As for the Jewish people's spiritual survival, that was the result of the vision of one man, the great sage Rabbi Yochanan ben Zakai. The Talmud recounts how, during the Roman siege of Jerusalem, Rabbi Yochanan ben Zakai smuggled himself out of the city walls and proceeded to the encampment of General Vespasian. Upon meeting the general, the rabbi greeted him with the words 'Hail Caesar'. The general explained that he was in fact not the caesar but merely one of the caesar's generals. No sooner had he finished explaining this to the rabbi when a breathless messenger appeared to inform Vespasian that the caesar had died and that he was being recalled to Rome to take his place.

Realizing at once that the old man before him was no fool, he granted him three requests. Rabbi Yochanan ben Zakai asked that, despite the terrors that lay in store for his people, the Roman must promise to preserve the descendants of the house of David; that he provide a physician to heal one Rabbi Tzadok (an elderly and saintly rabbi who made himself ill fasting for the sake of Jerusalem); and, finally, that he provide a refuge at Yavneh for the scholars and their disciples. One can imagine the Roman's surprise at these mild requests. Needless to say, he granted them.

Why did the courageous rabbi not demand more? Why did he not ask Vespasian to spare the Temple, Jerusalem even? Rabbi Yochanan knew that this was an impossibility. They were living on borrowed time. What he chose to do was to establish and protect the future spirituality of his people. This he did by establishing Yavneh. By ensuring that the teaching of Torah would never cease and that one generation would transmit to the next all that it knew he secured the spiritual future of Judaism through the long exile ahead.

70–475 CE – the Talmudic era

Rabbi Yochanan ben Zakai's request bore fruit: in the aftermath of the Temple's destruction and the banishment of the
Jews from Jerusalem, the academies of learning became the
central focus of the nation. It was during this period that the
Mishnah was formulated. Up to this point there was a very
clear demarcation between what is called the written Torah
and the oral Torah (see pp. 20–3.), which, as its name implies,
was transmitted only orally. During this period a major change
took place with the transcription of the Mishnah (see p. 248)
and the Talmud (see pp. 23–5.) Banished from Jerusalem,
Jewish scholarship moved to the town of Yavneh, and it was
here that the leading rabbinic sage, Rabbi Gamliel, presided
over the supreme rabbinic court known as the Sanhedrin,
which served as the last vestige of Jewish autonomy.

Rabbi Gamliel's position as president of the Sanhedrin,

The Sanhedrin

The Sanhedrin is the name of the supreme rabbinic court. During
the Temple period this court comprised seventy-one scholars
who would sit in a special stone chamber in the Temple precinct.
There were many smaller courts throughout the land, with a
minimum number of three judges each. These were called Battei
Din (sing. Bet Din) and their power extended to monetary cases
only. A capital case would be brought before a minor Sanhedrin
consisting of twenty-three judges. The Great Sanhedrin of
seventy-one judges served primarily as a legislative body, debating and producing Jewish law. It would also judge exceptional
trials, such as that of a king or false prophet. The president of the
Great Sanhedrin carried the title of Nasi, meaning 'prince' in
Hebrew. His deputy was known as the Av Bet Din, meaning
'father of the court'. While originally the Sanhedrin had great
power within Jewish society, it began to weaken with the Roman
conquest of Israel in the first century, when it lost the right to try
capital cases. Today, while there is no Jewish Sanhedrin, every
major Jewish community has a rabbinical court called a Bet Din
to deal with family and business law. Rabbinical courts have not
had the power to try capital cases for over 2,000 years.

otherwise known as the Patriarch or *Nasi* in Hebrew, was an inherited one. It went back to his grandfather Hillel the Elder, the first Patriarch, who assumed the position by virtue of his piety and scholarship. He was also chosen because his family claimed direct descent from King David. Thus, the position was seen as an extension of Davidic rule and as such it was passed on from father to son for almost four centuries. It was during this period of rupture and flux that Rabbi Gamliel asserted his authority to impose uniformity of Jewish law, practice and prayer. It was he who commissioned the first uniform text for daily Jewish prayer and insisted that it be adopted by all Jews. He also insisted that his calculations as to when the Jewish festivals fell be adhered to by all.

This was rather complicated, since Jewish festivals follow a lunar cycle and there could be different interpretations as to when the cycle begins. Rabbi Gamliel would not tolerate a multiplicity of views that led some to observe a particular festival on certain day while others would observe it on a different day. So insistent was he that he forced his deputy, Rabbi Joshua, to violate publicly the date that he calculated to be Yom Kippur because it conflicted with his own calculation as to when that holy day ought to fall. Rabbi Gamliel's harsh methods were resented by many of his colleagues, but his integrity and vision were never called into question. With hindsight Judaism owes him a great debt: he offered strong and confidant leadership when Judaism was at one of its weakest points. So influential was he that to this day the prayers he commissioned are at the centre of the Jewish service.

The decades that followed were extremely trying for the Jews in Israel. In 117 the Emperor Hadrian came to power. At first he treated his Jewish subjects in Israel rather well. He even promised to rebuild Jerusalem and the Holy Temple. For some unknown reason, his policies towards the Jews gradually began to change, however. Eventually his reign became repressive and cruel, where, not unlike Antiochus of the previous section, he outlawed most forms of Jewish practice and the study of the Torah.

This led the Jews to revolt, under the leadership of the charismatic warrior Bar Kosibah. Rabbi Akiva, who believed that Bar Kosibah was the messiah who would redeem his people from the oppression of Rome, nicknamed him Bar Kochba, meaning 'Son of a Star'. At first the revolt was very successful. Bar Kochba and his rebel army even managed to force the tenth legion to evacuate Jerusalem. Ultimately, though, the rebels were no match for the power of Rome, and three and a half years after it began the revolt was brutally crushed. The aftermath brought harsh reprisals from the Romans, and many Jewish leaders were tortured and executed, including Rabbi Akiva.

Towards the end of the second century the condition of the Jews in Israel improved considerably. The leading rabbi at the time was Rabbi Gamliel's grandson, Judah, known as 'Rabbi Judah the Patriarch' or simply 'Rabbi'.

It was Rabbi Judah who redacted the Mishnah, although the Mishnaic material had been accumulating for several decades. Jewish tradition records that Rabbi Judah enjoyed especially warm relations with a Roman Antonine emperor. It is hard to know for certain if this related to Pius Antoninus (86–161) or Marcus Aurelius (121–180). Some suggest it may have been Caracalla (198–217), who was a known Judaic sympathizer. Others suggest it may have been Alexander Severus (222–235).

This was a time of prosperity and economic growth for the Jews of Israel, which was reflected in the regal manner in which Rabbi Judah conducted his court. Jewish tradition looks back fondly on this period as one that, at least temporarily, reinstated some of the lost glory of the house of David when Jews were sovereign in their own land.

After Rabbi Judah's death a rift developed between his descendants who inherited the title and position of 'Patriarch' (a position formally recognized by the Romans) and the leading rabbinical scholars, represented by the Sanhedrin. The rabbis felt that the Patriarch exercised too much power, and they set about curtailing it.

The position of Patriarch continued to pass to the descendants of Rabbi Judah until the beginning of the fifth century, when it was abolished by the Romans.

Chapter 8

THE MIDDLE AGES TO
THE MODERN ERA

475–1038 CE – the age of Jewish scholarship in Babylonia
Jewish life in Palestine gradually began to decline and the
centre of gravity of Jewish scholarship moved to Babylonia,
which by now had become a great centre of Torah learning.
Under the relatively benign rule of the Persians Jewish life and
culture began to flourish. The Jewish community was treated
with respect by the Persians to the extent that they granted
them a form of self-rule – a sort of state within a state. The
political leader of the Jewish community was known as the
exilarch. The exilarchs were always chosen from the descendants of the Davidic family, and their office, upheld with much
pomp and ceremony, was seen as the last vestige of Jewish
royalty.

The other type of Jewish leader that emerged during this
period was the *gaon*, an honorific title, which translates as 'his
glory'. To be called a gaon one had to be the head of one of the
great academies of learning, the *yeshivot*. In an ideal world this

system of dual leadership, political and spiritual, should have worked well. This was not always the case. Particularly towards the end of this period there were occasions of major tension and controversy as exilarchs and gaonim clashed with each other over issues of power and authority.

It was during this period that study of the Talmud gave way to the writing of Jewish legal works by the gaonim. These primarily took the form of responsa literature, in which the gaon would respond in depth and in writing to a particular religious legal (*halachic*) query. These responses were preserved and served as the bedrock upon which a vast halachic literature was built. An interesting feature of this responsa literature is that the questions were often posed from distant Jewish communities. By this time Jews had spread far and wide from Babylonia to what is today western Europe. By the end of this period there were Jews as far away as North Africa and Spain. The Jewish people were perhaps the world's first global people and they perfected the art of global communication long before anyone else had even understood the term. What this says about the Jews is that despite their dispersion across many lands and cultures they saw themselves essentially as one people. Only this can explain the willingness of a Roman Jew, for instance, to submit to the authority of a sage from Baghdad.

Another important development during this period was the formulation of the first *Siddur* (prayer-book) by Rav Amram Gaon in the ninth century. While the basic structure of the daily prayers appears already in the Talmud, it seems that for the most part the prayers were committed to memory. That is why each service was led by a *chazzan* (cantor), someone himself fluent enough to recite the prayers out loud from memory. All those who could not pray for themselves would listen to the chazzan's prayers and respond Amen at the appropriate places, thus fulfilling their obligation of daily prayer.

Rav Amram not only fleshed out these prayers but he crucially committed them to writing, producing the Jewish people's first prayer-book. Although from a practical point of view the dissemination of the Siddur made the chazzan redundant, it was decided that the chazzan should continue to read the prayers aloud after the public had finished theirs. There are a number of reasons for this, the simplest being that the chazzan is required to pace the service so that it remains a communal prayer and not just a group of individuals gathered together reading prayers at their own pace.

It is important to point out here that while of extreme importance, Rav Amram's Siddur is not the only, nor the definitive, prayer-book. The unity of Diaspora Jews and their deference to the Babylonian sages did not preclude them developing their own distinct customs and orders of prayer. While the basic structure of Jewish prayer remains the same (it is, after all, recorded in the Talmud) the wording and often the order of particular prayers varies from place to place. Thus today, there are at least four prayer rites, the Italian, the Ashkenazi, the Sefardic and the Nusach Sefard, which, not to be confused with the much older Sefardic rite, only really developed in the eighteenth century. What is often confusing to the uninitiated is that each of these four branches of prayer has in its own right led to further variations and numerous prayer-books. All of these, in the end, must be seen as a tribute to Rav Amram Gaon, formulator of the first Siddur.

1038–1492 – the era of the Rishonim (early scholars)

One of the last of the great gaonim, Rav Hai Gaon, passed away in 1038. This accelerated the gradual decline of Jewish scholarship in Babylonia. At the same time, new centres and brilliant scholars arose in the west, in France and Germany (the original Ashkenaz) and Spain (the original Sefard). These scholars are today referred to as the Rishonim.

One of the most remarkable Jewish scholars of this period was Rashi. Rashi, the acronym by which he is universally known today, stands for Rabbi Solomon the son of Isaac. Rashi was born in France and studied under the leading Jewish scholars of his time. An accomplished scholar at a very young age, his greatest gift was an ability to simplify complex matters and to communicate in the most beautiful, elegant and concise prose. Although Rashi was one of the great halachic authorities of his time he is not thought of as much as Halakhicist as a teacher. His great work is a lucid and concise commentary on nothing less than the entire Tanakh and most of the Talmud. It is a task that no scholar had previously undertaken and it changed the way the Talmud and Tanakh have been studied ever since.

Rashi's main concern in his commentary is to elucidate the *peshat* or plain meaning of the text. This is no small feat for as any student of the Torah knows, the peshat is not always obvious. In the context of his search for peshat Rashi draws on his encyclopaedic knowledge of the entire Torah. What is truly remarkable about the author is his humility and intellectual honesty. When in his commentary he is unable to resolve a difficulty, he tells the reader bluntly that he does not know the answer. When a Jewish child is introduced to the Bible Rashi is his first guide and companion, and he remains so as the student progresses through the Talmud. Rashi has so influenced our way of understanding the Bible that we instinctively think about it through his commentary and it becomes difficult to differentiate between the text itself and Rashi's interpretation of it. As for the Talmud, given its cryptic and difficult style, it would be almost impossible to unlock it without Rashi's commentary.

Despite his great gifts Rashi lived a humble life earning his living as a wine merchant and teaching his three daughters (he had no sons) the Torah. His scholarly daughters went on to marry men of great intellectual calibre and their children contributed to Jewish scholarship by producing the Tosafot (literally, additions) commentary on the Talmud. In content and structure the Tosafot is almost the polar opposite of Rashi, introducing as it does a new genre of rabbinic writing.

Unlike Rashi, who is concerned with understanding the

plain meaning of the text at hand, the Tosafot raises complex questions on the text and offers ingenious solutions, often by drawing on many other Talmudic sources. To study the Tosafot is to travel on an intellectual journey. One begins with the Talmudic text as a departure point. A troubling question is raised and, in the context of answering it, the student is introduced to numerous other texts throughout the Talmud. In conclusion the problem is often resolved by discovering fine distinctions that were previously unapparent, or, on occasion, a new principle is established that casts the problematic text in a different light.

So popular were Rashi and the Tosafot and so integral to a proper understanding of the Talmud that when the Talmud was printed it incorporated Rashi and the Tosafot on either side of the text. To this day the layout is the same, consisting of a column of Talmud running down the middle of the page with Rashi's commentary along the inner margin and the Tosafot along the outer margin.

The Tosafot was not written by one man. Although it was started by Rashi's grandchildren, the commentary was not completed by them. That was to take another two hundred years and, when complete, it reflected the work of many rabbis, known as the ba'ale Tosaphot (authors of the Tosafot). These rabbis lived mostly in France, Germany and Italy, although a few lived in England. Sometimes the author of a particular Tosafot is identified, but most often the commentary is presented anonymously, reflecting a collaborative work. One of the most famous of the Tosaphists was Rashi's grandson, Rabbi Jacob, known more commonly as Rabbenu Tam. He is often cited in the work and on many occasions he takes issue with a point in his grandfather's commentary. In Jewish scholarship there can be no greater pleasure than when one's child or grandchild disagrees with one's point of view and presents his own dissenting opinion. This is apparent to any student of Rashi and the Tosafot, and it is a tradition that lives on amongst great Jewish scholars to this day.

It is amazing that Jewish scholarship flourished during this period, since shortly before Rashi's death the First Crusade swept through and shattered the Jewish communities of western Europe. This crusade, which was inspired by Pope Urban II who in 1096 called on the faithful to liberate the Holy Land from the Muslims, massacred entire Jewish communities along the way: the hardest hit were those in Germany; Worms, Cologne and Mainz, although many other communities, including some in France, also fell to the marauding crusaders.

It was during this tragic period that the concept of *kiddush hashem* (sanctification of God's name) was widely put into practice. This concept had been formulated during the Hadrianic persecutions in the second century. At that time the rabbis were faced with an unenviable dilemma. The Romans under the Emperor Hadrian had cracked down on Jewish life, outlawing the performance of mitzvot and the study of the Torah under pain of death. The questions the rabbis had to answer were these: what is more important, keeping the Torah or staying alive? May one abandon the mitzvot if the alternative is to die? In this context, are some mitzvot more important than others?

After debating this thoroughly the rabbis came to the conclusion that the preservation of life is paramount even if it means temporarily abandoning the mitzvot. However, even the lofty ideal of preserving life has its limitations. The rabbis set down an exception to their rule, stating categorically that it is forbidden to save one's life at the expense of idolatry, adultery and murder. The rabbis believed that these three cardinal sins were so evil and soul-destroying that a life that committed them would not be worth living. To die for this belief was to commit the holiest act of all, giving one's life for the sanctification of God's name, hence the term kiddush hashem.

After the period of Hadrianic persecutions this whole issue seems to have receded into the margins of Jewish life. It was the period of the crusades, beginning in the eleventh century, that once again turned it into an extremely unfortunate and relevant issue. Accounts from this period inform us that many Jews gave their lives for the sanctification of God's name rather than submit to the baptismal font. In recognition of their faith and courage, these martyrs are referred to as the Kedoshim, the holy ones.

In the following centuries countless Jews died for their faith, whether at the hands of future crusades, the Inquisition, the Cossacks or the Nazis. Although they were not always pre-sented with a clear choice of baptism or death, Jewish tradition treats as Kedoshim any Jew who was murdered as a result of being Jewish.

In addition to the crusades this period is also infamous for the blood libel. The first ever recorded blood libel occurred in Norwich, England, in the year 1144, and many more were to follow, not only in that country but across Europe. Eventually the blood libel would extend as far as Damascus, Syria, and as late as the nineteenth century. The basic libel was simple. The Jews were accused of procuring Christian blood for their Passover matzah by murdering a Christian child in the approach to the festival. As outlandish as this libel sounds today, its prosecutors achieved their objective of demonizing the Jews in the eyes of the ignorant Christian population. A Christian child would be murdered and the 'evidence' planted on Jewish property. Local Jewish leaders would have confes-sions tortured out of them and the entire community would be exposed to Christian hoards who would avenge the 'murder' by massacring the defenceless Jews. Time and again the truth of these libels was exposed, but this did little to prevent their happening again in the future.

The Middle Ages was a violent time, particularly for Jews living in Christendom. In 1298 in Germany incessant blood libels finally gave way to wholesale slaughter of the Jews in what has become known as the Rindfleisch massacres. These began when a German knight named Rindfleisch led a mob to massacre the Jewish community of Rottingen. The frenzied mob did not stop there but continued on to other Jewish com-munities in the region. Over the next few months they razed some 150 Jewish communities. When a few years later they had finally spent their fury, as many as 100,000 Jews had been killed. This was a huge blow to Ashkenazi Jewry and, in a sense, it never fully recovered. Some refugees, such as the great German Rabbi Asher ben Yechiel, made their way to Spain. Others made their way east to Poland and further still to Russia, where they brought with them their unique Jewish-German dialect, Yiddish.

While blood libels were increasing and the crusades were sweeping through Ashkenaz, the Jews on the Iberian Peninsula (Sefard) were living in relative tranquillity. Jews there had become assimilated into Spanish culture and yet managed to retain their distinct identity as Jews. It was in Spain that the balance between Jeremiah's call to civic responsibility and Daniel's example of religious commitment was achieved. It was into this culture that one of the greatest Jewish scholars was born. Moses Maimonides (son of Maimon) was born in Cordoba in the year 1135. He was to become esteemed as a physician, philosopher and halachist. Eventually his family moved from Spain and he settled in Fostat (now Cairo) in Egypt, where he earned his living as a physician and spent every moment of his spare time writing his great Jewish legal code.

Unlike many of the Ashkenazi rabbis who immersed themselves in Torah study to the exclusion of all else, Maimonides was also well versed in secular science and philosophy. It is a tribute to his brilliance that he was able to integrate all his learning and to produce a philosophical system of Judaism. He wrote this system in Arabic, in a book he called the *Guide for the Perplexed*. In this work he tries to align the belief and practices of Judaism with neo-Aristotelian thought. Apparently many young Spanish Jews were absorbed by the Arab rediscovery of classical philosophy. However, one of the problems with philosophical and rational enquiry is that it can undermine questions of faith, and it seems the young Jews of Maimonides' acquaintance were not immune to this.

Maimonides sought to address this problem with his *Guide*, in which he argues strenuously that matters of faith are not necessarily opposed to rational enquiry.

While to those with an interest and understanding of philosophy this was a most welcome and respected work, those who were suspicious of philosophy deemed Maimonides' work heretical. After his death a controversy raged between his supporters, who believed in subjecting the Torah to philosophical enquiry, and his detractors, who believed that any philosophical project was a waste of time, if not outright heretical. One of the main battlelines between these two camps was whether the Torah should be studied exclusively or whether it should be combined with secular study.

This debate continues to pervade the Jewish world. It crops up now and again in slightly different permutations but it is essentially the same debate. Today the lines are drawn between the Ultra Orthodox and the Modern Orthodox. The Ultra Orthodox believe that any time spent away from Torah study is a waste of time. They are also concerned, as were those of Maimonides' day, that secular studies will give rise to doubts and questions that the religiously committed can ill afford. The Modern Orthodox believe that one's understanding of the Torah can be deepened and enhanced through the lens of secular studies, particularly the humanities and that, in the end, such exposure only strengthens one's faith and religious commitment.

While Maimonides' *Guide* was a ground-breaking study in the philosophy of Judaism, his other great work, the Mishnah Torah, became central to the development of Jewish law. Until this point there had been no comprehensive code of the entire body of Jewish law. The Talmud, as described earlier, is the basis of all Jewish law but is not itself a code – the Talmud reads as a transcript of the various debates regarding Jewish law but it rarely tells us what the definitive outcome is. To extract this information from the Talmud one must be fluent in its entirety and well acquainted with the principles of Jewish legal jurisprudence. Needless to say, not many can claim such expertise, and so there is a need for a comprehensive halachic code that extracts the final law from the primary sources. One such code did pre-exist Maimondes, written by Rabbi Isaac Alfasi in the eleventh century. It was structured so that it followed the Talmudic tractates, extracting the law from each discussion. Yet while it was, and remains, an important work it has its shortcomings, the most important of which is that it is not very accessible to the layperson. To read Alfasi one has to have some training in the study of the Talmud. Also, while extremely ambitious, Alfasi did not cover the entire body of Jewish law and succeeded in writing on only some of the Talmudic tractates.

Maimonides produced a massive halachic code that spanned the entire range of Jewish law. In addition to its scope Maimonides' code differed from Alfasi's in its structure and style. Unlike Alfasi, Maimonides did not organize his code around the order of Talmudic tractates. Being a systematic thinker, Maimonides created his own structure from scratch: each of its fourteen books was broken down into sections, each section into further chapters and each chapter into individual laws. Whereas the Talmud begins with the laws of blessings and daily prayers, Maimonides starts his code with the basic principles of the Torah, ethical behaviour and the laws of repentance. The writing is unique and in extremely accessible Hebrew, in contrast to the more opaque rabbinic style of Alfasi.

Finally, and remarkably, he does not cite his sources. In fact in his introduction he writes that upon reading his work the reader will never have need to consult any other book to know the law. What he appears to have done is make his code as user-friendly as possible, with the intelligent layman in mind. To have cited copious sources would only have detracted from the work itself. While the layman no doubt appreciated the gesture, Maimonides' rabbinic colleagues were far less enthusiastic. They felt that it was arrogance on his part to record laws in a dogmatic fashion without providing the scholarly community the opportunity to check the sources. Indeed, one of the great challenges of studying Maimonides' code today is to try to locate the sources for his rulings. A number of these have defeated the best minds of the last eight hundred years. No one has yet been able to discover the sources for these rulings and it is unlikely that anyone ever will.

Yet despite the criticism of his lack of documentation very few could criticize his apparent scholarship. The code is a magnificent work and to this day it is unparalleled in halachic literature for its scope and clarity.

Real trouble started for the Jews of Spain in the second half of the fourteenth century, when thousands were massacred in Seville. Despite the prohibition against adopting another faith to save one's life, many of the wealthier Spanish Jews lacked the courage of their convictions. In order to protect their lives and their fortunes they publicly converted to Catholicism, remaining Jews in secret. These crypto-Jews provoked the disdain of both Jews and gentiles. It was in order to snuff out these Marranos (swine), as the Church called them, that the Spanish Inquisition was eventually formed in 1481.

Despite the rising tide of anti-Semitism in Spain many Jews remained there and tried to make the most of their lives. This came to end when in 1492 Queen Isabella expelled all Jews from her land. It is estimated that between 100,000 and 300,000 Jews were expelled. Many made their way to North Africa, Italy, Holland, Turkey and the Holy Land, thus considerably expanding the Jewish Diaspora. Many could not find the courage to start a new life and so remained behind, becoming crypto-Jews under the watchful of eye of the increasingly powerful Inquisition.

One of the leading figures of this period was Don Isaac Abrabanel (1437–1508). Born to a proud Sefardic family he was given a broad secular education and a thorough religious education. He spoke many languages and had considerable talent in the field of finance. He was also an accomplished

Map of Israel

A relief depicting the sack of Jerusalem in 70 CE on the Arch of Titus in Rome.

The Tomb of the Patriarchs in Hebron, the traditional resting place of
Adam and Eve, Abraham and Sarah, Isaac and Rebecca, Jacob and
Leah. It is one of the holiest sites for Jews.

An ancient *Mikveh* (ritual bath) in the ruins of Masada.

After close to 2,000 years of exile, Jewish sovereignty returns to the Old City of Jerusalem, when Israeli troops recapture it from Jordan during the Six Day War on 7 June 1967.

Jews praying at the Western Wall in Jerusalem. The wall, a remnant of the ancient Jewish Temple, is the holiest site in Judaism with the exception of Temple Mount itself.

(above) A family ushering in the Shabbat with the ritual lighting of candles.

THE JEWISH PASSOVER.

(left) An eighteenth century engraving showing a Jewish family celebrating the Passover festival.

(left) A medieval woodcut depicting the sounding of the Shofar on the Jewish New Year, Rosh Hashanah.

(right) The Altneu Synagogue in Prague, the oldest in Europe, built in circa 1270, and said to be the oldest functioning synagogue in the world. On the right hand side of the picture is the Old Jewish Community Council Town Hall with a Hebrew clock on its tower.

(above) The interior of a modern synagogue in Surfside Florida. The grating over the reader's desk is a motif borrowed from a Polish synagogue destroyed in the Holocaust.

A typical scene of a yeshivah (Talmudic academy).
The young men are studying the Talmud and codes of Jewish Law.

A young man celebrating his Bar Mitzvah in Israel by reading from the Torah.

Young men laying Tefillin in preparation for the morning service.

A page of Maimonides'
commentary on the
Mishnah.

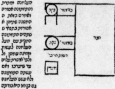

Lying on the desk is a Torah
scroll containing the Five
Books of Moses; Judaism's
holiest article. Standing above
the Torah is a highly decorative
case used for storage and
transport.

Torah scholar with an expertise in the Bible, on which he wrote a brilliant commentary which has become one of the great classics of Jewish literature.

Don Isaac served as a financier in the court of Queen Isabella. So valued was his expertise that he was given the right to remain after the 1492 expulsion. Don Isaac, however, chose to follow his people into exile. He spent time in Corfu and Naples, eventually ending up in Venice where he died. Towards the end of his life he wrote a trilogy on the nature of the messiah's arrival. He even set a date for it to happen, so certain was he that glory would be restored to his people. In the end, the date he designated came and went and the messiah was nowhere to be seen. Despite what could only be described as overwhelming disappointment at the messiah's failure to appear on the designated date, he did not die a broken man. He continued to live and practise as a Jew, to write on the Bible and to hope for a brighter tomorrow.

1492–1600 – the codification of Jewish law and the flowering of Kabbala

The result of the Rindfleisch massacres in Germany and the expulsion from Spain was the uprooting of entire communities. This affected not just the socio-economic plight of the Jews but also their religious practice. Each community had over the generations developed its own particular practices, rituals and customs. The order of service in a synagogue in, say, Mainz, was quite different from a service in a synagogue in Barcelona. Similarly, rabbis trained in Germany or France analysed Jewish law differently from the rabbis of Spain, leading them to different legal conclusions. This was acceptable provided there was consistency and unity among the various communities.

All this changed with the events in the fourteenth and fifteenth centuries. Suddenly an Ashkenazi Jew from Bavaria found himself in a Sefardic synagogue in Izmir, Turkey, and a Sefardic Jew from Saragossa found himself living amidst the

Ashkenazim of Amsterdam. What practices should be followed? Who did one turn to for rabbinic rulings? And what if various rabbis in the same community disagreed – whose authority was then binding and whose was not? This is the background to one of the most important Jewish literary projects, the formulation of the Shulchan Arukh.

As mentioned earlier, Alfasi and Maimonides had both written codes of Jewish law. The problem was that Maimonides' code was completed by the beginning of the thirteenth century, and by the sixteenth century Jewish law had developed considerably. Rabbi Jacob ben Asher, a fourteenth-century rabbi, sought to update the Halakhah with his code, called the Tur, meaning 'row', an allusion to the four rows of precious stones in the high priest's breastplate, since the priest was the fount of knowledge and authority in religious matters.

But even the Tur was outdated by the sixteenth century. It was time for a new code to be produced. It was also crucial that this code be accepted universally as the definitive guide to Jewish law, to put an end to the confusion thrown up by disparate communities merging into each other. The man who undertook this great task was Rabbi Yosef Caro (1488–1575), a Turkish Jew of Spanish extraction who eventually went to live in Safed, in northern Israel. Yosef Caro began by considering the structure his work would take. He decided eventually to follow the pre-existing structure of Jacob ben Asher's Tur, which is organized into four sections, each comprising a different area of Jewish law:

1) Daily, Sabbath and festival rituals
2) Dietary laws
3) Marriage and divorce law
4) Business law.

Unlike Maimonides' work, the Tur does not deal with the totality of Jewish law. So for example he did not write about Temple service or the laws pertaining to kings. Yosef Caro began by writing a commentary on the Tur. He envisioned a book that would have at its centre the text of the Tur with his updated commentary running alongside. This commentary, which he called the Bet Yosef (the house of Yosef), is hugely ambitious. It cites the Talmudic sources for each law as well as all subsequent works. In the process he does not just comment on the Tur but develops his own legal positions. The Bet Yosef is necessary reading for any student who wants to understand how the Jewish legal system works and how a definitive law is traced from its earliest source in the Mishnah or Talmud through centuries of rabbinic interpretation.

While Yosef Caro was working on his magnum opus in Safed, a younger contemporary, Rabbi Mose Isserles (1520– 1572) known by his acronym ReMA, in Krakow, Poland, was contemplating a similar work. By the middle of the sixteenth century Jews had prospered in Poland and with prosperity and relative tranquillity came a flowering of great scholarship in the two great centres of Lublin and Krakow. ReMA's own teacher was the famed Rabbi Shalom Shachna of Lublin, a man deeply respected by Jew and gentile alike for his scholarship and piety.

ReMA's father was a wealthy and scholarly man who spared nothing in his child's education. ReMA was not only taught the Torah to the highest level but he was also well versed in languages, science and philosophy. By the time ReMA began work on his super-commentary of the Tur, Yosef Caro was well on the way to finishing his. ReMA meanwhile continued on his project, unaware of the competition from Safed. This state was shattered one day when a traveller brought ReMA a copy of the first section of the Bet Yosef. ReMA was understandably devastated. Not only had the rabbi from Safed pre-empted his project but, in ReMA's own words, he had written it far better than ReMA himself could have done. After days of wondering if there was any way to salvage his work ReMA realized that there was still much that he could contribute to the codification of Jewish law. What he noticed upon closer inspection of Yosef Caro's work is that his methodology was decidedly Sefardic. That is to say, he tended to give weight of opinion to the great scholars of the past. ReMA, however, was taught a different methodology by Shalom Shachna, one that gives weight of opinion to the most recent authorities. This is based on the assumption that these latter scholars would have had the chance to read all the previous literature on the matter and as such, their decision would be better informed.

What ReMA discovered is that while Yosef Caro had written a great work for the Sefardic community it would not be accepted as definitive amongst the Ashkenazi community. Having identified his niche, ReMA continued writing, but less copiously, focusing instead on the areas of difference between Yosef Caro and himself, and in the process setting out the law for Ashkenazi Jews. Rema's commentary, which he called the Darkei Moshe ('paths of Moses', a reference to himself, Moses Isserles), was eventually published alongside the Bet Yosef.

It was not long before Yosef Caro decided to write another work, this time based on his Bet Yosef commentary. While the Bet Yosef was a mine of information for the scholar it was for the most part inaccessible to the layman. This always seemed to be the difficulty with halachic codes: they were either in-depth scholarly works like Alfasi's code or they were written with a broad audience in mind, like Maimonides' code, having to omit sources and discussion. Yosef Caro wanted to achieve both aims without compromising his work, and so he decided to write two separate works. While the Bet Yosef would serve the scholarly community, he would also write an accompanying work in which he would cite only the definitive law in the clearest and most concise of terms. This second work he called the Shulchan Arukh, meaning 'the set table'. The name reflects his hope that the reader would immediately gain access to the practical law without having to delve into the myriad sources, much as a hungry person can immediately sit down to eat at a prepared table. So, according to Yosef Caro, the Shulchan Arukh was to enable the lay person to locate easily whatever relevant law was required and also to serve as a source of review material for the accomplished scholar, who would review the Shulchan Arukh in its entirety at least once a month.

ReMA, in keeping with his agenda to present the Ashkenazi interpretation of Jewish law, wrote glosses on the Shulchan Arukh, which he aptly called the *mapa*, meaning 'tablecloth'. To this day every Shulchan Arukh is printed with ReMA's glosses, which are set into Caro's text with a different font so as to distinguish the two.

The Shulchan Arukh, while extremely popular, was not, at least initially, accepted by all. Yet, by the end of the seventeenth century, it was universally recognized as the definitive code of Jewish law, and, unlike previous works, it can rightly be called the Enduring Code. It remains the most authoritative code of Jewish law, surpassing even that of Maimonides. In fact, although the Bet Yosef is by far the more scholarly of Caro's works, he is best remembered as the author of the Shulchan Arukh.

How did the Shulchan Arukh come to be so authoritative? The answer is, as with so much in life, a matter of timing. It is of course a brilliant work, but so is Maimonides' code. Brilliance alone would not have established the Shulchan Arukh as the Enduring Code. Something else was at work here; there were many other scholars who wrote critical commentary. For some reason, possibly connected to the invention of the printing press, during the sixteenth and seventeenth centuries it became popular for great scholars to write on Jewish law in a new way. Much of this outpouring of literature emerged from Poland, written by the colleagues and disciples of ReMA. Like ReMA they felt it pointless to write a new halachic code from scratch, since Caro had already done so. Instead, they took Caro's code as a point of departure for their own commentaries, which were not entirely uncritical. Many of the writers take issue with the author and marshal sources to support their position. Over time, a second generation of legal scholars arose, who, in turn, wrote critical commentary on the commentators. By the end of the seventeenth century the Shulchan Arukh looked

nothing like its author had intended. Instead of a small reference guide to Jewish law it had become a vast body of work
with as many as a dozen commentaries debating the law. This
is precisely what gave the Shulchan Arukh its broad appeal.
Jews, it has been said, like options, and the newly expanded
Shulchan Arukh afforded them just that. No one rabbi,
however great a scholar he may be, will ever have his views
accepted by all. The beauty of the Shulchan Arukh as it developed is that on each page dozens of views are aired: this makes
it an unparalleled resource for scholars and rabbis researching
and applying the law.

Rabbi Yosef Caro is an interesting character because he
bridged two worlds, the world of Jewish law and the world of
Kabbala, Jewish mysticism. It is rare to find one man equally at
home in both these worlds, since by their very nature they
seem almost incompatible. Law is dry and analytical whereas
Kabbala is rich in poetry and imagination. An example of this
difference can be detected in the very language employed by
the two disciplines. The Talmud in its legal discussions will
draw the reader's attention to a new idea by using the words *ta
shema*, which means 'come and hear'. The Zohar, the most
important Kabbalistic text, employs a different phrase, *ta hazi*,
or 'come and see'. The difference is obvious: the law is something one *discusses*, its arguments and counter-arguments must
be *heard*; the Kabbala is something that one *experiences* and is
to be *seen* with the mind's eye.

The origins of Kabbala are ancient. According to Jewish tradition there are four levels of Torah knowledge. The first is
called *peshat*, which, as we have seen, means the plain or literal
meaning of the text. One must begin with the peshat before
even beginning to contemplate moving beyond onto the next
level. The second level is *remez*, which means hint. This refers
to interpretations of the Torah that are not stated explicitly but
are rather only hinted at in the text. An example of this would
be the verse in Genesis that describes Abraham sitting at the
entrance of his tent when God appears to talk to him. Oddly,

Abraham is sitting while the Almighty is standing. The *remez* is that this hints at the future, indicating that when a Jewish court decides Halakhah they are in God's presence and yet they must be seated while the Almighty stands above them.

The third level of Torah knowledge is *drash*; which can be roughly translated as homiletics. An example of drash is the story of Abraham discovering God at the age of three and having his faith tested by being thrown into a fiery furnace by King Nimrod. Nowhere is this story found in the text of the Bible, yet, as drash, it is an integral part of the Torah. Drash can be tricky. There is an entire literature of drash called Midrash which contains many fantastical tales relating to the Bible. The story of Abraham mentioned above is one, the story of Moses fleeing Egypt and becoming an African king years before he encountered God at the burning bush, is another. The tricky element is that the tales seem so simple and straightforward, but in truth they are not. Only an expert trained in the study of Midrash is able to understand their deeper meaning; and there is always a deeper meaning. Midrash is a form of allegory, and according to Maimonides only a fool would confuse the tale with the message.

The forth and highest level of Torah knowledge is *sod*, meaning 'secret'. Sod is the esoteric dimension of Torah that deals with matters of a higher world. It is concerned with the deepest questions regarding the Creator, the universe and the soul of man. It is this section of the Torah that is also known as Kabbala, meaning 'received tradition'. Unlike the other dimensions of Torah, Kabbala was never taught publicly. One had to be sufficiently well versed in all other aspects of the Torah before embarking on Kabbala. Even then, it was a very private affair passed on from master to disciple, who would in turn *receive* this ancient and secret tradition. The four dimensions *peshat*, *remez*, *drash* and *sod* give rise to the acronym PaRDeS which in Hebrew means an orchard. The orchard of the Torah is one unity, and just as both the written and oral Torah were given at Sinai, so too was the PaRDeS.

There is a story in the Talmud that serves as a warning to the uninitiated against entering the deepest levels of the PaRDeS. The Talmud recounts how four scholars, Rabbi Akiva, Ben Zoma, Ben Azzai and Elisha ben Avuya entered the PaRDeS, meaning that together they delved into the most hidden secrets of the Torah. As a result, Ben Azzai lost his life, Ben Zoma lost his mind and Elisha ben Avuya lost his faith. Of the four scholars, only Rabbi Akiva emerged unscathed. This cautionary tale is the backdrop against which the Talmud warns the masters of sod to exercise extreme caution before initiating prospective pupils.

The Zohar (the Book of Splendor) is the seminal text of Kabbala. It is traditionally ascribed to the second-century Talmudic master Rabbi Shimon bar Yochai, although modern scholars date it to Moses de Leon of thirteenth-century Spain. While Kabbala was taught and studied especially in the thirteenth century, it had a particular resurgence in the sixteenth century, at the time of Yosef Caro. During this period, in the aftermath of the Spanish expulsion of the Jews, many leading Kabbalists were attracted to the city of Safed in northern Israel, gradually turning it into the leading centre for the study of Kabbala. Yosef Caro belonged to this elite circle of leading Kabbalists, which, at this time, included Rabbi Moses Cordevaro (1522–70), Rabbi Shlomo Alkebetz (c. 1500–80) and Rabbi Hayyim Vital Calabrisi (1543–1620). The greatest Safed Kabbalist was Rabbi Isaac Luria (1534–72), known as the AriZal (the Holy Lion), who introduced an entirely new system of Kabbala, which is still called the Lurianic system.

One of the Lurianic innovations is the concept of *Shevirat ha-Kelim* (the shattering of the vessels) and *Tikkun 'Olam* (the repair of the world). This doctrine posits that God created two universes; this one and a previous one. The spiritual core of these universes consists of *Orot* (lights) and *Kelim* (vessels). Light is symbolic of God's creative energy while the vessels are symbolic of the receptacles that receive and harness the energy. In the first universe, which Luria calls Olam ha-Tohu (the world of chaos) the divine light was too intense for the vessels. This resulted in Shevirat ha-Kelim, the shattering of the vessels, and the implosion of that universe. In the second universe, the one we inhabit (called Olam ha-Tikkun), the divine light is much dimmer and thus suited to the limited vessels which, combined, create and sustain the universe. The real twist of this doctrine is that the shattered vessels showered sparks of the earlier light into the new universe, where they have become embedded. It is the purpose of life in this world (the world of repair) to uncover these holy sparks and release them back to their source. This, explains Luria, is achieved through the Torah and mitzvot. Once all the sparks are released and the *Tikkun* (repair) is complete, the messiah will arrive and the world will be redeemed.

An interesting feature of this Lurianic doctrine is the urgency it places on the study of the Torah and the performance of mitzvot. The Torah and mitzvot, according to Luria, are not a private affair between the Jew and God: they are in essence the key to the future redemption of this world and mankind. Every time someone does a mitzvah he is releasing a spark that brings redemption one step closer. This is a remarkable and radical idea, since it changes the very way one thinks about and observes the mitzvot. It also helped to make sense of a turbulent and difficult world, by seeing it as yet unredeemed, but at the same time empowering the Jew actively to change this reality through engagement with the Torah and mitzvot. The message that Jews could play a role in shaping not just their future but the future of the world was radical, bold and intoxicating, particularly to those who were still haunted by the Spanish expulsion.

In addition to the development of the study of Kabbala, the mystics of Safed also created new liturgies and practices. Rabbi Isaac Luria composed his own Siddur. He explained that there are twelve gates to heaven and that originally each of the twelve tribes had a particular prayer rite uniquely suited to their respective gate. As a result of exile and the dispersion, it is no longer certain who belongs to which tribe and thus which rite of prayer is to be used. Luria's Siddur purports to remedy this by incorporating the key elements of each of the twelve rites into one whole. Thus, Luria's Siddur is said to be the key to the thirteenth gate through which the prayers of any worshipper can travel.

One of the better-known rituals that developed in the mystical circle of fifteenth-century Safed was that of Kabbalat Shabbat, a beautiful Shabbat reception ceremony. The ceremony, based on the Jewish tradition that the Shabbat is likened to a queen, welcomes her arrival with song and prayer. In its original form, the mystics, late on a Friday afternoon as the sun began to set, would dress in white and go out into the fields to welcome the Sabbath Queen. They sang six psalms, each representing a day of the past week, and concluded with a seventh psalm in honour of the Shabbat. In due course one of their circle, a Kabbalist named Shlomo Alkebetz, composed a hymn called the Lecha Dodi. The hymn, which is full of longing, welcomes the Shabbat Queen and paints a picture of a world full of tranquillity and holiness, a world in which glory is restored to the Jewish people and to the Holy City of Jerusalem.

> Sanctity of the King, royal city,
> Arise, go forth from your ruined state.
> Too long have you dwelt in the valley of tears
> He will shower compassion on you.
>
> Come, my Beloved, to greet the bride;
> Let us welcome the Sabbath.
>
> Shake off the dust, arise!
> Put on your clothes of glory, My people
> Through the son of Jesse the Bethlehemite
> Draw near to my soul and redeem it.
>
> Come, my Beloved, to greet the bride;
> Let us welcome the Sabbath.

Wake up, wake up,
For your light has come: rise, shine!
Awake, awake, break out in song,
For the Lord's glory is revealed on you.

Come my Beloved, to greet the bride;
Let us welcome the Sabbath.

Do not be ashamed, do not be confounded
Why be downcast? Why do you mourn?
In you the needy of My people find shelter,
And the city shall be rebuilt on its hill.

Come, my Beloved, to greet the bride;
Let us welcome the Sabbath.

Those who despoiled you shall be despoiled,
And those who devoured you shall be far away
Your God will rejoice over you
As a bridegroom rejoices over his bride.

Come, my Beloved, to greet the bride;
Let us welcome the Sabbath.

So powerful was this ceremony that it has made its way into virtually every Jewish community. Although the vast majority of Jews would not proclaim themselves mystics, the Kabbalat Shabbat service has become part of their lives. Today, for practical reasons, the service is conducted in the synagogue, but one can almost imagine those mystics standing robed in white in the fields as the glowing sun dipped behind the mountains.

The Kabbalat Shabbat service has become extremely popular with the younger generation and nowhere is this more true than in Israel. Some young congregations have embellished the service with additional songs and dancing. I recall my first Friday night on sabbatical in Jerusalem. Having heard about a particular synagogue famous for its lively Kabbalat Shabbat services I was eager to witness it for myself. Upon arrival I got chatting to the fellow next to me and in the course of our conversation asked him what time the service would be over. 'If that is the kind of question you ask, you really don't belong here,' he answered. I stayed. The service lasted almost two hours and I returned every week for the rest of my sabbatical.

1600–1700 – Chmelnitzki's pogroms and the false messiah

The relatively safe and prosperous haven that Poland had become for the Jews came to an end in the middle of the seventeenth century. The Polish nobles of the time owned huge swaths of property on which thousands of serfs lived and worked. These nobles required middle men to run their estates and to provide goods and services to the serfs. This role was often filled by Jews, who bought these concessions from the nobles and earned a profit, if they were lucky, selling to the serfs. The problem is that the Jews were sitting on a tinderbox. The Polish nobles had for years been oppressing and humiliating the serfs, particularly in the south-eastern province, known as Ukraine. The Ukrainians, who considered themselves Russian, deeply resented their Polish overlords, whom they saw as conquerors and oppressors. Every now and then small-scale rebellions would break out which the nobles would put down with great force, only sowing the seeds of greater resentment amongst the serfs.

In 1648 tensions came to a head when a petty Ukrainian officer named Bogdan Chmelnitzki gathered around him large numbers of Cossacks and Tartars and began an invasion of Poland to avenge his people. The target of the Cossacks' wrath was of course the nobles, but it was also the Jews, who were seen by the serfs as complicit in their oppression. Although this was untrue, the Jews made a useful scapegoat. Chmelnitzki's Cossacks swept through south-eastern Poland destroying hundreds of Jewish communities. For two years they rampaged through Poland, torturing, forcibly converting and massacring tens of thousands of Jews.

This dark period in Jewish history became known as the years of *Tach* and *Tat* (the Hebrew equivalent of 1648–9). By the time it was over Polish Jewry was crushed.

An event occurred in 1656 that, although apparently almost insignificant against the backdrop of the Chmelnitzki massacres, is nonetheless a very important one. Baruch Spinoza (1632–77), a brilliant young Dutch Jew of Spanish extraction, was excommunicated by the rabbinical court of Amsterdam for heresy because he questioned, amongst other Jewish beliefs, the divine origin of the Torah. Baruch, who then became known as Benedict, continued to live, work and write in Amsterdam as a member of neither the Jewish nor the Christian communities. There were, of course, always small numbers of Jews who exchanged their faith and people for another. However, before Spinoza no one had actually left the Jewish fold in exchange for no faith at all. Throughout the Middle Ages in Europe one was either a Jew or a Christian. There was no possibility of remaining neutral. Putting aside religious beliefs, one had to belong to one community or the other just to survive. Belonging nowhere meant that one was an outcast from all societies, and from a purely social and economic perspective this was untenable. Seventeenth-century Holland was a different environment. In that country a new secular liberal age was dawning and Spinoza, it could be said, was the first secular Jew.

The Dutch rabbis who excommunicated him could never have foreseen the secular Jewish phenomenon of today, when there are numerous Jews who are not religiously committed in the slightest. Many of them may doubt the very existence of God, yet they identify as Jews and remain committed to the welfare of the Jewish people. They give generously to Jewish institutions and take an interest in the cultural development of Judaism and the well-being of the State of Israel. Rabbis these days do not have the power to excommunicate, and even if they did, it is unlikely that they would use it to push any Jew outside the bounds of Judaism. It is far more likely that they would reach out to secular Jews by trying to involve them in Jewish life and practice.

No sooner did the Jewish world emerge from the Khmelnytsky massacres than a new threat appeared on the scene. This took the form of a false messiah who emerged in Turkey. False messiahs were nothing new: as far back as the aftermath of the second Temple destruction there had been the occasional individual who claimed to be the messiah of the Jews and the redeemer of mankind. These false messiahs were for the most part local phenomena and their influence never spread far or lasted long. The actors invariably fell into two distinct categories, the unhinged and the unscrupulous. Their audience consisted for the most part of the unlettered and the simple, who, in dire circumstances, were prepared to believe anything as long as it meant that it would improve their lives.

There is a wonderful story about a simple Jewish peasant who comes home ecstatic from synagogue one Shabbat afternoon.

'Ok already,' says his jaded wife 'what is now?'

'Messiah is coming,' blurted out the man. 'Messiah is coming.'

'Oh and how do you know this? Are you a prophet all of the sudden?' challenges the wife.

'No, I'm no prophet, I heard this directly from the rabbi's mouth. This morning in synagogue he said messiah is coming and we will all return to the Promised Land, isn't that wonderful?'

'Well,' said the wife, 'I hate to put a damper on things but what exactly is so wonderful? We have a nice cosy little house here – what makes you so sure you'll find one in Israel? Besides, our calves are due to give birth in the spring. I don't suppose you think we can take them along to Israel? And what of the cucumber patch we just planted? We'd have to leave that behind as well. And the radishes, and the leeks, oh, and did I mention the chickens?'

All the air went out of the poor man's sails. He sat for a long time in deep concentration. Then with a great big smile he turned to his wife and said, 'You know what, my dear? We have a great and powerful God. He saved us from Pharaoh, he saved us from Hamman, and I'll be damned if he doesn't save us from this terrible messiah as well!'

The false messiah debacle of 1665–76 was altogether different. It lasted much longer than previous examples, spread much wider than ever before and, unfortunately, it caught up in its net not just the simple folk but, at least initially, many a scholar and rabbi as well.

It began in the city of Smyrna, Turkey, in 1626, on the ninth of the Hebrew month of Av (the anniversary of the destruction of both Temples in late summer), when a baby boy was born to Jewish parents of Spanish extraction. They named their child Shabbtai Tzvi, a common Sefardic name at the time. His birthday would later become most significant since the Talmud cites a tradition that the messiah will be born on the ninth of Av, an indication that within destruction are sown the seeds of redemption. Young Shabbtai was a most gifted child, precocious, intelligent and blessed with an abundance of charisma. He was also almost certainly manic depressive. Early on he began assiduously to study Kabbala and attracted a circle of devoted followers.

Nothing at this point seemed out of the ordinary, and his sphere of influence grew within the community. This came to an end when in the year 1648 (the same year the pogroms were raging through south-east Poland) he deliberately pronounced God's unspoken name before the Torah in the synagogue. This was seen as a display of blasphemy, and he was quickly excommunicated and exiled by the city's rabbis and elders. This only emboldened Shabbtai and his followers. He next appeared in Salonika, where in a public marriage ceremony he wed himself to a Torah scroll. More shocking still was his abolition of the fast of Tisha b'Av, commemorating the destruction of the Temples. Exiled and hounded from place to place he finally found what he was looking for in Egypt, where, under the patronage of a wealthy and influential Jew, Raphael Joseph Chelebi, he was treated as a lofty mystic. It was not long before Shabbtai visited the Holy Land, where he met Nathan of Gaza, who claimed to be the reincarnation of the prophet Elijah and the harbinger of the messiah.

Until this point Shabbtai did not see himself as the messiah but only as a mystic playing a role in the messianic drama. Nathan convinced him otherwise and began to publicize Shabbtai Tzvi as the messiah. The poor desperate Jews who survived the Chmelnitzki massacres were ready to believe anything that brought them comfort. Yet the belief spread far beyond the confines of Poland, as Jews and non-Jews all across Europe waited anxiously for events to unfold. Unfortunately, many rabbis were initially misled by the glowing reports and their support only contributed further to Shabbtai's credibility. Not all Jews were satisfied just to wait for events to happen and many, otherwise intelligent and responsible people, packed up their families and with a few meagre belongings made their way across Europe to the great ports to embark for the Holy Land.

One of the stranger characters in the Shabbtai cast was his wife, Sarah, an orphan girl who made her first appearance wandering through the desolate villages of Poland in the aftermath of the Cossack uprising. The story she told was that her dead father kidnapped her from the monastery where she was hiding from Chmelnitzki's hordes, and set her on her journey, telling her that she was destined to marry the messiah. Eventually word of the messiah's bride got to Shabbtai and he invited her to be his wife.

Shabbtai's career as messiah came to an end when he announced that he was making a journey to Constantinople to take the crown from the sultan, who would gladly give it up to the messiah, king of kings. Needless to say, as his ship pulled into the Turkish port he was arrested and imprisoned in a fortress at Gallipoli. He remained there for some time, living like a king with full freedom to receive visitors. Eventually his bluff was called when the sultan cleverly presented him with the choice between his life or conversion to Islam. Shabbtai chose the latter and was never heard of again. To those who doubted him all along his conversion was welcome proof; the many who followed him had to admit they had been duped. A small number of committed followers continued to believe in him, however, despite his apostasy, justifying his conversion in different ways.

What is interesting about Shabbtai is that underlying most of his actions was a coherent, if bizarre, doctrine, a gross corruption of the Lurianic idea of Tikkun 'Olam. Luria, as we have seen, teaches that embedded in this world are sparks of holiness which through the performance of mitzvot can be elevated back to their source, thus paving the way for the messiah. What was not mentioned earlier is that not all sparks can be redeemed by man but that some lie so deeply entrenched that it is only the messiah who will be able to release them. These entrenched sparks may be found in aspects of this world that are forbidden by the Torah. For example, if a spark of holiness exists in a kosher food item, say a piece of bread, then the act of reciting the proper blessing of grace thanking God for the bread will release the spark back to its source. If, however, there is a potential spark in a piece of pork, which is forbidden by the Torah, then no matter how many blessings one recites it will remain entrapped until such time as the messiah arrives and redeems the world of all of its impurity.

Shabbtai took this doctrine a crucial step too far by positing that through descending into the depths of the forbidden he could release the holy sparks trapped there and hasten the redemption. This gave rise to an extreme perversion of Luria's doctrine, what we may call sinning for a higher purpose. This is what was behind his eating on the ninth of Av as well as his many other sinful practices, which went far beyond the consumption of non-kosher food. Interestingly, before committing these sins he would recite a special blessing – the same blessing one recites first thing in the morning upon waking:

'Blessed are you God king of the Universe who has released the bound' (in Hebrew, *mattir assurim*). The meaning of the blessing is one of gratitude to God when, after a night of sleep, in which the human body is bound and restricted, one is able to once again walk about freely. Essentially it is a blessing thanking God for physical movement. Shabbtai perverted this blessing so that it had a very different connotation. For Shabbtai, releasing the bound is a reference to the sparks that were previously inaccessible. In the Hebrew there is also a significant play on the words as *mutar* also means religiously permitted and *assur* mean religiously prohibited. Thus *mattir assurim* can mean the one who permits that which is prohibited.

The Shabbtai Tzvi debacle was the result of many different forces merging at the same time. One was the massacre in Poland, which led many otherwise sober people to dream an impossible dream, that a charlatan from Turkey was the much awaited messiah. Another was the fact that most of Europe was in something of a messianic frenzy since Jewish mystics had already earmarked the year 1648 for the messiah's arrival. In addition, Christian mystics had calculated that the messiah would reveal himself in 1666. Added to this was the Lurianic doctrine of Tikkun, which was a relatively new and radical concept. Finally there was the character himself, brilliant, charismatic but deeply flawed, egged on by others like Nathan of Gaza for their own purposes. The result is one of the most unedifying chapters in Jewish history, a chapter that cast a long shadow into the next century, where it played upon developing events.

1700–1900 – weakening of rabbinic power, Jewish Enlightenment

In the aftermath of the Shabbtai Tzvi fiasco there was understandably a retreat from anything remotely associated with Shabbtai or his ideas. Closet followers of the false messiah, called Sabbateans, were smoked out and persecuted. This did not mean that everyone accused of being a closet Sabbatean was actually guilty. One of the most publicized cases of false accusations took place in the first half of the eighteenth century and involved two rabbis, Rabbi Jacob Emden (1697–1776) and Rabbi Jonathan Eybeschuetz (1690–1764).

The events unfolded in what was called the triple community of Altona, Hamburg and Wandsbeck. This was one of the most prosperous communities in Europe and the position of Chief Rabbi of the triple community was considered one of the most prestigious rabbinic positions. Jacob Emden was born into this community, where his grandfather was Chief Rabbi. Early on in his childhood his father, also a well-known rabbi, commonly known as the Chacham Tzvi, moved the family to Amsterdam. They moved several more times during Jacob's childhood, following his father's appointment to rabbinic positions in different cities. Chacham Tzvi was one of the few rabbis who from the outset were unconvinced about Shabbtai Tzvi. As the false messiah began to gain popularity Chacham Tzvi fought a campaign against him in Europe. The young Jacob worshipped his esteemed and courageous father and from a very early age tried to emulate him. Unfortunately for Jacob, his father passed away when Jacob was still in his teens and he was left having to fend for his mother and sisters. He married and for a while served as rabbi in the German city of Emden (hence his name) but eventually he gave this up and returned to his birthplace, the triple community, to live what he called 'the life of a free man'. As a sign of respect and in recognition of his esteemed father and grandfather he was afforded by the city elders the extraordinary privilege of being able to have his own small synagogue in his home.

Shortly after his arrival the position of Chief Rabbi became vacant. Emden would later say that he never wanted the post, but it appears he must have hoped that, considering his lineage, it would have been offered to him. It was not. Instead it was offered to a brilliant rabbi from Prague, Rabbi Jonathan Eybeschuetz, a learned halachist and also something of a Kabbalist. His Kabbala was not restricted to the theoretical or academic but took the practical form of his writing and distributing amulets for various illnesses. While this may seem strange to us, it was not strange or out of place at the time. Various rabbis engaged in this practice, in which they would inscribe on a piece of parchment some Kabbalistic formula, wrap it up and insert it in a small case attached to a chain to be worn around the neck. These amulets were popular with all sorts of people suffering from one ailment or another. Eybeschuetz, it appears, was just one expert amongst many in what at the time was considered a perfectly acceptable practice. However, it was his amulets that were to get him into trouble.

Emden, having had the chance to read one of Eybeschuetz's amulets, came to the conclusion that the writer could only be a closet Sabbatean. This, he claimed, was because the amulet contained hidden references to Shabbtai Tzvi. Charges were brought before Eybeschuetz, which he vigorously denied. The matter would have been settled there and then were it not for the fact that Emden then began to agitate against the rabbi from the pulpit of his private synagogue. The community elders deemed such behaviour unacceptable, revoked his privilege and gave him several months to move out of city. Emden complied but not before sending letters to a number of leading rabbis setting out his concerns about the Chief Rabbi. Eybeschuetz, for his part, also wrote to rabbinic colleagues arguing his innocence and appealing for their support.

Thus began a long and protracted battle, not just between these two men but eventually between most of the rabbis in Europe, who took one side or the other. The fact that Eybeschuetz took an oath in front of the open Ark in the Great Synagogue in Altona that he was no Sabbatean did little to convince his detractors. The controversy raged for several years, sweeping up entire Jewish communities until it was finally settled by the secular authorities, who backed Eybeschuetz in his position as Chief Rabbi, but not before he had to submit to re-election by the entire community.

One of the lasting legacies of this controversy is the irreparable damage it inflicted on rabbinic authority. Until then rabbis were revered as leaders of their communities, imbued with an almost mystical aura that put them in the unique and enviable position of being perceived as God's spokesmen. A rabbi's ruling was binding on his community and very few even thought of defying it. All this began to change with the Emden–Eybeschuetz controversy. This was not an issue that mattered to the average person: the Jew in the pew cared little what was behind the rabbi's amulets. All they cared about was strong rabbinic leadership to help guide them through a difficult time. Instead, all around them they saw their leaders, supposedly God's spokesmen, quarrelling and demeaning each other. The fact that the entire body of European rabbis could not resolve the matter but had to turn to the secular authorities was an indication of their moral bankruptcy. The people observed all this, and it changed the way they would think about their rabbis henceforth.

This weakening of rabbinic authority is the perfect backdrop to the next important episode during the eighteenth century, the rise of the Jewish Enlightenment. The father of the Jewish Enlightenment (known as Haskalah) was Moses Mendelssohn. Moses, the Son of Mendel the Torah scribe, was born in Dessau in 1729. He began life, like all Jewish boys of his day, studying the Talmud to the exclusion of all else. As he grew older he developed an unquenchable thirst for knowledge. He was first introduced to the philosophical work of Maimonides by his teacher, David Fraenkel, and this opened up a whole new world to him. When Fraenkel was appointed as rabbi in Berlin Mendelssohn followed him. In Berlin the young Moses studied and read anything he could get his hands on. He acquired a thorough knowledge of ancient and modern languages and a deep understanding of philosophy. Mendelssohn gradually made the acquaintance of many Christian thinkers, something almost unheard of for an eighteenth-century Jew, and he quickly won their respect.

Mendelssohn believed that it was time for the ghetto walls to come down; that non-Jews should welcome Jews into their society (even as he wrote this, Mendelssohn was, as a Jew, not entitled to Prussian citizenship) and that Jews should be open to assimilating the best of German culture. Mendelssohn believed that having spent centuries behind physical ghetto walls, the Jews had come to erect mental barriers as well as resisting all forms of non-Jewish culture. He argued that it is possible to retain one's Jewish identity and practice (Mendelssohn himself was an observant Jew until his dying day) while still benefiting from wider society. He also argued that the rabbis had too much of a stranglehold on the Jewish community and that people ought to be free in matters of religious conscience.

This had particular resonance with his audience in the light of the Emden–Eybeschuetz affair. Mendelssohn went on to publish a German translation of the Bible as a means of introducing Jewish schoolchildren to the beauty of the German language. He also founded a school that taught secular subjects alongside religious ones. While this seems mild and non-threatening by today's standards, it was not seen that way in the eighteenth century. The rabbis feared that exposure to the German language would open up to young Jews a whole range of secular subjects and that these subjects would corrupt their Judaism. As a result, Mendelssohn's Bible was banned in many communities and Mendelssohn himself was vilified by the rabbis. Mendelssohn died before Jews were granted emancipation in Europe, but his idea was a positive influence towards this.

Nevertheles, Jewish opinion is divided over Mendelssohn. Some hail him as a great emancipator who helped his people emerge from behind the ghetto walls so as to play a full part in society and reap the benefits of secular culture. Others see him as a destroyer of the faith who exposed the Jews to a life they would have been better without. As for Mendelssohn's own scrupulous observance of mitzvot, they cannot fault him, but they do point to the fact that not one of his children died a Jew. This, they say, is the price a Jew pays for admittance into non-Jewish society.

Hasidism

One of the most influential modern movements in Judaism is Hasidism. The term Hasid has several connotations, depending on where the term is used. It first appears in the Talmud and in that context a Hasid is someone who is exceedingly pious. This is generally measured by whether he is willing to go beyond the letter of the law. In this sense, the Hasid is on a higher level than the *tzadik*, the one who is righteous and follows the law to the letter. The term Hasid crops up again in twelfth and thirteenth centuries in Germany. Here it refers to a group of ascetic mystically inclined rabbis known as the Hasidei Ashkenaz. The Hasidei Ashkenaz influenced their society as religious leaders. They have also bequeathed to us a religio-ethical literature and some magnificent hymns. Thereafter the term Hasid refers to an ascetic individual usually belonging to a group of like-minded people immersed in the study of Kabbala and ascetic practices. These Hasidim were an elite whose primary goal in life was to pray and study undisturbed. The Hasidic movement of the eighteenth century was altogether different.

The acknowledged founder of the movement was Rabbi Israel Bal Shem Tov (Israel Master of the Good Name), Besht for short, whose early years are shrouded in mystery. Legend has it that his birth in 1698 was a miracle and that he was born to an elderly childless couple as a reward for their having committed an extreme act of charity. Not surprisingly Israel was orphaned at a young age. Before he died his father said to him, 'I leave you now before I can make you into a man that fears God and loves those who fear him. Never fear anything, remember that God alone is to be feared.' The young orphan spent long periods of time alone with nature in the forests, often sleeping the night there. As he grew older he took on various jobs such as teacher's assistant, synagogue beadle and ritual slaughterer.

No one thought much of this rather lonely boy, and he attracted little attention. Eventually he married a young woman, sister of a great Talmudist and Kabbalist named Rabbi Gershon Kitover. Rabbi Gershon was disappointed, if not a little embarrassed, at his sister's choice of husband and he did not welcome Israel. The young couple then spent many years living in the remote Carpathian Mountains, eking out a living selling clay. Finally, on Israel's thirty-sixth birthday, he 'revealed' himself as a mystic of the highest order. His brother-in-law was shocked by this revelation and subsequently became Israel's most ardent devotee. Israel eventually took up residence in the small Ukrainian town of Miedzyboz, where he gained fame as a resident mystic and healer. But he was more than just that; he was also a revolutionary thinker and his ideas changed the way many Jews perceived themselves and Judaism.

In less than a hundred years the Jewish world sustained considerable trauma. It saw the overwhelming destruction of 1648–9 and it experienced the euphoria and then extreme dejection with Shabbtai Tzvi. There were also great socio-economic gaps between the rich and the poor, the scholarly and the uneducated. While the rich could generally afford to send their children to school and marry their daughters to Torah scholars, the poor remained for the most part unlettered. All of this made for a very depressing life for many Jews living in or around Russia at that time. What was so radical about the Besht is that he reached out to the poor unlettered masses and taught them that in God's eyes they were as important as the scholars. He believed that a simple tailor or cobbler who recited psalms while at work was on a loftier spiritual level than the rich conceited scholar who was too proud of the many pages of the Talmud he had studied. The main thing, he taught, was to serve God with joy, something the austere Talmudist could not claim to do.

This seemingly simple idea was not at all simple at the time. It caught on like wildfire and many were drawn to this holy man who taught them not just how to love God, but that God loves them. In addition to the masses who were attracted to the

Besht's message of love and joy was an elite group of scholars who were attracted to his profound mystical teachings. Amongst this elite was Rabbi DovBer, who, after the Besht's death in 1760, became his successor.

Rabbi DovBer became known as the Maggid (the preacher) of Mezrich. He gathered about himself an elite corps of spiritually highly developed men who became known as the Chevraya Kadisha (the holy fraternity). Whereas the Besht will always be remembered as the founder of the Hasidic movement, Rabbi DovBer is remembered as its consolidator. He communicated his master's teachings to the holy fraternity and expanded on these with his own thoughts and ideas. In turn, he formed a generation of Hasidic leaders who, after his death in 1772, would go on to found their own Hasidic centres (courts, as they were called) and movements. Each of these leaders became known as a Rebbe (as distinct from a rabbi) or as a tzadik. Unlike the Talmudic term tzadik, which ranks beneath the Hasid, here it means a man of heightened spiritual qualities to whom the Hasid is bound and devoted.

Rabbi and Rebbe

The difference between a rabbi and a Rebbe is that the former is essentially a halachic authority whereas the latter is an authority on spiritual matters. There is also generally far more devotion in a Rebbe than there is in a rabbi. This can be illustrated by the following quip: the difference between a rabbi and a Rebbe is that when a rabbi speaks everyone thinks he is addressing someone else but when a Rebbe speaks everyone listening thinks he is talking to him alone.

One of these students, was Rabbi Shneur Zalman of Liadi (1745–1812), known as Rashaz. He was already a most accomplished Talmud scholar, halachist and Kabbalist when he arrived at Mezrich. After the Maggid's death RSZ developed his own particular brand of Hasidism which he called HaBaD. HaBaD is an acronym for Hochma, Bina, Da'at, which means wisdom, knowledge and understanding. According to RSZ it is not possible to develop a deep and sustained love for God unless it begins with the intellect.

RSZ taught that emotions can be misleading and, more importantly, fleeting. Even the belief in feeling very strongly about loving God is probably just a self-delusion. The proof is that the feeling cannot be sustained for any lengthy period of time. A Hasid may feel ecstatic in the presence of his master but the feeling is lost once he leaves his master's presence. It may be possible to feel love for God during a particularly moving prayer, but once the prayer is over the love invariably loses its intensity. The solution to this, argued RSZ, is for the emotions to be rooted in the intellect. But how does one contemplate the greatness and glory of God? How does one even begin to frame such thoughts? To this RSZ provides a solution, his theological works. He began to teach and disseminate his thoughts about theology and the Kabbala that had previously been within the purview of a select few. He believed that if only such powerful ideas were in the hands of the masses they would be able to use them in contemplating the greatness of God, leading them to a deep and sustained love of God.

This radical idea drew considerable criticism from his colleagues in the holy fraternity. Their criticism was based on two points. First, how could RSZ doubt the sincerity of the ecstatic Hasid who feels love for God? Second, how could RSZ have the audacity to disseminate to the masses the deepest teachings of Jewish mysticism? The masses do not need mystical ideas, argued one of RSZ's most outspoken critics, Rabbi Abraham Kalisher. What they need is a Rebbe who will inspire them. It is enough for the Rebbe to study such mystical texts: he will in turn inspire the Hasidim. RSZ's response to this criticism was that the job of a Rebbe is not to serve as the source of a Hasid's inspiration, it is to give the Hasid the intellectual tools so that he can achieve inspiration on his own. With neither side backing down, a creative schism developed in the movement, differentiating the intellectual Hasidut of RSZ (HaBaD) from the emotional Hasidut of his critics, called HaGaT (an acronym for Hesed Gevurah Tiferet; primary emotions).

One of the areas of distinction between the two schools of Hasidut is apparent in prayer. HaGaT Hasidim tend to engage in what can be described as ecstatic prayer. This includes lots of singing and shouting, accompanied by vigorous swaying and erratic body movements. HaBaD prayer is very different, as it is preceded by the study of mystical texts, followed by a period of deep contemplation or meditation called *hitbonne-nut*. Finally, after these preparations the Hasid begins to pray with deep feeling. It is a far more structured and goal-oriented prayer compared to the spontaneity of HaGaT.

As a little boy I had the privilege of observing real serious HaBaD contemplative prayer first hand. I grew up in a community that consisted of many elder Hasidim from Russia who had emigrated after the Second World War, and I regularly watched them pray. On a typical Shabbat morning they would rise at dawn, immerse themselves in a ritual pool of water, known as a mikveh, to cleanse themselves spiritually and then begin to study HaBaD Hasidut for several hours. Then would begin hours of contemplation where, wrapped deep in their prayer shawls, they would gently sway to and fro, occasionally humming a melancholy Hasidic melody. After all this preparation they would begin to pray. I would return to the synagogue hours later after having enjoyed Shabbat lunch and a nap and they would still be at it, sometimes until four or five in the afternoon. Very few people pray like this today, even within the HaBaD community, and I know that I saw something very special. Even if I may never pray with such devotion myself, at least I saw what true prayer can be.

By the late eighteenth century Hasidism had taken root, particularly in the Ukraine, which, from the perspective of Jewish scholarship, was a relative backwater. The Jewish masses embraced the Hasidic doctrine that taught of serving God through love and joy and they flocked to the many Hasidic masters who established their courts throughout the Ukraine.

Lithuania and White Russia offered a different picture altogether. Here was the bastion of Jewish scholarship. Many of the most accomplished scholars of the age lived in this region and they eyed the new movement with considerable suspicion, if not outright hostility. The opponents of the Hasidim, the *mitnagdim* as they would eventually become known, were led by the greatest scholar of the time, Rabbi Elijah of Vilna (1720–1797), known as the Gaon of Vilna or by his acronym, GRA, who, although he never held a public position, enjoyed incredible sway over Jewish life in that region.

The mitnagdim were opposed to Hasidism on several points. They were first and foremost troubled by the Hasidim's apparent lack of regard for Torah study. The mitnagdim felt that by elevating prayer to such an extent the Hasidim had, in the process, degraded the value of Torah study. They were also concerned that the Hasidim had exchanged the age-old Ashkenazi prayer rite for the Lurianic, developed in the sixteenth century. This, they felt, was an affront to their traditions. It also created the undesired effect of Hasidim setting up their own separate synagogues.

In addition, there was also a certain discomfort in the way Hasidim celebrated life, with lots of communal feasting and drinking which, to the austere mitnagdim, seemed inappropriate. These were the explicit reasons given at the time. There was then, as always, a deeper reason beneath the surface, and in this case it was loss of authority and control. By creating their own prayer rite, synagogues and rituals the Hasidim essentially formed an alternative community. This challenged those in positions of authority and may explain so much of the animosity directed towards the Hasidim.

Eventually the mitnagdim, under the leadership of the GRA, placed the Hasidim under a ban and collectively excommunicated them. This was particularly painful to RSZ and his Hasidim in White Russia: he tried together with some of his colleagues to meet the GRA to try to have the ban overturned. But the GRA refused to meet the Hasidic delegation, and the

persecution of the Hasidim continued. There were certain mitnagdim who accused the Hasidim of being Sabbatean, but this,
it seems, was never taken seriously. In fact RSZ himself was
pleased by this accusation; it was so ludicrous he hoped it
would expose the other accusations as equally false.

The struggle between the mitnagdim and Hasidim carried
on and even intensified after the GRA's death in 1797.
Eventually, it ran out of steam. The Hasidim for their part
made an effort to respond to some of their opponents' criti-
cisms, such as respect for Torah scholarship and Torah scholars, and the mitnagdim begrudgingly began to accept them. By
the second half of the nineteenth century the whole controversy was practically forgotten, especially since both the
Hasidim and mitnagdim realized that they had common
enemies to fight.

The legacy of Hasidism cannot be understated. It brought to
the Jewish experience a dimension of passion and fervour that
was previously lacking. It made Jewish practice exciting and
joyous and it taught the value of every individual. It also produced some of the most inspired leaders in Jewish history. RSZ
is just one of many Hasidic masters who, each in their own
way, changed the way Jews lived and practised their Judaism.

One of the greatest of the Hasidic masters was Rabbi Levi
Yitzchak of Berdichev (1740–1809), who had the most outstanding quality: he was never able to see bad in another. The
story is told that once, on the fast of the ninth of Av, the good
rabbi was walking in the street when he beheld a young Jew
eating.

'Young man,' said the rabbi, 'it must be that you don't know
that today is a Jewish fast day.'

'Wrong,' replied the young man, 'I know full well what
today is.'

'Well then, it must be that you are unwell, in which case it is
permitted for one to break their fast.'

'Wrong again,' replied the young man, 'I am in rude health.
... Don't look so surprised,' added the fellow when he saw the

rabbi's reaction. 'I am eating because I want to, and that's the end of it.'

The rabbi's face broke out into a smile, he turned his gaze heavenward and proclaimed to the Almighty: 'Master of the universe, look at your children; even when they violate your law in the most shameful way, still, they cannot bring themselves to tell a lie.'

Rabbi Levi Yitzchak was also well known for calling God to account for his people's suffering. One year on Yom Kippur, the holiest day of the year, Rabbi Levi Yitzchak interrupted the service. 'Master of the Universe,' he said, 'I am halting the prayers right here. So long as you continue to ignore them, there is no point in us continuing to say them.'

While to someone unfamiliar with Judaism this may seem blasphemous, the idea of arguing with God is as old as Judaism itself. Abraham argued with God to save the inhabitants of Sodom and Moses argued with God to save his people. Rabbi Levi Yitzchak of Berdichev simply took this further than anyone else had done. Yet no one accused him of disrespect for God. This, explains the Jewish writer Ellie Wisel, is because Judaism allows man to say anything to God provided it is on behalf of one's fellow man. Besides, despite all his railing against God, Rabbi Levi Yitzchak never sulked for long. He got the matter off his chest and returned to serving his Creator with awe and joy.

By the second half of the nineteenth century the German Jewish Enlightenment which started with Moses Mendelssohn began to make its way into Russia. The early Jewish *maskilim* (adherents of the Haskalah) believed that if only they could demonstrate to the Russian authorities that the Jews were capable of culture this would pave the way for their emancipation and equal rights. The Tsar's government went along with the programme of introducing Jews to secular culture and learning but, as became evident, never had any intention of emancipating them.

As in Germany, the Haskalah initially came up against opposition in Russia. This came from the many rabbis, both Hasidic and mitnagdic, who felt that the educational reforms proposed by the maskilim would corrupt the Jewish youth and turn their hearts and minds away from Judaism. Thus began a battle between the maskilim and their detractors. In the end the maskilim appealed to the government for support, which was granted, and they gradually began to put down roots in Russia.

While the first generation of maskilim were essentially, like Mendelssohn, religious Jews who were primarily interested in broadening their culture, the second generation had little interest in their Jewish roots. To a certain extent this was the fault of the Russian government who, despite the maskilim's best efforts, refused to grant Jews equal rights. The second generation felt duped. The young Russian maskil had, after all, a good broad education and had done much to acculturate himself, yet as far as the Russians were concerned he was still just a zhid. This caused a great sense of bitterness and resentment amongst these young Jews who, as a result, became aggressively secular.

In addition to this, many young Jews were drawn towards the various underground revolutionary movements in the hope of overthrowing the oppressive tsarist regime.

This sudden secularization of the youth took their elders by surprise. For generations children followed their parents in both matters of religion and occupation; suddenly, in the space of less than one generation, all this had changed. Parents could not understand their children's resistance to their Jewish faith, and this caused much concern and upset. From the rabbis' perspective a crisis was brewing, since many of the sharpest young minds were being drawn away from Torah study to the great universities and many of the natural-born leaders were investing their energy in the socialist cause. Where would the next generation of leaders come from if this flow continued? The solution to this problem was to create higher institutes of Talmudic learning called yeshivot, which would attract highly intelligent and idealistic young men. A number of such yeshivot blossomed towards the end of the nineteenth century. Each one had its own unique philosophy and goals and attracted the type of student to whom such a philosophy and goals appealed.

Perhaps the most famous of the great nineteenth-century yeshivot was the Yeshiva of Velozhin. Velozhin itself was a small sleepy town in White Russia. The yeshiva was founded there in the first half of the nineteenth century by Rabbi Chaim Velozhiner (1749–1821), the most outstanding disciple of the Gaon of Vilna. The yeshiva began for a small group of elite scholars handpicked by Rabbi Chaim. Gradually the yeshiva's reputation grew and the centre attracted students from all over Russia. By the late nineteenth century it had become the premier centre of Torah study in Russia, with a student body of some four hundred young men. Rabbi Chaim Velozhiner had since passed away and the yeshiva was now headed by Rabbi Naftali Tzvi Yehudah Berlin (1817–93), known as the Netziv. But the real attraction was a young lecturer, still in his twenties, Rabbi Chaim Solovietchik (1853–1918), known as Rabbi Chaim Brisker, who completely revolutionized the study of the Talmud.

Talmud is an extremely challenging discipline, and to master it requires years of study. It involves highly developed analytical skills and an ability to unravel extremely opaque texts written in Aramaic. However, for hundreds of years young bright Jewish minds were doing just that. A budding scholar would first be introduced to the Talmud at about eight or nine. If he was clever, he would be able to navigate his way around it unaided by the time he was bar mitzvah. He would then spend the rest of his life assiduously studying the Talmud and its commentaries, broadening his knowledge base. The problem for exceedingly bright students was that once they had learned how to master the Talmud, further such study could be rather boring and unexciting. This is because while the Talmud contains thousands of pages dealing with legal questions the logic pattern is quite limited. There are perhaps two or three dozen patterns of argument applied in slight variation throughout the entire Talmud. Once these patterns have been mastered, there is little further intellectual challenge for the student. This problem was first addressed in Poland as early as the fifteenth century in the school of Rabbi Jacob Pollack, the leading rabbi at the time. Rabbi Pollack introduced a system of thought called *pilpul*, which in Hebrew means pepper, symbolizing his hope to sharpen the flavour of Talmud. The nature of pilpul is that it raises questions about the Talmudic text and then takes the student on a tour of numerous other texts that either support or demolish the question. In the end an entire intellectual edifice is created out of these efforts. This method enabled students to let their creativity run wild as they built more and more elaborate structures of argument and reasoning. The method was not without its critics, however. Their criticism was that these intellectual structures were in essence nothing but houses of cards; the entire exercise was merely splitting hairs for the sake of splitting hairs. The journey was not a quest for a deeper understanding of the text but rather just a way of engaging in pointless mental gymnastics.

Often the masters of pilpul were so busy raising questions that they had not bothered to understand the meaning of the text in the first place, and so they built their structures on false premises. While many criticized pilpul for its pointless nature and intellectual dishonesty, no one before Rabbi Chaim Solovietchik had produced an exciting alternative. Rabbi Chaim developed a school of thought that is the polar opposite of pilpul. Whereas pilpul starts with a text as a point of departure, fanning out in all directions, Rabbi Chaim's method goes inward, seeking the truth of the text itself. He does this by breaking the text down into its constituent parts and then subjecting them to intense critical analyses. Through this rigorous process, the text is illuminated and the student is able to detect new principles and ideas underneath it.

His method borrowed heavily from philosophical and scientific thought patterns, which in the late nineteenth century was extremely new and exciting. Rabbi Chaim and the Velozhin Yeshiva offered the student a real intellectually challenging alternative to going to St Petersburg to study philosophy, law or science. Rabbi Chaim's method has become so popular that it is taught in virtually every yeshiva today and most well-trained yeshiva students instinctively subject any text to the brisker method of analytical scrutiny.

While, Rabbi Chaim and the Velozhin Yeshiva appealed to the bourgeois student, the Mussar Yeshivot appealed to the budding young revolutionary. Mussar was a school of thought that developed in the nineteenth century by Rabbi Israel Lipkind Salanter (1810–83). The main thrust of Mussar (which means moral instruction) is character development. Rabbi Salanter found that while there were a great many Torah schol- ars and a high level of intellectual achievement in the Jewish community there was a decided lack of moral and ethical stand- ards. He found that people were not sensitive to the needs and feelings of others, that people were often rude and impatient and that they were not always scrupulous in their business dealings. He set out repairing this by writing and teaching about the importance of character development, impressing upon his students the virtues of humility, punctuality, patience, industry, honesty and personal cleanliness. He drew many stu- dents and adherents and his ideas began to spread. Eventually some of his students opened up yeshivot where, in addition to the traditional study of the Talmud, they also offered classes and guidance in the area of character development. Each of these yeshivot had its own particular emphasis.

One of the most interesting was the Yeshiva of Navardok, which emphasized humility. Navardok was a radical place, where students were encouraged to defy social convention, to act out in socially unacceptable ways and to be scoffed at. The idea behind this was that pride is an obstacle that interferes with life. If only one can build a resistance to humiliation one would be free to live and act as one saw fit, unencumbered by social convention or the judgement of others. An example of the behaviour at Navardok would be for a student to enter a pharmacy and ask for a box of nails, or go into a hardware store and asking for medicine. The proprietor and other customers would of course laugh at the fool, but that was the whole point. After enough practice the student would become immune to the opinion of others. Unlike their clean-shaven and smartly dressed bourgeois contemporaries at Velozhin, the Navardok students deliberately dressed shabbily and grew unkempt beards.

This nonconformist attitude struck a chord with the young potential social revolutionaries, and many who would otherwise not have considered studying in a yeshiva were attracted to Navardok.

A third yeshiva which emerged at this time was a Hasidic yeshiva called Tomchei Tmimim. The founder of this yeshiva was Rabbi Shalom DovBer (1860–1920), the fifth HaBaD Rebbe and a direct descendant of Rabbi Shneur Zalman of Liadi. He founded what was at first a small yeshiva in the White Russian town of Lubavitch for the express purpose of training the next generation of spiritual leaders for the Jewish community. As with all yeshivot, the curriculum consisted mainly of Talmud study but he also included the study of Hasidut. There was also great emphasis on prayer; some select students were allowed to pray for hours each morning. Rabbi Shalom DovBer was cognizant of the various secular ideologies, particularly revolutionary ideas, competing for the minds of his young students. He sought to combat this by lecturing his students on the importance of a spiritual revolution at hand and encouraging them to play their part. The spiritual revolution was of course a reference to combating rising secularity and apathy amongst the Jews of Russia. He even borrowed ideas from revolutionary ideology, such as telling his students to forget their families and to sacrifice every fibre of their being for the sake of the spiritual revolution.

Each of these yeshivot played their part in managing to attract and train future leaders for the Jewish community. That

is not to say that they were able to turn the tide. This they were
clearly not able to do. The vast majority of young Jews became
absorbed in the new exciting ideologies of the late nineteenth
century, socialism, Bundism and secular Zionism.

1900–2000 – Zionism, the Holocaust and the State of Israel
Zionism
The land of Zion, or Tziyon in Hebrew, had never been forgotten by the Jews in exile. While for centuries it changed
hands between Christians and Muslims, Jews formed a steady
if small presence there. There was also a constant trickle of
Jews who left their homes in the Diaspora and made their way
back to the Holy Land. For centuries the concept of Jewish
national independence in the Holy Land was linked to the
arrival of the messiah, which, despite the many disappointments and setbacks of exile, the Jews continued to believe in. In
the nineteenth century the concepts of messiah and Jewish
nationalism were gradually separated from each other. The
argument made was that Jewish nationalism was not necessarily dependent on the arrival of the messiah; Jews had it within
their power to achieve an independent state in Israel if they
only put their minds to it. As for the messiah, that depended on
whether one was a religious or a secular Zionist.

The religious Zionists believed that the messiah would
arrive, rebuild the Temple and usher in a universal age of peace
and spiritual enlightenment. This did not preclude the Jews
from beginning the work by returning to Israel en masse and
building a national Jewish homeland. In fact, the messiah's
arrival, according to many religious Zionists, depended on the
Jews taking this crucial first step; they saw Jewish nationalism
in Israel as a necessary step in the messianic process. Secular
Zionists held no such beliefs. For them the messiah was just a
myth to keep the Jewish people from losing hope during their
years of exile. If there was redemption it was not going to be
spiritual but political. Their goal was to establish a secular
Jewish state within Israel. While these two ideologies are quite

far apart, the religious Zionists nonetheless partnered with the secular Zionists. Each needed the help of the other and, as they shared an overarching objective, they were able to make allowances for each other's particular beliefs.

However, not all religious Jews took such a kind view of Zionism. In fact, the vast majority were opposed to it. From their perspective the notion of Jews rebuilding their national homeland before the arrival of the messiah was sheer blasphemy. In addition, they harboured fears that the religious Zionists were being used by the secular Zionists to create a secular state without any religious character. This debate raged on during the last decade of the nineteenth century and into the second decade of the twentieth. Through the efforts of many ardent Zionists inspired by Theodore Herzl, the driving force behind political Zionism, they managed to settle a considerable number of Jews in the Holy Land, creating a significant Jewish presence there. This led to the British Balfour Declaration in 1917 and eventually, after the crushing of European Jewry in the Holocaust, to the United Nations' creation of the modern State of Israel in 1948.

Now, more than half a century after Israel's independence, the ideological debate between the religious pro- and anti-Zionists still continues. On one extreme end of the religious spectrum there are a tiny minority of Ultra Orthodox Jews who believe that the creation of the Jewish state before the messiah's arrival was sinful. They are particularly critical of the fact that the state is for the most part secular. As a result they do not recognize the validity of the State of Israel, and although many of this group live there, they refuse to participate in Israeli society. From their perspective, they are living in Eretz Yisrael, the Holy Land, which the modern secular state has nothing to do with. There is another, larger group who question the wisdom of the establishment of the State of Israel, but accept it as a fait accompli. They do not believe that the state has any religious significance, though they do appreciate it as a haven and refuge for Jews around the world. This fact alone, in their mind, is reason enough to give the state their tacit support. Moving along the spectrum, there are national religious Jews who believe that the State of Israel is a crucial first step in the messianic process. The state, according to this group, although currently secular, possesses intrinsic spiritual and religious significance. They play a full part in its society and serve with distinction in the army. At the farthest end of the spectrum is a subgroup within the national religious faction. This group believes that Jewish conquest and control of every last bit of biblical Israel is necessary in order to precipitate the arrival of the messiah. Much has been written about this group, particularly since Israel's withdrawal from Gaza in 2005.

In addition to the religious spectrum there is a secular perspective. Jews at one extreme of the secular spectrum question the very need of a Jewish state. At the other extreme are secular Jews who believe passionately in the history and destiny of their people and they see the secular state and Jewish nationhood as the final stage of a 2,000-year exile. In between these extremes are those who support the state because it happens to be there and it serves as a haven for Jews.

The above account is a very rough guide to the main groups. Of course, each of these groupings contains many subgroups and there are various hybrids as well who combine particular aspects of different ideologies. The vast majority of Jews, both in Israel and in the Diaspora, fall somewhere in the middle. They support the State of Israel, although not necessarily a particular government's policy. They do not think in deep ideological terms. They see the state as a means of preserving Jewish identity and as a haven for Jews from around the world.

The Holocaust

One of the darkest periods, if not the darkest, of the 2,000-year exile was the Nazi Holocaust. In little over six years the vast majority of European Jewry, six million in total, was wiped out. I once heard an eminent rabbi and psychologist say that to this day the Jewish people suffer post-traumatic stress disorder as a result of the Holocaust. So much of the post-Holocaust Jewish experience is coloured by that event that it is almost impossible to emancipate ourselves from its influence.

One obvious result of the Holocaust is the creation of the State of Israel. The world finally woke up to the realization that had the Jews had a homeland, the Holocaust would never have occurred, or if it had, its effects would have been far more limited.

Another effect is what I can only describe as profound insecurity and paranoia, the Jews' feeling that they cannot trust anyone, that anti-Semites are everywhere and that given half a chance they would wipe out all Jews. It should be noted that while this feeling is certainly prevalent in the Jewish community, it is primarily so amongst the older generation. Younger Jews on the whole do not bear the same fears and insecurities as their parents and grandparents, and, if they do, it is to a far lesser extent. This was brought home to me when several years ago I led a synagogue trip to Poland to visit various sites of Jewish interest including the Majdanek concentration camp just outside Lublin. Throughout our trip we encountered Poles in one context or another. With the notable exception of being spat upon and cursed by an elderly Pole walking through Lublin, I found everyone else to be kind and helpful. This was not the experience of many of our group, who were of an older generation. They saw insults and threats, which from my perspective clearly did not exist. The fact that some of their parents were Holocaust survivors while mine are not certainly had something to do with it.

The Holocaust has also pervaded the way Jews think about Jewish continuity. The tremendous drive to build schools, synagogues and Jewish centres is in no small measure due to the fact that Jews feel they must replace what was lost.

The Holocaust affects even such personal decisions as how many children to have, as parents feel they must make up for the six million lost Jews.

Assimilation and intermarriage, two of the greatest threats to Jewish demography, have for years been portrayed as a second holocaust. Today most communal leaders realize that this type of comparison is unhelpful and often backfires, but that does not mean that, deep down, they do not see a correlation.

The Holocaust also throws up profound theological questions. How is it that God could allow such a thing to happen? Since it did happen, where does that place God? For some the question is simply, is there a God after the Holocaust?

I recall as a little boy accompanying my father and his good friend, a Holocaust survivor, as they went around our neighbourhood during the festival of Sukkot offering people the chance to say a blessing on the *lulav* and *etrog* (the palm branch and citrus fruit over which Jews recite a prayer during the Festival of Sukkot: see p. 199). We knocked on one door and a woman answered in a terrible state. 'How dare you go around telling people to do mitzvot after the Holocaust?' Apparently she was a writer and had retuned from Poland. The research she unearthed deeply disturbed her and she could not abide the sight of two Jews blissfully serving the God who had abandoned six million of His people. My father's friend spoke to her softly telling her that as a fifteen-year-old boy he had been deported to Auschwitz where he lost every single member of his once large family. The woman was speechless and I remember to this day how she cried. There in front of her stood a man who had lost everything yet he still managed to retain his faith in God.

These questions preoccupied many Jewish thinkers in the aftermath of the Holocaust, giving rise to very different outlooks. Amongst these various philosophies two stand out in particular. The view of one influential Ultra Orthodox leader, Rabbi Joel of Satmar, was that the Holocaust was a punishment from God and that Hitler and the Nazis were His instrument. The punishment was for the sin of secular Zionism and assimilation. The Lubavitcher Rebbe took strong issue with this view, arguing that it offers no explanation as to why so many pious and innocent Jews, not to mention one and a half million children, were killed. On a more theological level, he argued that to give any reason for the Holocaust is to trivialize it. Ultimately, the question is too great for us to even think of answering. We can only be silent in the shadow of the Holocaust and somehow learn to live with the question.

Chapter 9

DIASPORA JEWRY TODAY

> The Lord did not set his love upon you, nor choose you, because you were more in number than any people; for you were the fewest of all peoples.
>
> (Deuteronomy 7:7)

In the preceding chapter relating to the last five hundred years I have focused almost exclusively on the Jewish experience in Europe. This is because it was there that most of the ideas that shaped world Jewry first surfaced. This chapter very briefly gives an overview of the development of major Jewish centres across the world. The list is not exhaustive, merely illustrative of the geographical and cultural range of Jewish communities today.

Israel

Despite the Roman expulsion and exile in 70 CE, remnants of the once proud Jewish community remained in Israel. In the years immediately following the exile, the Jews were primarily concentrated in the north of Israel, known as the Galilee.

Throughout the centuries and millennia that followed a small but steady trickle of Jews found their way back to the Land of Israel and ensured a continuous Jewish presence there. In the sixteenth century many leading scholars and rabbis made their way to Safed in the north of Israel where they disseminated the mystical teachings known as the Kabbala. In the eighteenth century groups of both Hasidim and their opponents left Russia and Poland to immigrate to Israel. They established yishuvim, Jewish settlements primarily in the cities of Safed and around Lake Tiberias in the north and Jerusalem and Hebron in the centre of Israel. Jewish immigration picked up towards the end of the nineteenth century with the advent of political Zionism. During the Second World War numerous Jews fleeing the Nazi Holocaust sought refuge in what was then British Mandate Palestine. On 14 May 1948 the United Nations established the modern State of Israel, then with a Jewish population of 655,000. Over the years many Jews have returned to their ancestral homeland. There were particularly large waves of Jewish immigrants from North Africa in the 1950s, from Ethiopia in the 1980s and from the former Soviet Union in the 1990s. Today Israel's Jewish population stands at five and a quarter million. (This and subsequent figures given in this chapter are taken from the *Jewish Yearbook* published in association with the *Jewish chronicle*.)

United States of America

The second largest Jewish population is found in the United States of America, currently with almost six million Jews, 1,720,000 of whom live in the New York metropolitan area. Although there had been individual Jewish settlers in what is now America before 1654, it was not until that year that a group of Jews first settled in what was then New Amsterdam, later to be renamed New York. The first immigrants were Sefardic Jews, some of whom came by way of Cuba and Jamaica. The next wave of immigrants followed in the eighteenth century. These were primarily German Jews. The largest wave came from Russia and Poland at the end of the eighteenth and beginning of the nineteenth centuries. Fleeing poverty and religious persecution they found America to be hospitable and a land of opportunity. To this day American Jews are extremely patriotic and proud of being American. My maternal grand-father was born in Indiana in 1901, the son of Russian immi-grants. One of my earliest childhood memories of visiting him is the American flag he always flew from his porch on the fourth of July.

Canada

It is not exactly clear when the first group of Jewish immi-grants entered Canada, although by the second half of the eighteenth century the first synagogue, a Sefardic one, was established in Montreal. The first Ashkenazi synagogue was established in that city by the first half of the nineteenth century. The number of Jewish immigrants increased, and by 1832 Lower Canada Jews received full civil rights. By the end of the nineteenth century many more Jews immigrated to Canada following religious persecution in Russia and Poland. During the 1970s large numbers of North African, particularly Moroccan Jews, emigrated to French-speaking Montreal. The overall Jewish population in Canada today stands at nearly 350,000.

Brazil

Brazil has a Jewish population of a quarter of a million. Jews fleeing the Spanish Inquisition sought refuge in Dutch-con-trolled Brazil in the early part of the seventeenth century.

Argentina

Like the early Jewish immigrants to Brazil, the early Jewish settlers in Argentina were fleeing the Spanish Inquisition. By the middle of the nineteenth century the Jewish population began to grow through immigration from Germany, the Balkans and North Africa. It was not until the end of the nineteenth century that Eastern European Jews began to emigrate in large numbers to Argentina. Most of the Jews living in Argentina today are Ashkenazim. The total population of Jews in Argentina is nearly a quarter of a million.

The former Soviet Union

Russia boasted the world's largest Jewish population before the First World War. The result of poverty and religious persecution led masses to emigrate across the world by the late nineteenth century. Despite this mass emmigration Russia still maintained a sizeable Jewish population. The official 1989 Soviet census put the Jewish population in that country at just under one and a half million. Since 1989 some 400,000 more Jews have left Russia. Today there are an estimated 440,000 Jews remaining in Russia, some 300,000 in the Ukraine, 40,000 in Moldova, 28,000 in Belarus and 10,800 in Latvia.

France

The first Jewish settlers in France arrived with the Greek founders of Marseilles in about 500 BCE. The Jewish community in France grew after the destruction of the Temple in the first century. Throughout the Middle Ages France was a centre of the highest level of Jewish scholarship. French Jews were emancipated in 1791. During the Second World War 120,000 French Jews were deported or massacred by the Nazis. Postwar immigration from central and Eastern Europe as well as North Africa has increased the numbers of French Jewry to just over 600,000, some 380,000 of whom live in the greater Paris area.

United Kingdom

Jews first settled in England during the Norman Conquest, from 1066. These were French Jews who lived in the continental possessions of William the Conqueror and followed him across the Channel. By the mid-twelfth century Jewish communities could be found in Lincoln, Winchester, York, Oxford, Norwich, Bristol and London. In 1290 King Edward I banished the Jews from England. Small numbers of Spanish and Portuguese Jews began to trickle back to England in the sixteenth century. By the middle of the seventeenth century Jews began to settle in larger numbers. The first waves of Jews to resettle England were of Spanish and Portuguese extraction. Eventually, by the end of the seventeenth century, they were joined by a small Ashkenazi community, primarily from Germany and Holland. This Ashkenazi community steadily grew so that by the end of the eighteenth century it overtook the Sefardic community in numbers and influence. The mass immigration from Eastern Europe that began in 1881 dramatically affected the size of the Anglo-Jewish community. The community, which stood at a population of 65,000 in 1880, had increased to 300,000 by 1914. By the middle of the twentieth century Anglo-Jewry peaked at over 400,000. Since then it has been on a gradual decline in terms of numbers. This is a result of the combination of assimilation and emigration to Israel as well as to other countries, notably the United States and Canada. Today the Anglo-Jewish population stands at about 270,000.

Germany
The Jewish presence in Germany goes back to Roman times. As in France, the Jewish community of Germany produced during the Middle Ages some of the greatest rabbinical minds. Before 1933 the Jewish population was more than half a million, 160,000 of whom lived in Berlin. Today there are about 100,000 Jews in Germany, many immigrants from the former Soviet Union. It is said that Germany is Europe's fastest-growing Jewish community today.

Italy
The Jewish presence in Italy goes back to ancient times, expanding considerably at the time of the Roman exile in the first century. Italian Jews have their own prayer rites and rituals that are neither Ashkenzi nor Sefardi. They call these rites

Italki and claim that this is one of the oldest and most authentic prayer rites in the Jewish world. The Jewish community of Italy today is rather small, numbering some 35,000, to be found mostly in Rome and Milan.

Australia

The earliest record of a Jewish community in Australia is from the early nineteenth century. By the middle of the nineteenth century the first synagogue was erected in Sydney. The community numbers were boosted in the second half of the twentieth century by the immigration of Holocaust survivors. Australian Jewry today stands at nearly 100,000.

South Africa

The Jewish presence in South Africa goes back to the earliest period of South African history. Today the Jewish population numbers some 75,000.

Sefardic lands

Most of the once glorious Sefardic communities have dwindled considerably since the establishment of the State of Israel in 1948 and the outbreak of Arab hostilities. The current populations for some of what were once the most significant Sefardic communities are as follows:

Egypt	240
Libya	50
Morocco	5,800
Tunisia	1,500
Yemen	1,000
Syria	1,500

A notable exception is Turkey, which during the Ottoman Empire was a destination of refuge for many Jews fleeing the Spanish Inquisition. The Jewish population in Turkey today numbers some 25,000.

Other locations

Singapore: the Jewish community in Singapore dates back to the first half of the nineteenth century. Its current population stands at 240.

Surinam: this is one of the oldest Jewish settlements in the western hemisphere, dating back to the first half of the seventeenth century. Its Jewish population today numbers 300.

Curaçao: the first Jews to come to this country were Sefardic and they established their community in 1651. The synagogue established in 1732 is the oldest synagogue in continuous use in the western hemisphere. The Jewish population today numbers 350.

Fiji: Jews from Britain and Australia settled in the islands as early as the nineteenth century. Today about twelve Jewish families reside in Suva.

Malta: Jews have lived in Malta since pre-Roman times. Before the Spanish expulsion of 1492 one-third of its capital city, Mdina, was Jewish. A small Jewish community was established there in the nineteenth century and survives to this day. There are currently some fifty Jews in Malta.

Zaire: during the period of Belgian rule there were some 2,500 Jews living in this country. Today they number 100.

All in all the total world Jewish population hovers around thirteen million. Of that figure some 1,600,000 are found in Europe, about 6,483,900 in North America, five million in Israel and 90,000 in Africa.

It could reasonably be said that the Jewish people understood globalization long before anyone else had even heard of the term. Despite the wide-ranging gaps of geography, language and culture, Jews perceive themselves as one people. This point is driven home to me whenever I travel and meet another Jew on a train, at a hotel or in a departure lounge. Despite language barriers, we immediately connect, and if we are lucky we may discover that we have a mutual friend. History has not always been kind to us and we have been forcibly dispersed over many years. Yet somehow we have managed to retain our unity. This unity has always been our greatest strength and source of comfort. It is also the key to understanding Jewish history and survival.

PART 3

Practice

Chapter 10

A DAY IN THE LIFE OF A PRACTISING JEW

A season is set for everything, a time for every experience under heaven.   (Ecclesiastes 3:1)

Jewish observance and practice is bound to time. It is not just the performance of the ritual that matters but also its timing. Every Jewish ritual has its own timing be it seasonal, monthly or daily. Moreover, many rituals must be performed within prescribed hours. On a certain level this seems to rob Jewish ritual of spontaneity. How spontaneous can one's prayers be when they have to be recited daily between the hours of, say, 7 a.m. and 12 noon? Yet from a theological perspective the notion of a time-bound ritual gives expression to the idea that godliness is not limited to the spiritual realm but that it can be found in our physical world, defined by time and space. Jewish ritual bridges heaven and earth by recognizing that the infinite Creator can be found, and related to, in finite time and space.

The Jewish day begins at nightfall, or, to be precise, at the moment of *tzeit ha-kokhavim*, that is, when at least three stars emerge, which is roughly an hour after sunset. Many Jewish calendars will carry the exact time of tzeit ha-kokhavim on any given date, and so there is little need today to actually step outside and count the stars. I recall a summer holiday in a tiny Italian village on the Adriatic coast and not having a calendar with me, gazing at the darkening sky each evening in search of the stars that would signal the beginning of a new day and the time for evening prayers. This simple act brought me to a deeper appreciation of Judaism's link with nature and time, something I had previously not given much thought about while checking the printed times in a calendar.

The first ritual of the day following nightfall is the recitation of *ma'ariv*, the evening prayers. The central prayers in this service are the *shema*, consisting of biblical verses pertaining to the oneness of God, and the *amidah*, a series of joined blessings composed by second-century rabbis. Framing these two prayers are several blessings that incorporate the themes of God's love for his people and of redemption.

> Help us lie down, O Lord our God, in peace, and rise up, O our King, to life. Spread over us your canopy of peace.

> Shelter us in the shadow of your wings, for You, God, are our Guardian and Deliverer; You, God, are a gracious and compassionate King.

> Guard our going out and our coming in, for life and peace, from now and forever.

> Blessed are You, who guards His people Israel for ever.

In general, prayers ought to be recited in the presence of a *minyan*, a quorum of ten male Jews above the age of thirteen. It is for this purpose that many observant Jews will go to the synagogue each evening. If it is not possible to pray with a minyan one may recite the prayers alone, with certain omissions.

Upon entering one's home it is customary to touch with one's hand the *mezuzah* affixed to the right doorpost and then to kiss one's fingertips. The mezuzah is a small parchment scroll containing the biblical verses of the *shema* which Jews are commanded to affix to the doorposts of their homes. It is a reminder to the Jew of God's continuous presence in his life and home. Displaying a *mezuzah* on one's front door is a rather widespread practice even amongst Jews who do not consider themselves religious.

A common misconception is to confuse the mezuzah case with the actual mezuzah scroll, which traditionally is rolled up and placed in a small decorated cylinder case and then affixed to the doorpost. Since mezuzahs are often sold already rolled up in their cases many people never actually see the scroll inside. Some are unaware of the presence of the scroll altogether. The fact that the decorative case often has Hebrew lettering on it only compounds the confusion. I recall a rabbi once telling me that he was asked by a woman in his community if he could come over to her house and help her affix a new mezuzah she had bought. When he arrived she handed him an empty mezuzah case. Perplexed, he asked her where the mezuzah scroll was. 'Oh,' she responded, 'you mean the Hebrew instructions? I threw it away with the packaging. I figured that as a rabbi you wouldn't need them.'

Mealtime has its own set of rituals, consisting mainly of blessings of thanksgiving to God both before as well as after eating. If the meal consists of bread, a ritual washing of the hands is required before sitting down to eat. This ritual consists of pouring water over one's hands from a large ceremonial cup symbolizing the ritual washing of the priests' hands before serving God in the ancient Temple. The ritual cleansing of hands before eating symbolizes that even an act as mundane and material such as eating can be infused with holiness. This is especially so if one eats in a dignified manner cognizant of the fact that one is, through this act, keeping body and soul together.

The holiness of eating is compounded when the table conversation is elevated and refined. This idea is beautifully expressed by the Talmudic sage Rabbi Simeon who said that when a group of people who have eaten at a table over which words of the Torah were spoken it is as if they had eaten from God's table.

After the washing of the hands one is not permitted to speak until one has said the blessing over the bread and had a piece to eat. While the blessings before eating are brief, consisting of one sentence blessing God for creating the food we are about to eat, the grace after meals is much longer, running to several pages in the prayer-book. It has become customary in many circles to sing the grace after meals, which means that most observant Jewish children learn it by heart by the time they are six or seven years old.

> Blessed are You, Lord our God, King of the Universe, who in His goodness feeds the whole world with grace, kindness and compassion. He gives food to all living things, for His kindness is for ever. Because of His continual great goodness, we have never lacked food, nor may we ever lack it, for the sake of His great name. For He is God who feeds and sustains all, does good to all, and prepares food for all creatures He has created. Blessed are You, Lord, who feeds all.

While this highly regulated form of eating suits a domestic setting it can be somewhat challenging when eating away from home. Planning an outing, any outing, an observant Jewish family must take into account not only packing kosher food, but also water and cups with which to ritually wash their hands before eating bread. Travelling abroad to places without a sizeable Jewish community able to provide kosher facilities means that one must travel with a reasonable amount of kosher food. I have visited cities famous for their cuisine only to return to my hotel room to dine on matzah crackers and canned tuna fish. Experience has taught me that when travelling it always pays to be prepared and that even if a city boasts a kosher restaurant there is no guarantee that it will be open when you wish to eat.

At some point in the evening an observant Jew will study some Torah. The mitzvah to study the Torah is one of the most important, and in an ideal world one should study it assiduously. For those who spend the bulk of their day working this is not possible, and so they set aside time each evening and/or morning for the purpose of study.

A set of prayers is recited before going to bed. These include the shema as well as meditations and reflections on one's behaviour during the day and resolutions to improve tomorrow. The final prayer is a request that God grant us a restful sleep and that he guard our soul until such time as we wake.

> Blessed are You, Lord our God, King of the Universe, who makes the bonds of sleep fall on my eyes, and slumber on my eyelids. May it be Your will, Lord my God and God of my fathers, that You make me lie down in peace and arise in peace. Let not my imagination, bad dreams or troubling thoughts disturb me. May my bed be flawless before You. Enlighten my eyes lest I sleep the sleep of death, for it is You who illuminate the pupil of the eye. Blessed are You, Lord, who gives light to the whole world in his glory.

An abridged version of these bedtime prayers are recited by children, and most parents make a point of teaching it to them at an early age. In fact the first Hebrew words a child is taught to speak is the first sentence of the shema prayer, 'Hear oh Israel, the Lord is our God, the Lord is one.'

The first words uttered upon waking are a short prayer of thanksgiving to God for restoring our soul and giving us another day of life. Morning prayers, known as shaharit in Hebrew, are the most lengthy of all the daily prayers, taking a little under an hour to recite. The time for these prayers is from sunrise until late morning, although the shema prayer must be completed even earlier. In the dark winter months they can be recited even before sunrise. As with the evening prayers, these should ideally be recited along with a quorum at the synagogue. If this is not possible they may be recited alone, with certain omissions. One of the noticeable characteristics of morning prayer is that male worshippers over the age of thirteen are required to wear tefillin (see page 20). Many will also be wrapped in a *tallit* prayer shawl, although in some communities prayer shawls are worn only by married men. On Monday and Thursday mornings the Torah is read and the prayers are slightly longer.

After morning prayers most people will rush off to work, while some may remain behind for a while studying some Torah before starting the day.

The regulated times for prayer mean that even after a late night or on weekends there is a limit as to how late one can sleep in. A late synagogue service on a Sunday morning will typically be at eight o'clock. This can be extremely challenging, particularly for teenagers as they train themselves to rise at the appropriate time so as not to miss morning prayers.

Most challenging for those at work are the afternoon prayer, or *mincha*. By definition, the time for mincha is in the middle of the working day. Although it is a relatively short prayer – it can be read in about ten minutes – finding the time to break away from a busy schedule can prove difficult. It is for this very reason that the Talmud states that of all the prayers, the one most beloved by God is the mincha prayer. This is because God appreciates the gesture made by one who prioritizes his time so as to include this prayer.

In the summer, when the days are long, the time for mincha can extend from early afternoon until as late as eight in the evening; in the winter it may extend from midday until only about four o'clock. Unlike the morning and evening prayers, which can be recited in synagogue or at home before or after the workday, mincha is difficult to plan. In large metropolitan cities with sizeable Jewish populations, one can find daily mincha services at various places of work, enabling one to pray with a quorum. For a couple of years I gave a weekly Bible class at a prestigious law firm in the city of London followed by mincha. At least twenty people attended regularly. Without such facilities one has to find some quiet place to pray, be it in an office or deserted boardroom. For those with great commitment it may mean interrupting an important phone call or even excusing oneself from a meeting to ensure the prayers are recited on time. Travelling presents its own challenges, as one must remember to factor in mincha. Sometimes a journey takes longer than expected and one finds oneself praying in the strangest places such as a car park, a shopping centre, the forecourt of a petrol station or even inside a phone booth.

I could probably write a chapter about my most interesting mincha experiences, but the one that stands out took place at the departure lounge at Budapest airport in the summer of 1998. I was returning to London from a weekend in Hungary with a group of some fifty members of my synagogue. Our plane was delayed by several hours, and as the afternoon began to drain away we decided it was time to pray mincha. We stood up to pray and remained standing in a loose formation for the next ten minutes. After prayers we turned back to our seats only to find an enormous queue stretching back through the departure lounge. Were these all co-religionists who had joined us for mincha? Not exactly: they were overtired and impatient travellers who saw fifty people get out of their seats to stand along the wall, and just assumed it was the queue for boarding the plane.

The Sabbath

The Jewish Sabbath, known in Hebrew as Shabbat, begins at sunset on Friday evening. Preparations for Shabbat in most homes begin on a Thursday night as families begin to shop, cook, bake and clean their homes for this very special day. Preparations continue throughout Friday. In predominantly Jewish neighbourhoods the excitement on a Friday afternoon is palpable as Jews rush about running last-minute errands. In the winter, when the days are short, observant Jews will make a point of leaving work early so as to be home in time to get ready for Shabbat.

By sunset the table will be set and all the family will have bathed and dressed up. The women will then light the special Shabbat candles. Originally these were lit in order to ensure that the home had light and that the Shabbat dinner would as a result be a pleasant experience. Today our homes are illuminated by electricity, yet the practice of lighting candles, or in some homes oil lamps, continues, as it has come to represent the spiritual illumination of the Shabbat. There are different customs relating to the amount of candles lit. The minimum is two candles per household. Yet others have the custom of lighting a candle for each member of the family. When large extended families celebrate the Shabbat together the result can be quite beautiful and dramatic.

The candle-lighting is accompanied by a special blessing and often followed by a short meditation or silent prayer in which the woman of the house may make specific requests of God asking Him to bless her family. As a child I was always fascinated by my mother's silent prayers, which at times seemed to go on for an eternity. I used to sneak up and try to listen as she prayed silently with her eyes tightly closed, but I could never make out her words. I knew that whatever she was saying was important, and that God was listening to her.

Candle-lighting is followed by a synagogue service consisting of some of the most uplifting prayers known as Kabbalat Shabbat, welcoming the Shabbat. These prayers have their origins in sixteenth-century Safed. It was the custom of the mystics of that holy city to dress in white and to go out into the fields at sunset to sing and welcome in the Shabbat (see pp. 138–9). These prayers have now become universal Jewish practice, although going out into the fields has been replaced by the custom of turning around at one point in the service towards the synagogue door in a symbolic gesture of greeting the Shabbat. After Kabbalat Shabbat the evening ma'ariv prayers are read. These are mostly similar to the weekday ma'ariv except for some changes reflecting the Shabbat theme.

There is a Jewish tradition that one is accompanied home from synagogue on Friday night by two angels. It is in deference to this tradition that immediately upon returning home we recite a hymn welcoming them into our home. This is followed by reading chapter 31 from the Book of Proverbs extolling the woman of valour, as an expression of gratitude to the woman of the house for the central role she plays in the Jewish family. It is then customary to bless one's children. The traditional blessing involves placing both hands on the child's head and reciting an ancient blessing from the Torah. As with the prayers after candle-lighting, parents may wish to add their own specific blessings as well. When I bless my children on Friday nights I make a point of whispering something additional to each of them, acknowledging their own unique personalities and talents.

The kiddush, a prayer sanctifying the Shabbat, is then recited over a cup of wine and the meal can then begin. The meal will always start with the ritual washing of the hands followed by a blessing over two loaves of specially braided bread known as *challah*.

Jewish law does not prescribe the Shabbat menu other than stating that it must be more elaborate than that served on an ordinary weekday. The average Jewish family will serve several courses, though what these consist of depends very much on one's cultural background. Ashkenazi Jews will traditionally serve chicken soup, *gefilte* fish, a hot potato pudding called *kugel* and roast chicken, while Sefardic Jews will have more exotic fare involving liberally spiced fish and meat dishes. Both traditions serve a special stew for lunch. This stew, known as *cholent* for Ashkenazim or *hamin* for Sefardim, is cooked before the Shabbat and left to simmer on the fire all through the night. It was originally conceived as a way of ensuring a hot lunch despite the prohibition against cooking on the Shabbat. It remains a much enjoyed staple on Shabbat afternoon.

My wife, who is an Italian of Sefardic extraction, did not grow up with Ashkenazi food as I did, and so to an Ashkenazi, her Friday night dinners can seem rather unconventional. I recall we once invited a non-observant Ashkenazi couple to a Friday night dinner and the woman was absolutely scandalized when instead of chicken soup Dina served gazpacho. Despite my best efforts to explain that Jewish law does not require the consumption of chicken soup on a Friday night she remained doubtful. To this day I am convinced that she thinks her rabbi let her down by serving gazpacho on the holy Shabbat.

Gefilte fish is made out of ground carp, whitefish or pike, and sometimes all three, mixed with breadcrumbs, onions and spices. They are rolled into balls, boiled and garnished with carrots or parsley. There is some debate as to the origin of this dish. Some say that grinding the fish was a way to circumvent a complex Shabbat law prohibiting the extraction of bones from meat or fish. Others suggest that grinding the fish down and mixing it with breadcrumbs was a way for poor Jews to stretch the dish to feed their large families. Whatever the reason, Jewish law or plain home economics, some anonymous but ingenious Jewish housewife created a classic Shabbat dish that has withstood the test of time.

As with any meal, only more so, it is customary to share ideas from the Torah at the Shabbat table. Traditionally these ideas relate to the weekly Torah portion read in synagogue each Saturday morning. Children who attend Jewish schools will inevitably bring home ideas or stories to share at the table. It is also customary to sing. Many Shabbat hymns have been composed over the years, and these are published in special booklets. Each hymn can be sung to many tunes and every family will have its own favourites.

The length of the Friday night meal depends on each family, although it will generally proceed at a much more leisurely pace than one during the week. After dinner a family may sit down together to read or study, or, particularly during the long winter nights, they may go out to visit friends or family.

One of the Shabbat pleasures on Friday night is marital intimacy. It is a time for married couples to reconnect with each other after a hard working week. That Judaism sees sexual intimacy as not only compatible with the holy Shabbat but even as a way of celebrating it speaks volumes about the Jewish attitude toward sex. The sexual urge itself is seen as neither good nor evil; rather, its worth depends on how the urge is channelled. While extramarital sex is prohibited, Judaism appreciates the value of sex in a loving marriage, so much so that the Torah considers it a mitzvah, particularly on Friday night. The fact that an act as carnal and sensual as sex can be counted as a mitzvah highlights the key idea that we keep returning to, namely, that Judaism seeks to elevate the physical and to bridge heaven and earth.

It is customary to sleep in a little later on a Shabbat morning, as sleep is considered another one of the special Shabbat pleasures, although some people will rise early anyway, either out of habit or in order to study some Torah before prayers commence. As a child I recall my father rising extremely early on a Shabbat morning, sometimes before six, to study uninterrupted for several hours before praying.

The Shabbat morning service is the longest of the week, lasting from two to over three hours, depending on the nature of the congregation, the proclivity of the cantor, the length of the particular Torah reading that week and if there are additional causes for celebration such as a bar or bat mitzvah. It is common for most rabbis to deliver a weekly sermon, although this seems to be a rather late nineteenth-century development as rabbis originally preached only two or three times a year, before major festivals.

The service itself consists of a lengthened version of Shaharit, followed by the Torah reading and sermon. This is then followed by the *musaph* or additional service, which is much shorter than Shaharit. Many congregations will host a kiddush after the service. Kiddush, as mentioned earlier, is the special blessing recited over a cup of wine before Friday night dinner or Shabbat lunch. The term can be confusing because, particularly in the context of Shabbat lunch, kiddush can also refer to the lunch or snack itself. Hence when a synagogue 'hosts a kiddush', or when one 'attends a kiddush', the reference is to the meal not the wine. The staples served at a synagogue kiddush can range from dry biscuits and soda to a full hot lunch. In my experience, the British incline towards the former while the Americans tend towards the latter.

Shabbat lunch is something of a repeat of Friday night dinner, usually followed by a long nap. During the long summer afternoons friends and family will get together. Synagogues generally provide educational activities for children, while adults may attend a lecture or study session.

Later in the afternoon a third Shabbat meal is served. Unlike the first two this one is not preceded by the recital of kiddush. According to some authorities it is not even necessary to eat bread. In general this meal, called *se'uda shlishit*, or the third meal, is more of a snack than a full meal.

Many synagogues will host the se'uda shlishit after the mincha prayers. In mystical circles this last period of Shabbat is seen as the holiest part of the holy day and the mystical songs composed in its honor reflect a deep yearning for communion with God. It is also a bittersweet time, as the Shabbat slowly slips away. Many of the traditional tunes sung at this time are tinged with melancholy, reflecting our sadness at the passing of the holy Shabbat.

One of the most moving hymns was written by the sixteenth-century Safed Kabbalist Rabbi Eliezer Azikri. Below are just a few stanzas:

Glorious, beautiful, radiance of the world,
My soul is sick with love for You.
Please God, heal her now
By showing her your tender radiance.
Then she will recover her strength and be healed,
and have everlasting joy

Ancient of days, let Your mercy be aroused
And have pity on Your beloved child.

How long have I yearned
To see the glory of Your strength.
These things my heart passionately desires –
Have pity; do not hide yourself.

Once three stars have appeared the evening prayers are read and the Shabbat is formally brought to a close in a ceremony known as *havdalah*. The ceremony consists of special prayers and blessings recited over wine, a flame and spices. It is only befitting to bid the Shabbat farewell over a cup of wine just as she was welcomed in on Friday night. The creation of fire, prohibited on the Shabbat, represents the start of the creative working week. Lastly, the spices are to revive us lest we feel faint with yearning for the Shabbat, and to fortify us for the week ahead.

This is traditionally followed by a post Shabbat meal, known as *melaveh malkah*, (escorting the Shabbat queen) in honour of the departed Shabbat. As it follows two earlier meals, it is often not much more than a light snack. Here again, there is a large repertoire of special hymns, this time reflecting our hopes and prayers for a blessed and successful week.

Chapter 11

THE JEWISH YEAR CYCLE

September–October

Rosh Hashanah (Jewish New Year)

The Jewish year begins on the first of the Hebrew month of Tishrei, which in most years will fall some time in September. The festival of the New Year is called Rosh Hashanah, which translates literally as the Head of the Year. The term *head*, according to Hasidic tradition, reflects not just the start of the year, but, more importantly, its direction. As the head (brain) governs the body and determines its movements similarly Rosh Hashanah contains the spiritual energy that determines the type of year about to unfold.

Although Rosh Hashanah is technically a festival, its celebration is somewhat muted. This is because it is primarily a day of judgement in which the Almighty weighs up our deeds of the previous year. It is a festival of reflection and introspection in which we resolve to improve ourselves and pray to God for a healthy and prosperous year to come.

The festival begins at sunset on the eve of Rosh Hashanah,

when services are read in the synagogue. Upon returning home
the kiddush prayer is recited over a cup of wine. It is customary to follow kiddush by partaking of an assortment of fruits
and vegetables which represent various blessings, such as prosperity, fertility and security. This is then followed by the ritual
washing of the hands and the blessing of the challah bread. In
many homes it is the custom to replace the oblong-shaped
braided challahs, used throughout the year, with circular ones.
This symbolizes the circle of life and the passage of a new year.
It is also customary to dip the challah in honey as a symbol for
a sweet year. A festive meal follows in which various types of
rich and sweet food are served, again symbolizing our hopes
for a good sweet year. Synagogue services the next morning
start earlier than usual as the prayers of Rosh Hashanah are
amongst the lengthiest of the year. It is not uncommon for
them to begin at 8 a.m. and to conclude not much before 2 p.m.
As on Shabbat, the services consist of *Shaharit*, the morning
prayer and *musaph*, the additional prayer, with the reading of
the Torah in between. The highlight of the Rosh Hashanah
service is the sounding of the shofar, an unadorned ram's horn,
after the reading of the Torah. While the Torah simply states
that a shofar be sounded, the Talmudic rabbis interpreted this
to mean a series of blasts of differing lengths. The minimum
number of blasts required, or *kolot* in Hebrew, is thirty, but
traditionally at least a hundred are sounded and in some congregations even more. The shofar blasts have come to represent
many themes. My favourite is that it represents crying. Indeed,
the crude sounds produced by blowing on a ram's horn are
remarkably similar to the sounds of human wailing or sobbing.
This crying represents the soul's yearning for God, a theme
that plays itself out in much of the liturgy of the day. Yet while
the liturgy is beautiful and poetic it lacks the raw expression of
the sounds emitted by the shofar. The sobbing of the shofar
expresses an honesty and urgency that words cannot, and it is
in transcending words that the shofar comes to express the
deepest longing of the soul.

One of the greatest honours is to be asked to sound the shofar for the congregation. This is also an awesome responsibility: not only must one have the technical skill to produce the requisite sounds, but ideally one must also be a man of heightened spiritual stature. To this day when I hear the shofar a scene plays out in my mind in which I am a nineteen-year-old yeshiva student in Brooklyn New York at the court of late Hasidic master Rabbi Menachem Mendel Schneersohn (who died in 1992). I recall thousands of Hasidim packed into the synagogue all eager to hear, and if lucky, to catch a glimpse of this holy man sounding the shofar. The Rebbe was almost ninety years old. He stood robed in white on the elevated reader's desk, at either side of him stood two men with Torah scrolls. On the desk itself were eight or nine bulging sacks of post, each one full of letters sent to the Rebbe in the weeks leading up to Rosh Hashanah from Jews all over the world. Each letter, known as a *kvitel* in Yiddish, was essentially a petition to the Rebbe to pray to God on the sender's behalf for a good and sweet year. I watched as, moments before sounding the shofar, the Rebbe threw his prayer shawl over the desk, covering himself and the petitions. He remained there for many long minutes. Not a sound could be heard in the vast synagogue except for the muffled sobbing of the Rebbe as he poured out his heart to God. Then suddenly, without warning, he threw back his prayer shawl revealing a face burning with intensity. He recited the blessings with deep feeling, put a small ram's horn to his trembling lips and produced the most haunting and moving sounds I have ever heard. They were soft, barely above a whisper, but so full of longing it was as if I heard the soul itself calling out to God. This was without doubt one of the great religious experiences of my life and one I return to in my mind each year as I hear the shofar.

The services are followed by a festive lunch. Later in the afternoon, just before or after the mincha service, it is customary to recite a special prayer at a body of water, often a brook or stream, and to recite verses from chapter 7 of the Book of

The concept of the kvitel and intercession in prayer
While Judaism believes that great spiritual people are able to intercede before God and request His blessing for others, it does not absolve individuals from praying on their own behalf. No one can pray *instead* of you, they can pray *with* you. The aim of the kvitel is not that the Rebbe prays *instead* of the supplicant but rather *with* him. This idea is beautifully illustrated by a story concerning the Hasidic master Rabbi Levi Yitzchak of Berdichev.

It once happened on the eve of Yom Kippur, the Day of Atonement, that Rabbi Levi Yitzchak announced to his community that this year he would not accept their kvitel without payment of the princely sum of a silver rouble each. Of course there was a lot of grumbling, for who could easily afford to part with such a sum? On the other hand, who could even conceive of not presenting the Rebbe with a kvitel? In the end, all the townspeople somehow managed to scrape together the extortionate fee. Towards the very end of the afternoon, just as the Rebbe was about to leave for synagogue, a young widow came rushing into his house with a kvitel, begging the Rebbe to pray for her sick child. The Rebbe motioned to the large pile of gleaming coins on his desk indicating where she should place her rouble, but, alas, the wretched woman had nothing to give. She broke down and pleaded with the Rebbe, explaining that she spent the entire day scrounging around for the money but to no avail. The Rebbe was resolute. He would not agree to pray for the child unless his mother could pay his fee. Exasperated, the poor woman stormed out of his house but not before shouting over her shoulder, 'You think I need you, Rabbi Levi Yitzchak, to pray for my child? I don't need you at all. I will myself pray to our Father in Heaven. He will no doubt be merciful to me.' Upon hearing this, the Rebbe's face broke into a wide smile. 'Come back!' he called after her. 'I am not at all interested in the silver roubles, I was waiting for someone to challenge me and realize that a prayer cannot be bought. Come now with me, let us go to synagogue and there we will pray together for your child.'

Micah. Included is verse 19: 'He will take us back in love; He will cover up our iniquities, You will hurl all our sins into the depths of the sea.' This practice, called *tashlikh*, meaning 'casting away', symbolizes our hope that as we cast our sins away (metaphorically into the sea) God will overlook them and allow us to start the new year afresh.

Rosh Hashanah is a two-day festival and all the rituals and services with the exception of tashlikh are repeated on the following day.

Rosh Hashanah ushers in what is known as the ten days of repentance. These include the two days of Rosh Hashanah, the Day of Atonement; Yom Kippur, and the seven days in between, which are seen as a period of repentance leading to the ultimate day of repentance and atonement; Yom Kippur. During this period additional prayers are recited early each morning before the Shaharit service and certain additions are made to all three of the daily services themselves.

One of the important aspects of the days of repentance is apologizing to people we may have hurt or insulted in the past year. Judaism divides sins into two distinct categories: sins between man and God and sins between fellow men. The former involve laxity in observing religious rituals, whereas the latter involves any type of crime that we may have committed against our fellow man. Judaism teaches that while God has the power to forgive sins committed against Him, He does not have the power to forgive sins committed against one's fellow. That is to say, there is no point in praying to God for forgiveness for the sin of insulting or defrauding one's neighbour. One must seek forgiveness from the victim, since only this can lead to God's forgiveness and atonement.

It is inevitable that one of these seven days of repentance will be a Saturday. This is known as Shabbat Shuvah, the Shabbat of return or repentance. It is given this name because of the opening lines of the prophetic reading in synagogue that morning: 'Return (shuvah), O Israel, to the Lord your God, for you have fallen because of your sin' (Hosea 14:2).

Yom Kippur (Day of Atonement)

Yom Kippur is the holiest day of the year in the Jewish calendar. It is the culmination of the ten days of repentance and, as such, it is a Day of Atonement and forgiveness. It is the one day a year in which Jews are required to try to transcend the material and to strive, if only for a short while, to emulate the spiritual quality of angels. This is achieved through self-denial in five areas: food, drink, anointing the body with oils or perfumes, the wearing of leather shoes and sexual intimacy. These denials, known as *innuyim*, literally, afflictions, begin at sundown on Yom Kippur eve and remain in place until nightfall the next day, some twenty-five hours later. Yet, somewhat paradoxically, Yom Kippur is preceded by a festive meal eaten late in the afternoon and concluding shortly before the fast begins. This is partly in order to give strength to those who are fasting and partly to honour the day of Yom Kippur itself, which is technically a festival. Thus the feasting is brought forward a day as it is not possible to eat on Yom Kippur itself.

There are five prayer services throughout Yom Kippur. According to kabbalistic tradition these represent the five levels of the soul, each level deeper than the previous one. The fifth level is the quintessence of the soul, its very heart and core. Accordingly, the services of Yom Kippur take the worshipper on an inward spiritual journey of self-discovery leading to a connection with one's very essence. The climax of this intense spiritual journey is the closing service at the very end of Yom Kippur. By then the worshipper has connected with his spiritual core and emerges spiritually cleansed and revitalized.

As there is no festive meal to go home to and the purpose of the day is to pour out one's heart to God in prayer, the services last all day. Many people arrive at synagogue early in the morning and do not return home until after dark.

At the heart of each service is the confessional prayer, consisting of a general listing of common sins. The list is illustrative and not exhaustive, and so each individual is required to add confessions for their own particular sins. The confessions are made to God alone and any confession to particular sins, as opposed to the general list in the prayer-book, is recited silently so that others may not hear it. The confessional prayer is recited whilst standing, bent slightly forward, and as each sin is enumerated one lightly strikes one's chest with one's fist.

At certain points in the Yom Kippur service the worshippers will prostrate themselves. Prostration was common practice during the ancient Temple rites. Whenever God's name was proclaimed aloud by the priests the congregation of onlookers would bow to the ground in reverence. It is not Jewish practice to bow to the ground in prayer today, with the exception of Yom Kippur, when the bowing takes place during the part of the service that recounts the Temple rites.

Of all the innuyim on Yom Kippur the most difficult is fasting. The rule is that any healthy person above the age of twelve for a girl and thirteen for a boy must fast for the duration of Yom Kippur. Fasting here means that nothing is allowed to pass one's lips, neither food nor drink for twenty-five hours. Exceptions are made for women who have just come out of childbirth and for pregnant women who are exceedingly weak. However, there is no blanket dispensation for pregnant women per se. While there are dispensations for the seriously ill, the laws governing such dispensations are complex and generally a rabbi ought to be consulted. Although girls under the age of twelve and boys under the age thirteen are exempt, most children from the age of nine or ten will try to fast for at least part of the day.

The conclusion of Yom Kippur is signalled by a single long

blast on the shofar. At that point the weekday *ma'ariv* service is read and everyone goes home to celebrate with yet another festive meal. This festive atmosphere reflects our firm belief that God has heard our prayers, accepted our sincere repentance and will bless us with a good year.

Sukkot – the Festival of Booths

Sukkot, the Festival of Booths, comes four days after Yom Kippur. Falling in the autumn each year, Sukkot is essentially a harvest festival in which we thank God for His bounty. It is therefore a festival of great joy, particularly coming so soon after the spiritual cleansing of Yom Kippur.

There are two main features of Sukkot, the *sukkah* and the lulav. The sukkah, after which the festival gets its name, means a booth. This is based on the verses in Leviticus (23:42–3): 'You shall live in booths seven days; all citizens in Israel shall live in booths, in order that future generations may know that I made the Israelite people live in booths when I brought them out of the land of Egypt, I am the Lord your God.' The definition of a sukkah is any shelter with a minimum of three walls and a roof covered by organic material leaving enough open space to see the stars peaking through. Sukkahs today come in all sizes and materials and there are thriving pre-fab sukkah businesses in most large Jewish communities that do a brisk trade in the weeks leading up to this festival. In warm climates people will sleep in their sukkah for the entire week. In colder climates they will at least take all their meals there. The nature of the organic material covering the roof, the *sekhakh* in Hebrew, also varies from country to country. As a child growing up in Montreal we always covered our sukkah with pine branches and to this day I associate the sweet smell of pine with the sukkah festival. As a teenager I spent a couple of years in South America, where they use palm branches.

The idea behind sitting in this rather exposed booth is, on a very basic level, to recall the journey our ancestors made through the desert to the Promised Land during which they

dwelt in makeshift huts or booths. On a deeper level the
sukkah's exposure to the elements symbolizes man's vulnera-
bility. This is a particularly important idea to bear in mind at a
harvest festival when one reaps the benefits of a year's work.
The sukkah's exposure to the elements reminds us that we are
not the masters of our own destiny and that all our success is
due to God's blessing. The lulav is a palm branch on which are
bound myrtle and willow twigs. This is then held together
with an etrog; a citron fruit and a blessing is recited. Following
the blessing the palm branch and citron are then waived in
every direction. It symbolizes our joy and thanksgiving to the
Almighty, whose presence is everywhere, blessing us with
abundance.

The following story about Sukkot highlights the theme that
Judaism is about reaching God through the physical.

One year in Berdichev it was impossible to obtain a lulav and
etrog (see p. 168). As the festival drew nearer, the townspeople
began to grow concerned. How would they fulfil the mitzvah
this year? The day before Sukkot Rabbi Levi Yitzchak took
decisive action. He appointed several townspeople to take up
positions on the main road with instructions to intercept any
passer-by who might have a lulav and etrog. It was not long
before they found a Jew who was passing through Berdichev
on his way home to another town and, behold, he had a lulav
and etrog. They begged him to spend the festival in Berdichev
so as to enable them to fulfil the mitzvah with his lulav and
etrog. However, the traveller was adamant; he had been away
from home for several months now and nothing was going to
part him from either his family or his precious lulav and etrog.
Eventually Rabbi Levi Yitzchak offered the man a deal he could
not refuse. In exchange for spending the festival in Berdichev
the rabbi would promise him a guaranteed place in paradise.
This was too good an offer to refuse. One could spend one's
entire life doing good deeds in the hope of a place in paradise
and here, just like that, he was being offered a guarantee. It was
surely worth the small sacrifice of spending the festival away

from home. Besides, his wife would certainly understand once he told her what he had received in return.

The traveller went happily on to a small inn to bathe and prepare himself for the festival. In the meantime, unbeknownst to him, the rabbi secretly sent word to all the townsfolk that under no circumstances were they to permit this traveller to enter their sukkahs to enjoy the festive meal. Strange as the order seemed, the townspeople were used to their rabbi and his unconventional ways and so they obeyed without question. After the evening prayer the traveller, now quite hungry, made his way to the nearest sukkah, hoping to join the family for the evening meal. To his surprise the door to the sukkah was locked. He knocked and waited, but there was no response. After several minutes he thought he would try his luck elsewhere and went to the next sukkah; but the same thing happened. In fact he could hear the family inside reciting the kiddush prayer, yet they could not or would not acknowledge his presence on the other side of the locked door. On to the next sukkah and again the same thing happened. After trying several sukkahs it began to dawn on him that the rabbi might have something to do with his inability to gain entry to even a single sukkah. Off he went to the rabbi's sukkah and was not surprised when there too he was confronted by a locked door. 'Rabbi,' he called out 'is this any way to treat a guest? Do not I deserve to eat in a sukkah like every other Jew? This will be the first time in my living memory that I will have missed out on the mitzvah of eating in the sukkah.'

The rabbi's voice could be heard from the other side of the door. 'So, tell me, you want to eat in a sukkah? That can easily be arranged. In fact you can join me right here, on one condition.'

'Anything you ask,' said the desperate traveller.

'You must first agree to release me from the deal I made with you earlier today. Release me from my promise to secure for you a place in paradise and I will open up the door of my sukkah to you.'

'Release you from the deal? But that was the only reason I agreed to spend the festival here in the first place!'

'So be it,' said the rabbi. 'I am afraid you will have to miss out on eating in the sukkah.'

'Why, this is sheer blackmail!' shouted the astonished man.

'Call it what you will, but that is the deal I am now offering. Decide what you want to do.'

'Well,' said the man, 'let it be on the record that I protest at the way in which you have manipulated and blackmailed me. Yet, having said that, there is really only one option open to a Jew on the first night of Sukkot and that is to eat in a sukkah.' Having said this, the traveller released the rabbi from his promise and the rabbi, for his part, graciously welcomed him into his sukkah to enjoy the festive meal. The rest of the festival passed unremarkably.

At the end of the festival, as the man was preparing to leave, the rabbi sent for him. He entered the rabbi's study and the rabbi said: 'I know how sore you are about the way you have been treated so before you leave I'd like to explain my actions to you. You see it is not really in the gift of any man to promise his fellow a place in paradise. Paradise must be earned in this world through toil and sacrifice. You were a fool to believe otherwise. However, when you were prepared to trade what you believed was a place in paradise for the possibility of fulfilling a mitzvah in this world, namely, the mitzvah of eating in a sukkah, at that moment you earned yourself a true place in paradise. Now go home to your family and rest assured that your time here was well spent. You have indeed gained for yourself a place in paradise.

Shemini Atzeret and Simchat Torah (the Rejoicing with the Torah)

Immediately following the seven-day festival of Sukkot is another festival, called Shemini Atzeret. On this festival special prayers for rain are recited and in Israel the year-long cycle of reading the Torah is completed and restarted. In the Diaspora

the Torah is not completed until the next day, which is celebrated as the festival of Simchat Torah (rejoicing with the
Torah.)

While Shemini Atzeret and Simchat Torah are excessively
joyful festivals I always found them to be rather bittersweet.
They are the last moments of an entire month of celebration
and one is conscious of the routine of the daily grind just
around the corner. As a child I felt this particularly keenly as
the autumn school term would really begin in earnest the day
after Simchat Torah.

The main feature of the Simchat Torah celebration is the
singing and dancing with the Torah scrolls, which are normally
kept in a special closet called the Ark. They are only removed
for the purpose of reading from them. The one exception is
Simchat Torah, where the scrolls are removed primarily to
dance with. The dancing with a closed scroll symbolizes that
each Jew, regardless of their scholastic ability, is able to connect
with the Torah on the most basic level.

Of all the major festivals, Simchat Torah is the rowdiest.
This is in large measure due to the rather unstructured prayer
service of that day, combined with all the dancing and singing.
Another contributing factor is that many of the adults enjoy a
stiff drink or two.

December

Hanukkah (Festival of Re-dedication)

Hanukkah has always been my favourite festival. It commemorates the Macabean uprising against the Seleucid Greeks in
the second century BCE.

The uprising began when King Antiochus Epiphanes
forbade the observance of the Jewish religion in Judaea. In
response to this, a priestly family known as the Hasmoneans
led a successful revolt and managed against overwhelming odds
to defeat Antiochus' armies and to gain control of Jerusalem
and the holy Temple, which the Greeks had defiled. Hanukkah
is both a celebration of the Hasmoneans' military victories as

well as a festival marking the re-dedication of the defiled Temple. It was during this period of re-dedication that the 'miracle of the oil' occurred. One of the daily rituals in the Temple was the kindling of the menorah, a giant seven-branched candelabrum. This was faithfully carried out each afternoon just before evening by the high priest. The flames would burn in the giant menorah all through the night, symbolizing the radiance of God's glory.

When the victorious Maccabees entered the Temple after defeating the armies of Antiochus they found to their dismay that the Greeks had sacked the Temple and defiled all the olive oil, rendering it unfit for use for the menorah ritual. They dispatched messengers to Galilee with instructions to obtain freshly pressed olive oil, realizing that it would be at least eight days until they returned. Then someone found a small cruse of pure olive oil lying in the Temple compound with the holy seal of the high priest. It was enough to fuel the menorah for only one night. They poured it into the giant menorah, which miraculously burned for eight days until the messengers returned from Galilee with a supply of fresh oil. This miracle is celebrated in Jewish homes by kindling an eight-branched menorah, otherwise known as a hanukiah, on each night of Hanukkah. We begin by kindling a single light on the first night and add one more flame on each subsequent night so that by the last night of the festival all eight flames are kindled. Menorahs or hanukiahs come in all shapes and sizes, from magnificent silver to the bottle cap and Popsicle stick concoctions children bring back from school. While it is acceptable to use candles it is preferable to use olive oil, which is more reminiscent of the miracle.

Candle-lighting ceremonies differ slightly from family to family but essentially they all involve family and friends gathering around for the lighting followed by the singing of traditional Hanukkah hymns. It is also traditional to enjoy foods fried in oil to commemorate the miracle of the oil. Doughnuts are an all-time favourite, as well as a special savoury potato

pancake known as a *latke*. It is also customary to give monetary gifts, known in Yiddish as Hanukkah *gelt* (or Hanukkah
money) to the children. The appeal of a joyous festival in the
midst of an otherwise bleak winter is evident in the popularity
of Hanukkah amongst Jews of all levels of religious commitment and observance.

February
Tu Bi-Shvat (New Year of the Trees)
The fifteenth of the Hebrew month of Shevat is celebrated as
the New Year of the Trees. This is significant in that it relates
to the Jewish laws of tithing produce. In ancient Israel a certain
tithe was taken from each year's produce and given to the
Kohanim (the priests). It was important that the tithe given
was actually from that particular year's produce and not from
the following year. The rabbis determined that the year in this
respect begins and ends on the fifteenth of Shevat, for that is
when, at least in Israel, the sap in the trees begins to run. While
it would seem that this festival would not have the same mass
appeal as, say, Hanukkah or Purim, in recent years it has
become quite popular. This is especially so amongst those who
care deeply about ecological matters. There is no prescribed
method of celebrating Tu Bi-Shvat other than sampling a new
fruit (that one has not eaten for at least a season) or a fruit from
the Land of Israel. As this festival becomes more popular many
are turning to a sixteenth-century mystical practice of hosting
a Tu-Bishvat Seder, which consists of drinking four cups of
wine of different shades, representing the four seasons and the
sampling of various fruits and nuts, representing different mystical ideas. This is accompanied by scriptural recitations and
singing.

March
Purim (Festival of Lots)
The festival of Purim celebrates the redemption of the Jewish
community of Persia in the fourth century BCE. The story

behind this festival is recounted in great detail in the scroll of Esther, which is part of the Jewish Bible. The story in its most basic outline is this: a weak and insecure king Ahasuerus kills his wife Vashti in a drunken rage. He sobers up and, feeling very lonely and sorry for himself, holds a beauty pageant to select the most beautiful woman in his empire as his new queen. Esther, a Jewish orphan, gets swept up in the pageant and rather reluctantly ends up as Persia's new queen. Esther's uncle (others say cousin) Mordechai advises her to keep her faith a secret. In the meantime, Haman, one of the king's advisors and a rabid Jew-hater, convinces the king to annihilate all Jews in the Persian Empire. The king agrees and Haman goes about making the technical arrangements for this wholesale slaughter. Amongst these preparations was the casting of lots to determine the date of the massacre. Esther comes to the rescue by revealing to the king her true faith and, but for the fact that she is queen, Haman would have her slaughtered as well. The king, who is prone to temper tantrums, has Haman executed and replaced with Mordechai the Jew. The story ends on a high note, with the original date earmarked for destruction being converted to a day of redemption.

Jews celebrate this redemption on Purim in several ways:

1. By reading the scroll of Esther in synagogue both on Purim eve as well as on Purim day. The scroll is not short: it takes a seasoned reader almost an hour to read through the whole story. One of the reasons for this is that at every mention of Haman's name (fifty-four in total) the reader pauses and the congregation erupts with booing, hissing and the loud banging of special noisemakers called *gragers*.
2. Monetary gifts to the poor are encouraged. The minimum is a coin each to two needy people. However, generosity is encouraged on this special day, and people are exceedingly generous. In London one finds queues of people collecting charity outside certain well-known and prosperous Jewish

homes waiting for their turn to get inside. No one is turned away empty handed.

3. In addition to the monetary gifts to the poor, gifts of food are given to friends and family.

4. In the afternoon a special Purim feast is enjoyed. One of the features of Purim is that it is acceptable, indeed one is practically encouraged, to get inebriated. This ensures that the Purim feast is always a lively affair, often lasting way into the night.

5. It is also customary to wear masks and fancy dress. This is said to highlight the notion that things are not always as they appear – a theme that runs throughout the Purim story.

The drinking, costumes and gifts all contribute to a carnival atmosphere. Purim is a welcome break from the long dull winter and signals the approach of spring.

April
Passover (Festival of Redemption)
One of the best known Jewish festivals is Passover, or Pesach, commemorating the Jewish people's exodus from slavery in Egypt in the fourteenth century BCE.

As it is forbidden to eat or possess any leaven during the festival, Jewish families spend much time cleaning their homes in preparation. It is not uncommon for pre-Pesach cleaning to begin a month beforehand, usually immediately after Purim.

In a faith that is generally child-oriented, Passover stands out as particularly so. The central ritual meal of Passover; the Passover seder, begins with the children asking a series of four questions relating to the theme of Passover. In addition to the formalized recital of these fixed questions (dating back some 2,000 years) children are encouraged to ask about the exodus and the meaning of Passover. The Passover seder begins after nightfall and routinely lasts several hours. Our seder is rarely over before one in the morning and I know of others that carry on right until daybreak.

The main features of the seder are the eating of matzah, an unleavened bread, and, interspersed throughout the evening, the drinking of four cups of wine. It is also customary at certain points in the seder to recline, symbolizing the freedom that is celebrated on Passover. Towards the end of the seder a cup of wine is filled in honour of the prophet Elijah, who is believed to visit every Jewish home on the seder night. This is followed by opening one's front door symbolically to welcome the prophet in.

One year, the great Hasidic master Rabbi Menachem Mendel Morgenstern (1787–1859), otherwise known as the Kotzker Rebbe, after the Polish town Kotzk in which he resided, asked the students around his table if they would like to see the prophet Elijah. They responded in the affirmative, and he promised them that at the particular point in the seder when Elijah enters they would indeed behold the prophet with their own eyes. Needless to say the remainder of the seder was a blur. The students, eagerly anticipating Elijah, could not wait to get through the seder quickly enough. Their master, however, seemed oblivious to their yearnings as he took his time, pausing at each point in the seder to explain some deeper meaning and to teach words of wisdom. Finally the long-awaited hour arrived. The students filled Elijah's cup of wine and rushed to the door, tearing it open in breathless anticipation. And they saw what they had become accustomed to see each year, namely, nothing. They rubbed their eyes in disbelief. Had not their master promised them that this year would be different? That they would for once, have the great privilege of actually seeing the prophet? Dejected, they returned to their seats. So disappointed were they that they barely managed to muster the energy to finish the seder. Yet the Kotzker seemed in another world. His eyes tightly closed his face aflame he sang the concluding hymns and prayers with intense devotion and joy. When he finally concluded and opened his eyes he was met by sad dejected faces all around. 'What is the matter?' he asked. 'Did you not see the prophet Elijah?'

'No,' they responded sadly. 'We saw nothing, nothing at all.'

'Well, where did you look for him?' he asked. 'Why, in the doorway of course!' they answered.

'Fools!' thundered the Kotzker. 'What makes you think Elijah enters through the doorway? Elijah does not enter through a doorway, Elijah enters through the heart.'

May
Lag ba-Omer
In Hebrew, letters and numbers are written with the same characters. This means that every letter or word has a numeric value and that two or more numbers spell words. Lag ba-Omer is an example of the latter. The number 33 makes up the word lag, thus lag ba-Omer means the thirty-third day of the Omer period. The Omer period consists of the seven weeks between Passover and Shavu'ot, representing the journey the ancient Israelites made from the depths of slavery to the spiritual heights of receiving the Torah. Each night after nightfall Jews recite a special blessing and count the passage of one more day leading to the climax, Shavu'ot. The thirty-third day of this period is the anniversary of the death of the great second-century rabbi and mystic Rabbi Shimon Bar Yochai. In his honour the day is marked by celebrations, outings and bonfires. Another reason for the celebration of Lag ba-Omer is that during the second century many of the disciples of the famous Rabbi Akiva died as the result of a plague. This tragedy was seen as divine retribution for the lack of respect these scholars had for each other. On the thirty-third day of the Omer the plague miraculously stopped and so this day was set aside as a day of celebration.

Yom ha-Atzma'ut (Israel Independence Day)
After nearly 2,000 years of exile the modern Jewish state came into existence on 14 May 1948. This is celebrated each year on its corresponding Jewish date of the fifth of the Hebrew month of Iyyar.

Unlike other Jewish festivals, the nature of Yom ha-Atzma'ut celebrations is not uniform. Secular Jews see it as a purely secular holiday, no different from, say, the way Americans see the fourth of July. This is manifested in parades, barbecues, family outings and fireworks. Amongst religious Jews there are those who see Yom ha-Atzma'ut as a genuine religious festival. They will of course join in the same parades and outings as secular Jews but they will also attend special prayers in honour of the festival. There are others in the religious Jewish community for whom Yom ha-Atzma'ut has no real religious significance. They do not see the establishment of a secular state as anything to celebrate and certainly not on a par with any of the traditional festivals.

June
Shavu'ot (Pentecost or the Festival of Weeks)

Seven weeks after Passover Jews celebrate the giving of the Torah on the sixth of the Hebrew month of Sivan. There is a tradition that when God gave the Torah on Mount Sinai the mountain, otherwise desert, burst into bloom. To commemorate this it is customary to decorate the home as well as the synagogue with flowers and greenery. It is also customary to eat milky food on this festival, and so cheesecake features prominently on the lunch menu. So strong is the association between Shavu'ot and cheesecake that when my brother was five years old the teacher asked the class what God had given the Jewish people on Shavu'ot. Expecting to hear one of the brighter pupils to respond 'the Torah', she was taken aback when my little brother responded, 'On Shavu'ot God gave us cheesecake.'

Numerous explanations are offered for dairy consumption on Shavu'ot. One of the more popular reasons is that upon receiving the Torah, with all its dietary laws and complex rules regarding the preparation of kosher meat, the Israelites opted for something easy and simple – a dairy lunch. Jews have been enjoying cheesecake ever since!

Another tradition is to stay up all night on the eve of Shavu'ot studying the Torah in preparation for the reading of the Ten Commandments in synagogue the next morning. This practice originated amongst the mystics of the sixteenth century and until fairly recently was confined to a small element within the Orthodox community. Lately this practice, known as *tikkun*, has become extremely popular and is now observed by a wide range of Jews of varying levels of religious commitment. Many synagogues will host a tikkun by providing a full programme of lectures and workshops lasting all through the night, fuelled by lashings of black coffee and refreshments. This is often preceded by a communal dinner.

One of the most memorable Shavu'ot experiences I have is from my sabbatical in Jerusalem several years ago. The neighbourhood we were staying in was buzzing with activity all night as people were coming and going to various lectures and study sessions. Shortly before dawn we woke up our young children and proceeded to the Western Wall in the old city. Along the way we were joined by others and by the time we reached Damascus Gate one could see throngs of Jews making there way to the old city from all over Jerusalem. At the crack of dawn we began to pray and we concluded just as the sun began to rise. Looking out over the Western Wall plaza, now gleaming in the early morning sunlight, and seeing thousands of fellow Jews united in prayer after a night of intensive Torah study was an experience that will remain with me for ever. Utterly exhausted though spiritually elated we made our way back home to enjoy a well-earned rest.

July–August
The Fast of Tammuz
The seventeenth of the Hebrew month of Tammuz is a fast day. This is because a number of calamities befell the Jewish people on this date. Perhaps the best known calamity was the breaching of the walls of Jerusalem by the Romans in the first century. This was the beginning of the destruction of Jerusalem

and the subsequent exile of the Jewish people. As with all fast days, food and drink are forbidden and special prayers are read in the synagogue.

Bein ha-metzarim (Between the Straits)

Between the Straits is the name given to the three-week period between the Fast of Tammuz and the Fast of Av, which commemorates the destruction of the Temples. These three weeks are considered a mourning period, and so celebrations such as weddings are not held during this time.

The last nine days of this three-week period are treated even more stringently and so travel, music, swimming, the eating of meat or consuming of wine are all prohibited as a sign of mourning over the destruction of the Temple.

Tisha b'Av (The Fast of the ninth of Av)

The ninth day of the Hebrew month of Av is the date on which both Temples were destroyed, the first by the Babylonians in 423 BCE and the second by the Romans in 70 CE. It is the saddest day in the Jewish calendar, marked by fasting and prayer. Prayers begin in the evening with a public reading of the Book of Lamentations, at which participants sit on the floor or on low stools as a sign of mourning.

Paradoxically, while Tisha b'Av is a day of mourning it is also a day of hope as there is a tradition that the messiah (the redeemer of the Jewish people) will be born on this day. In a sense, it means that within the destruction there exists the seed of redemption. This paradox is reflected in the practice of omitting the daily supplication prayers. These prayers are otherwise only omitted on festivals or happy occasions.

One of my abiding Tisha b'Av memories goes back to when I was a child in Montreal. In our synagogue there was a certain individual who had a heart of gold and went out of his way to help people; but he could also be a real nuisance as he frequently disrupted synagogue services for one reason or another.

One year he got it into his head that the messiah was going to arrive at the end of Tisha b'Av. To mark this momentous occasion he prepared a sumptuous feast in the synagogue. Throughout the day as the community prayed and fasted this fellow, with lots of help from my friends and I, laid out tables with a tantalizing assortment of delicacies. This drew sharp critical glances from many of the worshippers, for not only was the laying out of a feast a violation of the spirit of this sad and tragic day, it was also a source of torment to those fasting who were doing their best not to think about food. Critical glances aside, no one was able to summon up the courage to denounce the activity, which was just as well as it would have been futile. As the day progressed our friend grew increasingly excited. Finally the moment he had been waiting for arrived. Night had fallen, the fast had terminated and the messiah would grace his feast any moment now. Needless to say, the messiah did not grace his feast that year. Two hundred fellow congregants did, however, and after their fasting all day the food disappeared within minutes. The feeding frenzy over, people quickly wished their host well, thanked him for his generosity and hurried to get back home to their families. In my mind's eye I can still see the image of him sitting forlorn at the head of an empty table strewn with empty plates, casting his gaze at the heavens and swearing never again to put himself out for the messiah.

August–September
The month of Ellul
The last month of the Hebrew calendar is the month of Ellul. As this immediately precedes the month of Tishrei and the high holy days, it is essentially a month of repentance and a time of spiritual preparation for the New Year. It is also a time in which God's presence is more keenly felt and when prayers are more readily heard. It is customary to sound several short blasts on the shofar each morning after prayers to draw attention to the forthcoming New Year.

Chapter 12

THE JEWISH LIFECYCLE

Birth

The beginning of life is marked and celebrated by various rituals. One of the first is the naming of the baby. According to Jewish mystical tradition, a person's name is the spiritual conduit for all God's blessings throughout one's lifetime. Bearing in mind, then, the enormous pressure the selection of a name has on the parents, tradition also teaches that they (specifically the mother) are given divine inspiration at the time they choose a name. Often the name of a deceased relative, usually a grandparent or great-grandparent, is chosen for the newborn. This is a mark of respect for the deceased and a way of ensuring that their memory is perpetuated. In Ashkenazi communities as well as in many Sefardic communities it is taboo to name a child after one who is alive. However, in some Sefardic communities naming after the living is widely practised and is seen as a mark of the highest respect to the one whose name is chosen for the newborn baby.

The naming ceremony itself differs according to whether the

infant is a boy or a girl. A baby boy is given his name at his circumcision. Baby girls are named at the first Torah reading following the birth, usually on the Shabbat.

Brit (Circumcision)

At eight days old, health permitting, a baby boy is given his *brit*. This Hebrew term is often inaccurately translated as circumcision. While it is true that the brit *involves* the circumcising of the foreskin, it *means* something else entirely. Brit means a pact or covenant; in relation to circumcision it refers to the covenant that God made with Abraham, whereby through circumcising their male children, his descendants would be worthy of being God's people. So strong is the connection between circumcision and Jewish identity that tradition has it a baby's soul does not fully inhabit the body until the time of circumcision.

The person who circumcises the baby is known as a *mohel*. *Mohelim* (the plural of mohel) are highly trained and are occasionally, though not necessarily, physicians themselves. One of the first things a mohel must determine before proceeding with a brit is the baby's level of health. In this respect, Jewish law is far more conservative than modern medicine. If the baby suffers the slightest ailment the brit will be postponed. One of the most common ailments, which is becoming increasingly common, is jaundice. Jewish law determines that circumcision cannot be performed on a jaundiced baby and so the brit must be postponed until it clears up. Usually this takes a week or so, but sometimes it can take significantly longer. I recall a family that lived on our street when I was a child who had to postpone the brit of their newborn baby for nearly a month. Since a baby boy is not named before the brit, this little fellow was nameless for all that time – that is, until one of the local children began referring to the baby as 'Jaundice'. Somehow this caught on, and for years the poor child tried to convince people that his name was not Jaundice.

My own experience with jaundice and a postponed brit

occurred with our eldest child. Dina and I were delighted with
our healthy bouncing boy and we excitedly prepared for his
brit. These preparations included extending invitations to all
our family. We were living in New Jersey at the time and so
Dina's parents flew in from Italy, my parents drove down
from Canada and my elderly grandfather drove in from
Massachusetts. The mohel we booked was highly recom-
mended. He was so popular in fact that he didn't have the time
to make a house call shortly after the birth to examine the baby
and determine if the brit could go ahead. We spoke by phone
and he seemed so relaxed about it that we assumed everything
would be all right. A day before the brit Dina began to notice
that our son had developed a yellowish tinge. 'Not to worry,'
said the two proud new grandmothers, 'he looks just fine.' The
next day, two hours before the brit, with tables set and over a
hundred guests waiting in eager anticipation, we had to call it
off. So high was our baby's biliruben count that he had to be
rushed to the hospital to spend the next forty-eight hours
bathed in UV light in a special incubator. That was the last time
Dina would ever ignore her maternal instinct.

The brit can take place either in the synagogue or at home. I
have attended some with hundreds of guests in the synagogue
and others with only immediate family at home. The actual
procedure is very quick and involves the removal of the foreskin on the baby's penis. Yet there is much colourful ceremony
surrounding this otherwise dry clinical procedure. Once all the
guests have gathered around and the mohel is prepared to
proceed he calls out for the godparents to bring the baby into
the room. Being asked to serve as a godparent is a great honour
and mitzvah; it is believed that in reward for this act the godparents themselves will be blessed with children. It is for this
reason that it is often young newlyweds who are chosen in the
hope that they, too, will one day, be parents. The godparents,
who must be a married couple, divide the honour by having
the wife carry the baby halfway and then passing it to her
husband, who in turn, passes it to the mohel. The mohel then

places the baby on a special designated chair, called the Chair of Elijah. This is because it is believed that the prophet Elijah is present at the brit of every Jew to offer his blessing. After formally welcoming the prophet Elijah, the mohel will then place the baby on the lap of the *sandek*, who holds the baby during the actual circumcision. Traditionally the role is given to a grandparent, though which grandparent to honour can often be a difficult decision to make.

Strictly speaking it is the father's responsibility to circumcise his own son. Since for obvious reasons this is unlikely to happen, the father formally appoints the mohel to act on his behalf. Some even have the custom of the father handing the knife to the mohel. As the mohel conducts the procedure, which lasts seconds, the father recites a special blessing out loud. The baby's wound is dressed and he is then handed to another honoured person to be held during the naming ceremony. According to Jewish mystical tradition the honour of holding the baby during his naming is even greater than holding him during the circumcision. In any event, it is convenient to have this additional honour, often given to the other grand-parent as something of a consolation prize. A blessing is then recited over a cup of wine and the baby is given his Hebrew name. At this point the mother recites a blessing of thanksgiving and the ceremony concludes with the godparents carrying the baby out of the room, straight to his mother, to be fed and cuddled.

This ceremony is then followed by a festive meal. So important is this meal that if one leaves before partaking of it one is considered to have caused grave offence to the mitzvah. Often the brit will be held first thing in the morning and as people are keen to get to work they will at the very least take a mouthful to honour the mitzvah and their hosts. Some consider it particularly fortuitous to partake of such an important meal and will make a point of taking some cake or biscuits to share with others who were not present at the brit.

Another interesting feature of the brit is that one does not normally issue invitations. This is because it is deemed unfair to put someone in the position of possibly having to turn down an invitation to such a religiously significant event. Instead, the parents will *notify* their family and friends that the brit will be taking place at such and such a time and at such and such a place. It is taken for granted that you are more than welcome to join them for the celebrations if your schedule permits.

Finally, there is a tradition that the heavens open when the baby cries. It is therefore an opportune time for those present to request of the Almighty blessings for the baby and his family.

Pidyon ha-Ben (Redemption of the first-born son)

It is a biblical command for a father to redeem his first-born son from the *kohen* (priest). The rationale of this practice is that when God smote the first-born Egyptians just before the exodus, he spared the first-born Israelites. As a result God has claim to every first-born Jewish child, until the child is redeemed by his father. In essence this mitzvah teaches us never to take anything for granted, certainly not the birth of a first-born child.

The redemption involves the father giving the kohen a sum of money in exchange for his son. This is done on the baby's thirty-first day of life. The ransom fee is set in the Bible at five *selah*. This is not a currency but a specific weight of silver coins. Over the years and throughout the various countries where Jews lived, the rabbis would determine the sum in local currencies. The sum in the United States was determined at five silver half-dollars. Today in Israel one can purchase a set of specially minted silver Pidyon ha-Ben coins with the appropriate biblical verses etched into them.

Pidyon ha-Ben is a somewhat rare occurrence. This is because only first-born males are subject to this ransom. This would exclude a first-born girl or any sons born after a daughter. Furthermore, the baby must be born naturally, and so a baby boy born through caesarean section would not need to be ransomed. Finally, if either the father or mother is from the tribe of Levi (that is to say they are Kohanim or Levi'im) they are exempt.

The procedure begins with the mother bringing her son in and passing him to his father, who in turn places him in front of the designated kohen. It is customary to bring the baby in on a silver tray, and for the women to drape him with their jewellery. Once the baby is laid before the kohen a dialogue ensues between the kohen and the father in which the kohen asks the father if he is prepared to part with five silver coins in exchange for his son. The father responds that he is indeed prepared to part with the money in exchange for the baby and proceeds to hand over the coins to the kohen. The father recites two blessings, and the kohen in turn places his hands on the baby's head and blesses him. The baby is returned to his mother and everyone enjoys a festive meal.

Once the kohen accepts the coins he may do with them what he likes. Often he will return them to the father as a gift. A family will hold on to these coins, attributing to them great sentimental value. Sometimes they will be used again for the next generation if another Pidyon ha-Ben presents itself. I consider my family particularly privileged in that my father, myself and my eldest son were all redeemed. Not only that, but the same coins were used for all three of us. The pressure on my son to produce a first-born male is, understandably, enormous. He could of course spite us all by falling in love with the daughter of a kohen, or, even worse, producing a first-born daughter.

Opsherin

Opsherin, a Yiddish word for haircut, is a reference to a young boy's first haircut at or around the age of three. While the origins of this custom are shrouded in mystery it is today widely practised amongst Hasidim and Sefardim. It is considered that at the age of three a child is mature enough to begin to understand Jewish rituals and practices. One of the most personal ritual practices for a Jewish male is having *peyot* (side-locks). It is therefore customary to wait until the child is old enough to appreciate his unique Jewish haircut.

There are other, deeper interpretations of this ritual, linking it to the biblical prohibition against eating fruit of a new tree for the first three years. Only after three years have passed can one benefit from the fruit. The parallel message for parents is that when it comes to children one must give unconditionally without any expectations. Only after an initial stage of such selfless love can parents begin to see the fruits of their labour in their child. I might add that three is a rough figure; if you find yourself waiting for some payback from your teenage child, know that you are not alone.

The actual haircutting ceremony itself is straightforward. Everyone present takes a turn to snip a tiny lock of hair. Most mothers stand guard zealously to ensure that the locks sniped are indeed tiny, so that the rest of the haircut can be completed by a professional. The locks just above the forehead are usually reserved for either the father or the rabbi to cut. This is the spot on which, ten years later, the boy will place his tefillin.

The haircutting is followed in good Jewish style by a festive meal, although as the opsherin is a late custom, special blessings over a cup of wine are not recited. Some have the practice of making the opsherin at the tomb of the second-century rabbi and mystic rabbi Shimon bar Yochai in Meron, northern Israel, on Lag ba-Omer, the anniversary of his death. It is a remarkable sight as thousands converge around the great sage's resting place, and amidst bonfires and singing proceed to cut their little boys' hair for the first time.

One of the occupational hazards of letting your little boy's hair grow untrimmed until the age of three is that people constantly mistake him for a girl. My youngest looks and behaves as boyishly as is humanly possible, yet without fail when I am walking with him in the street some one (usually a kind old woman) will invariably approach as and say 'my, my what a pretty girl you have there'. By now I know better then to do anything other than smile back politely, thank the well-meaning stranger for her compliment, tousle my little boy's mane and go on my way.

While an opsherin is nowhere nearly as traumatic as the brit, the lead-up to the ceremony may bring with it certain anxieties for the little boy. One of my sons does not appreciate being in the limelight and he found the idea of strangers lining up to take snips of his hair rather disturbing. One of my own earliest childhood memories is of my mother reading me a book about a young lion that refused to have his mane cut and how, in the end, after submitting to the dreaded haircut, he could see so much better. Apparently I harboured some anxieties about my first haircut and my wise mother addressed them through this fictionalized tale.

As a parent there is something truly remarkable when one sees one's little boy for the first time after his haircut. A transformation has occurred and a whole new little person emerges. Yet it can be a bittersweet moment. On the one hand your baby has now become a little boy, the cause of great pride and celebration. On the other hand you know that you are deeply going to miss that baby and that you can never go back. No doubt all parents experience this in one form or another, but with the opshern it happens so suddenly and the transformation is so physically apparent that you can never truly be prepared for it.

Bar mitzvah

One of the better known Jewish rites of passage is the bar or bat mitzvah. So popular is it in the United States that in certain sectors it has become trendy for non-Jews to have them as well. Unfortunately, for many Jews the bar/bat mitzvah is nothing more than an opportunity to celebrate a child's coming of age. For them it is no different from, say, a sweet sixteen party. It follows logically that there is no reason why a non-Jew should be excluded from celebrating in the same way. Yet a bar/bat mitzvah has a profound religious meaning, and for those willing to make a religious commitment it can be a truly spiritual experience.

The origin of bar mitzvah (which, as a celebration, dates to the middle ages) is based on the fact that according to Jewish law a boy ceases to be a child on his thirteenth birthday, from which point onwards he is considered a man. This manhood is to be understood in the context of being responsible for observing all the mitzvot. Until the age of thirteen it is the father's responsibility to ensure that his son is educated in their performance so that once he reaches thirteen he will know what to do. From this age the onus falls squarely on the young man's shoulders, which is why he is called a bar mitzvah, meaning 'the son of the mitzvah'.

It is interesting that Judaism does not recognize the phase of adolescence. One goes from being a child to being a man, literally overnight. This does not mean that the thirteen-year-old is in any emotional or intellectual sense on a par with, say, a thirty-year-old. It does mean, though, that from this age Judaism recognizes his ability to make choices and so to be responsible for the choices he makes.

One of the misconceptions about bar mitzvah is the belief that the young man must engage in ritual, such as reading from the Torah, in order to be considered bar mitzvah. Even worse is the misconception that the rabbi somehow bar mitzvahs the boy, much like a priest through powers vested in him declares a couple to be husband and wife. The reality is far less dramatic. A child becomes a man on his thirteenth birthday regardless of how he chooses to spend it. As soon as he is thirteen, with or without a synagogue service, with or without a party, he becomes responsible for observing mitzvot and hence, a bar mitzvah. On more than one occasion I have been approached by congregants nervously confiding in me that they were never bar mitzvah. They usually add in self-defence that this was due to no fault of their own. What they are trying to tell me is that due to the war or some other misfortune their parents were unable to *celebrate* their thirteenth birthday in a traditional manner in synagogue. Sadly, they have been led to believe that the absence of any such ritual means they are not bar mitzvah. When I explain to them that they are bar mitzvah simply by virtue of being over the age of thirteen, they become visibly relived, if bewildered as well.

What people tend to confuse is the *actual* bar mitzvah with the rituals and celebrations that *characterize* the bar mitzvah. One of the earliest bar mitzvah rituals, dating from the Middle Ages, is the young man's delivery of a complex Talmudic discourse known as a drasha. Ironically, this venerated custom is barely practised today outside very Orthodox circles. Two of the most common rituals associated with bar mitzvah today are the laying of tefillin and the reading of the Torah. The reason these two particular mitzvot stand out in relation to the bar mitzvah is that, unlike many other mitzvot, these are not permitted to children. Therefore a public display is made of these mitzvot, to indicate that the boy has now become a man.

Reading from the Torah can be challenging, as it involves memorizing all the vowels as well as the musical cantallations. It takes a boy on average six months to learn the Torah portion for his bar mitzvah. My own bar mitzvah was unconventional in the sense that I did not read from the Torah, although I did give a discourse. The reason was that my father felt it would be a better use of my time to study Jewish law and Hasidic thought in preparation for my bar mitzvah. In hindsight he was right and I learned how to read the Torah anyway, a year later.

Bat mitzvah

Whereas Jewish law considers a boy to have reached manhood at the age of thirteen, it considers a girl to have reached womanhood at the age of twelve. This reflects the conventional wisdom that in both a physical and emotional sense girls generally mature sooner than boys.

Despite the religious significance of a girl's twelfth birthday it was not until the early twentieth century that it was marked by any ritual. While the ritualization of the bat mitzvah

originated in non-Orthodox circles, it has today spread to the
Orthodox community as well. Given the limitations of
women's participation in Orthodox services the bat mitzvah
girl will not read from the Torah in mixed company, though in
some Orthodox congregations she might read from the Torah
at an exclusively women's service. However, in most congregations the ritual will consist of the girl delivering a discourse
before the congregation.

The bar/bat mitzvah party has religious significance in that
it reflects and celebrates a religious milestone. Extravagant and
ostentatious parties devoid of any spirituality may be common
amongst many Jews. Sadly, they do not reflect the ideals of
Judaism or an appreciation of the bar/bat mitzvah. They are, to
borrow a well-worn phrase, all about the bar and nothing
about the mitzvah.

The Jewish wedding

Marriage is a Jewish ideal rooted in two concepts. The first is to
procreate. This is expressed in the first chapter of Genesis,
when God commands Adam and Eve to be fruitful and to multiply. The second is the intense love and bonding that can be
achieved between husband and wife. This is also expressed in
Genesis, when Adam calls Eve 'Bone from my bone, flesh
from my flesh'. A loving marriage enables both partners to
grow emotionally, intellectually, even spiritually.

It is therefore not surprising that marriage occupies such an
important place in the Jewish community. This, of course, has
given rise to endless jokes about over-eager relatives doing
their utmost to 'set up' their niece, granddaughter or cousin
with a nice Jewish boy they just happen to know.

Jokes aside, marriage holds great spiritual significance and
this is alluded to in the Hebrew term for the marriage ceremony, *kiddushin*, which translates as 'sanctified'. Whenever I
meet a young couple planning a Jewish wedding I ask them
why they want to get married. When they tell me they want to
marry because they are in love I gently point out that two

loving people could cohabit for their entire lives without necessarily getting married. At this point the couple begin to look perplexed. They give it some more thought and then say that in truth they could just cohabit without getting married but that is not what their parents and friends expect of them. 'So,' I say, 'you are going through with this entire ceremony, not to mention expense, just so that you meet other peoples' expectations?' At this point the couple begin to start having serious doubts, not about their future or marriage but about me. I can almost read their minds: 'Honey, did you say this guy is the rabbi you want to marry us? How would your parents feel if they knew their rabbi was trying to convince us to elope?'

I let them have this mental dialogue with each other for a few minutes and then I explain to them the concept of kiddushin. Jews marry neither out of social conformity nor as a means to ensuring fidelity. Jews marry because it is a holy act and a mitzvah and it is a way of drawing God's presence and blessing into one's marriage and home.

The Jewish marriage ritual begins a week before the wedding when, on Shabbat, the groom is called up to read a portion from the Torah. This is traditionally referred to as the *Aufruf*, the German/Yiddish for 'call-up'. The idea behind this call-up to the Torah is both to honour the groom and to offer him the blessings inherent in reading from the Torah. It is customary to throw bags of sweets at the groom after he finishes his reading and for his family to host the kiddush, or even lunch, after the service for the congregation.

On that same Shabbat the bride celebrates with her friends. This takes the form of a party, called Shabbat Kallah (the bride's Shabbat), usually hosted by her parents or very good friends. There is no particular religious ritual to follow at this party although some brides will share some Torah thoughts and invite others to do likewise. It is rare for men to attend these parties unless they are family or close friends.

The wedding day

It is customary for both bride and groom to fast on their
wedding day, beginning at daybreak and concluding after the
chupah (the wedding canopy) ceremony. The reason for this
fast is that the wedding day is so holy that it is considered like
Yom Kippur (the Day of Atonement) for the bride and groom.
Just as Yom Kippur wipes the slate clean and allows the individual to enter into the New Year a changed person for the
better, so too the wedding day is a new beginning for the bride
and groom, opening fresh possibilities for a new future
together. Needless to say this fast sets the tone for the couple,
which, far from being sad, is nonetheless somewhat sombre
and reflective. While it is important to fast it is also important
to ensure a healthy bride and groom stand under the chupah
later that day. If either of them feels particularly faint there are
grounds for them breaking their fast. I remember going to a
good friend's wedding and while she was fine with the fasting
her groom was not. An hour before the ceremony was to begin
he almost passed out. The rabbi told him to break his fast but
he wanted to soldier on. I can still hear his mother-in-law
telling anyone who would listen what she thought of her young
son-in-law, who almost passed out at his wedding.

Most Jewish weddings are held in the afternoon and so they
are preceded by the afternoon mincha prayers. In keeping with
the Yom Kippur theme the groom and bride silently recite part
of the confessional Yom Kippur prayers during this service.

After mincha the presiding rabbi will ensure that the marriage document, known as the *ketubbah*, is read by the groom
and signed by two witnesses.

The ketubbah is essentially a pre-nuptial document in which
the groom promises that, if he were to divorce or pre-decease
his wife, then she would be entitled to a financial settlement.
This dates back some 2,000 years, when it was highly unusual
for a woman to have financial independence. Most women
depended for their support on either their father or husband.
The Talmudic rabbis recognized the implicit risk a girl took

leaving the financial security of her father's home and so they devised the ketubbah as a legal means for her protection. Although the socio-economic situation has changed radically since then, as today in many cases the bride earns more than the groom, nonetheless the ketubbah has become an integral part of the marriage ceremony, and one cannot get married without it. A by-product of the ketubbah is that it provides a written record of the marriage. This can come in handy in all sorts of ways, not least as a historical record, years later, for those researching their family trees.

Once the ketubbah has been signed by two witnesses the groom will be escorted to meet and veil the bride. In this ceremony, known as the Badekin (German/Yiddish for 'covering'), the groom places a veil over the bride's face.

There are many reasons offered as to why the bride must wear a veil. My favourite is a mystical tradition that teaches when a bride stands under the wedding canopy her face radiates such an intense spiritual beauty that it is too pure for mere mortals to gaze upon. The veil protects and preserves this beauty. There are varying customs as to how opaque the veil must be. For some it is practically transparent. In other circles, particularly those who subscribe to the mystical tradition above, the veil is entirely opaque so that it is impossible to see the bride and the bride cannot see beyond it.

I recall my own wedding, standing under the chupah watching eagerly as Dina made her way down the aisle carefully supported at each elbow by our two loving mothers. Suddenly she stopped for what seemed like hours. Dark thoughts began to swirl through my head: 'is she having cold feet?' Well I was right about the foot thing. Apparently her heel caught on a grate in the ground (our wedding was outdoors) and she couldn't break it free. The two mothers, who could not see her expression, kept on urging her forward while Dina, desperate not to lose her shoe, pulled back. In the end the bride, the mothers and the both shoes made it to the chupah.

It is customary for the rabbi and the parents to bless the

bride and groom just after the Badekin. This is an intensely emotional moment, and although I have officiated at numerous weddings, it never fails to move me.

After the Badekin the bride and groom, escorted by their parents, proceed to the chupah. The ceremony under the chupah comprises two parts, the Kiddushin, or betrothal, and the Nissu'in, or marriage. Originally, 2,000 years ago in the time of the Mishnah, the two parts were actually two separate ceremonies. First would come the betrothal, at which the groom would give the bride a ring and declare that she is henceforth betrothed to him. A rabbi would sanctify the betrothal by reciting a blessing over a cup of wine. This ensured that they could go their own separate ways and leisurely plan for the wedding without the groom having to fear that in his absence another man may woo his bride. Betrothal meant that the two were bound to each other legally and morally. Once the wedding was prepared the bride and groom would once again stand under the chupah and under the guidance of a rabbi seven blessings, known as the Sheva Brachot, were recited over a cup of wine. At the conclusion of this second ceremony the bride and groom were deemed husband and wife. Today both ceremonies are rolled into one, which explains for the observant onlooker the reason for two cups of wine. In addition to the betrothal and blessings the ketubbah is read out loud in its original Aramaic. Finally, a glass is broken at the end of the chupah to symbolize the destruction of the Temple in Jerusalem. This practice highlights the Jews' eternal connection to Jerusalem, giving pause to reflect on its destruction at the most joyous of occasions.

After the chupah the newlyweds retire to a private room to break their fast and to spend the first moments of their married life in each other's company. There is a halachic aspect to this practice as well. Jewish law demands that two witnesses observe the couple going into their new home together. As this is highly impractical, as well as obtrusive, the private room in the synagogue or wedding hall is designated as their symbolic home. Two witnesses are posted outside to attest to this.

Each night during the week following the wedding a special feast is held in honour of the newlyweds. The same seven blessings recited under the chupah are repeated during grace after meals. It is customary for family or close friends to share the hosting of these parties.

Death and mourning

While Judaism demands that we do all we can to preserve and prolong life, it also recognizes that death is inevitable. There is a very moving story in the Talmud about the great Mishnaic sage Rabbi Judah, known simply as Rebbe. Towards the end of his life he fell ill and suffered agonizing pains. His disciples, desperate not to lose their revered master, engaged in around-the-clock prayers for his full recovery. A wise woman working as a servant in the rabbi's household realized that the students' prayer was a selfish act. She understood that they did not want to lose their master but that they had no idea of the pain he endured just by being kept alive. She finally took matters into her own hands and disrupted the students' prayers long enough for the master's soul to slip away from this world. The Talmud records her act in a positive light. This is not to say that Judaism endorses euthanasia: it most certainly does not. The point of the story is not to cause premature death but rather to accept death as inevitable and to know when to step aside and let nature take its course.

In an ideal world a dying person leaves this life in his own bed surrounded by family and loved ones, lucid enough to give final instructions and be able to recite the final prayers. But life and death are rarely so neat, and one has to deal with circumstances as they are, not as we would like them to be. Jewish law prescribes that a dying person recites confession. This confession is not to a rabbi or any other human being but rather to God alone. It is the same confession that Jews recite each year on Yom Kippur and the same one a bride and groom recite on their wedding day. If this proves too onerous for the dying person a shortened version is suggested. At the very least a

dying person should recite the first passage of the shema, a
Jew's declaration of faith in one God. This is the first prayer a
child is taught to say and it is the last prayer on one's lips
before departing for a better world.

As a rabbi I have been called to deathbeds. It is never a pleasant experience and afterwards it takes me some time to regain
my equilibrium. Almost without fail, I am called too late and
by the time I arrive the dying person is either no longer of this
world or comatose. Only once did I arrive on time. I was called
to the hospital by a woman who was sitting with her dying
mother. As far as I could tell the dying woman was aware of
her surroundings. As she was unable to speak, her daughter
and I chanted the shema, which takes only a couple of minutes.
When we had finished we looked over at the old woman: her
face was relaxed and serene. She had stopped breathing.

Once a loved one has passed away it is important not to
leave the body unattended until the time of burial. This is a
mark of respect for the body created in God's image and the
earthly vessel for the divine soul. Amongst religious Jews it is
customary for the close relatives to sit with the body and to
recite psalms until it is removed for burial. Judaism's concern
that the body be treated with respect generally precludes
autopsies. Cremation is prohibited in the strongest terms.
Anything other than gently laying the body to rest in the earth
(in fulfilment of the verse 'For thou art dust and to dust thou
shall return') is proscribed by Jewish law.

Before burial the body undergoes a purification rite known
as the *tahara* (the cleansing or purifying). This involves a group
of highly dedicated men or women (depending on the gender
of the deceased) ritually washing and then dressing the body in
special linen shrouds. The body is then placed in a simple pine
casket ready for burial. Jewish law does not permit lavish
funerals with expensive coffins and flowers. There are at least
two reasons for this, one religious, the other socio-economic.
The religious reason is that in death all are equal. Whatever
one's wealth and position during one's lifetime, it counts for

nothing in the world of truth. It is said that a child is born with clenched fists, displaying the ingrained human instinct of acquisitiveness, while the dead pass from this world with their palms open, a sign that one must leave behind all material acquisitions. Ostentatious funerals make a mockery of this truth and, in turn, of the deceased.

The socio-economic reason goes back to the time of Rabbi Gamliel in the second century. Rabbi Gamliel was the Nasi, the president of the Great Sanhedrin and the *de facto* leader of the Jews in the Holy Land after the destruction of the Temple. It was a position that he inherited from his father and grandfather before him. Rabbi Gamliel observed that while the rich buried their dead with all sorts of finery, pomp and ceremony, the poor, embarrassed that they could not afford such a display, ended up leaving their dead unburied outside the city walls. In a wise and sympathetic gesture Rabbi Gamliel, who was himself a man of substantial means, instructed that he be buried in simple linen shrouds. The result was an end to the distasteful display of wealth at funerals which had become such a source of social competition.

Jewish funerals can be described as harsh, blunt and final. There is no effort to try to shield the mourners from their loss; on the contrary, Jewish law ensures that they face their loss directly. Barring any extraneous circumstances, Jewish funerals are generally held on the day after death. Occasionally, if time permits, it may be held on the day of the death itself. This does not give the mourners much time or space gradually to come to grips with their loss. At the funeral the mourners are expected to make an incision in their garments (usually the lapel of a jacket) to express their grief. After the eulogy the body is unceremoniously lowered into the grave and the mourners lead the assembled in covering the coffin with earth. Once the grave is filled the mourner's prayer, kaddish, is recited along with a memorial prayer and the service is concluded.

While the easier option is to protect the mourners from some of the harsher aspects of the funeral, Jewish law in its wisdom understood that the sooner the bereaved are able to accept the reality and finality of their loss the sooner they can begin to grieve and eventually heal.

What must be said of Jewish bereavement is that the mourners do not mourn alone. Almost as soon as the funeral is over, friends and family will move into action. It is traditional that the mourners do not prepare their first meal. This simple fare of bread and egg and a beverage (usually tea) is supplied by friends. However, it does not end there. Entire communities sweep into action, cooking and delivering for days on end more food than anyone could possibly eat. During the week of mourning, known as *shiva*, the mourners are rarely left alone. Ideally the three daily services are held at the mourner's home, at which special prayers are recited for the deceased. In addition to this, people pay visits to the mourners all through the day and often late into the night. Sometimes this can be too much, as all the exhausted mourners want to do is to rest and to be left alone. They may try to ask people to limit their visits, but in the Jewish community such requests are rarely treated seriously, and if they are noted, people generally think they must refer to someone else.

I recall once paying a shiva visit to a colleague in the middle of the day. As I approached I noticed a note attached to the door. The note kindly asked that guests refrain from visiting between the hours of 2 and 5 p.m. I looked at my watch: it was 4.00. I hesitated, and then not without an element of guilt, pushed open the unlocked door. I was only half surprised to see my colleague holding court in the centre of a packed room of visitors. All along the periphery friends and family were serving hot drinks and snacks. The last vestige of guilt slipped away from me when a kind lady appeared at my side, asking 'coffee or tea?'

The mourning observances are detailed and fairly restrictive. The spirit behind them is the notion that life cannot immediately carry on as before in the absence of a loved one. This is both a mark of respect to the deceased as well as a coping mechanism for the bereaved. The observances begin with the week of shiva. During this period it is forbidden for mourners to leave their home. It is certainly not permitted to resume working. During this first week the mourners will wear the same garment they tore at the funeral, sit on low stools and forgo leather footwear. Additionally, any mirrors in the house are covered for the duration of the shiva and one is not allowed to have a haircut, shave or bathe.

The common theme shared by these restrictions is that it is inappropriate to be concerned with one's own comfort and vanity at a time of such loss. Certainly music or any form of revelry is forbidden. The shiva gives way to the thirty-day period known as the *shloshim*, during which some of the harsher restrictions are put aside. The mourners are now permitted to bathe, wear leather shoes and resume their daily activities. The prohibitions against shaving and haircuts remain in force until the close of this period. This gives way to the final and longest mourning phase, the first year. Until a full year has passed the restrictions on music and revelry remain in force.

A closing thought on this chapter, and indeed on this entire section, brings us back to the theme of bridging heaven and earth. Jewish law prohibits the manifest display of mitzvot when visiting a cemetery. Practically, this means that, eulogies aside, it is forbidden to discuss words of the Torah. It is also forbidden to display one's tzitzit fringes and so one must ensure they are neatly tucked away under shirt and trousers. The reason for this is that it is unfair to remind the dead of the life of the Torah and mitzvot they are missing.

I never really contemplated or understood this law until one summer when I was visiting the Ukraine. Whilst there, I took the opportunity to visit the resting places of some of the greatest eighteenth-century Hasidic leaders. Upon entering the cemetery I instinctively hid my tzitzit away. It then occurred to me that in whatever heaven these lofty souls were, and whatever they were preoccupied with there, its value could not compete with my pair of tzitzit. This, in a nutshell, is the whole essence of Judaism. It is about people bringing godliness into the physical world through physical mitzvot. 'The Torah is not in heaven,' as Moses said to the Israelites on his last day on earth. It is here on earth right in your midst. The Torah with its physical mitzvot is more than just a moral guide to our small insignificant lives. It is what gives them meaning and purpose far beyond their diminished capabilities. It is the bridge between heaven and earth, enabling limited man to draw the limitless Creator into his world.

Epilogue

JUDAISM IN THE TWENTY-FIRST CENTURY

Judaism in the nineteenth century was passionate. Indeed, from the second half of the nineteenth century and into the first half of the twentieth, society at large was passionate about any of any number of 'isms', capitalism, communism, fascism, nationalism and socialism. The Jewish community was not immune to this frenzy of ideologies and, in it's case, one could add to the long list of 'isms' Hasidism, Secularism and Zionism. If the late nineteenth and early twentieth centuries were characterized by passionate ideological debates, nowhere was this more true than in Judaism. It would have been rare to find a disengaged Jew; almost everyone had a view or an opinion about the best path for Judaism to take. What is more, many ideologues were actually willing to put their lives on the line in pursuit of their ideologies.

The second half of the twentieth century was coloured by two of the most monumental events in Jewish history, the Holocaust and the establishment of the State of Israel. These two events shaped and defined Jewish life for the following decades, making it difficult for even the most apathetic Jew to entirely escape his Judaism and its consequences.

As we enter the first decade of the twenty-first century much has changed. Society in general is uninterested in ideology. More important today is the ability to earn a living, educate one's children and pay the mortgage. There are also fears of global terrorism that previous generations did not have to contend with. The widespread use of the Internet and mobile phones has ensured that we have less, not more, leisure time to reflect on life, its meaning and direction. Judaism is not immune to these realities and pressures, and while there is, at its centre, a core of deeply committed Jews, the vast majority along the periphery can be best described as apathetic.

This huge gap between the core and the periphery exists not only in terms of Jewish religious knowledge and observance but also in commitment to the future of the Jewish people. In the past, even Jews who considered themselves atheists still took a strong interest in Jewish culture and its future; some also took a keen interest in the fledgling Jewish state. While there are still many such Jews today, their numbers are decreasing. Jewish culture and identity are less important to many young Jews today than they once were to their parents. While many still see the Holocaust as a unique event in Jewish history, it has become just that, a tragic event in history, without any particular impact on their lives. Similarly, the State of Israel is no longer young and fresh. Young Jews today take the middle-aged state for granted and for many, particularly in the United States, it simply does not feature prominently in their lives.

Another interesting change in Jewish life is organizational. Until about the 1980s Judaism was neatly divided up between Orthodox, Conservative and Reform congregations in the USA and Canada, and its equivalents in the United Kingdom and elsewhere. At the risk of simplifying the philosophies of each of these movements, Orthodoxy adheres to the strict interpretation of Halakhah, Conservatism adheres to Halakhah but sees it as far more flexible than do the Orthodox, and Reform gives Halakhah and Jewish tradition a vote but not a veto on how Jewish life ought to be practised in the modern world.

This neat, and admittedly oversimplified distinction, is not necessarily applicable any more as these once large denominational movements begin to break up into smaller groupings with particular flavours and ideologies. Two such examples are the UTJ (Union of Traditional Judaism) and Chovevei Torah.

In the mid-1980s UTJ broke away from the Conservative movement in the United States over, amongst other things, that movement's decision to ordain women rabbis. The Conservative movement itself is more liberal than Orthodoxy in its interpretation of Jewish law. However, the decision to ordain women rabbis was a step too far to the left for some in this movement. To its founders, UTJ recaptures the spirit of the true Conservative movement of the 1950s with a much greater emphasis on Halakhah. By the same token, UTJ does not sit easily within mainstream Orthodoxy, and it does not pretend to.

An almost mirror image of the Conservative–UTJ split occurred in Orthodoxy. For at least a decade, though perhaps longer, an element within the Orthodox community felt that Orthodoxy was becoming too extreme or 'too far to the right' in common parlance. They began to challenge this in various ways, most notably, by seeking to involve women to a greater extent in Orthodox ritual. A number of egalitarian Orthodox services (an oxymoron to those on the right) began to sprout up in Jerusalem and New York City in the mid-1990s. At about the same time, a new rabbinical seminary, called Chovevei Torah, was established in New York City to rival the more right-wing Orthodox Yeshiva University rabbinical seminary. Ironically, one of the differences between the right wing and the emerging left wing of Orthodoxy is over the appointment of women rabbis. For halachic and political reasons no one in the Orthodox world is so far suggesting the ordination of women *rabbis*. But the left wing has already begun to appoint female educational and spiritual *leaders* to some of its otherwise Orthodox congregations.

An interesting point to which there is no adequate answer to date is what is the difference between UTJ to the right of the Conservative movement and Chovivei Torah to the left of the Orthodox movement? Do they overlap? Where are the ideological lines drawn? Is it possible that UTJ, with its refusal to ordain women, is more Orthodox than Chovivei, with its desire to promote female spiritual leaders?

The answer to this question is for our purposes not so important. What is important is to appreciate the sense of rupture and fluidity within established movements. At the moment, in the early twenty-first century, this is still work in progress and it is by no means clear what the end result will look like in, say, a quarter of a century from now.

Another fascinating phenomenon linked to the distinctions of movements is what has become known as the post-denominational Jew. Reflecting the consumer-oriented society in which they live, many young Jews are not satisfied with buying all their religious goods from one supplier. No one religious denomination offers all its adherents exactly what they want all the time. In the past this was not a problem. You simply put up with the less attractive aspects of your chosen denomination, be they social, spiritual or ideological, because on the whole you were comfortable there. Today this is no longer the case. In the marketplace consumer loyalty is fickle to non-existent. Everything is about choice, and customers will flit around in search of the best products at best value. The post-denominational Jew does just this in a religious or ideological sense. There are young Jews who wish to retain their Orthodox practice yet, for various reasons, often ideological, feel more comfortable in a non-Orthodox synagogue. Similarly, there are Reform Jews who are attracted to the fire and passion of Hasidism, yet they are not prepared to adopt an Orthodox lifestyle. Each of these post-denominational Jews will pick and choose a Judaism that suits them perfectly without any concern as to where these disparate elements originate.

The post-denominational Jew is both advantageous and threatening to the future of the Jewish community. The advantages are passion and commitment, something that is in short supply today. The post-denominational Jew thinks about his Judaism. He does not just take it for granted. He is a highly discerning consumer and it is exactly this type of serious and committed Jew that the Jewish community could use more of.

On the other hand, the post-denominational Jew poses a threat, at least from an organizational point of view. Because choice is paramount he flits between various congregations and denominations without particular loyalty to any of them. Post-denominational Jews will often prefer not to belong to a synagogue, choosing instead to pray in small groups of similar-minded Jews in private homes. The potential loss to the organized denominations is not just financial but also in terms of human capital. These organizations depend on young talent for their future; and if they cannot attract the young, talented and committed, their future is uncertain.

A related feature of this post-denominalization is the lack of authority in Judaism today. Community leaders, particularly rabbis, used to have considerable authority over their communities. Today this is no longer the case. Most young Jews today relish their personal autonomy at the price of religious authority. The exception to this is the Ultra Orthodox community, which, on the whole, invests greatly in rabbinical authority, often at the expense of personal autonomy.

One of the most exciting areas of development in Judaism today is Jewish learning. There are more yeshivot and institutions of higher Jewish learning today than in pre-war Europe and possibly in Jewish history. There has also been a huge surge in informal Jewish learning, provided by various institutes and synagogues. Much of this informal learning is text based. In the past, such learning, also known as adult education, involved to a large extent the student listening to a lecture by an expert on a Jewish topic. While this format still takes place today, many of the emerging informal Jewish educators are involving their students in textual reading and analysis. The idea behind this shift is the awareness that despite the lack of formal Jewish education many of those attending informal Jewish learning are highly educated and fairly intelligent. By asking them to join in the reading and analysis of a text they are empowered to make it their own. This has very positive ramifications for the development of Jewish learning and the spread of knowledge, although it should be stated that some more traditional educators look askance at novices imposing their own interpretations on an ancient Torah text.

Technology has also revolutionized Jewish learning. Where it was once necessary to sift through dozens of books to find an elusive source, today this can be accessed on a number of computer discs. The most outstanding example is the one produced by Bar Ilan University, which has most of Jewish legal literature on a single disc. This not only saves space in the home but enables one to locate the most obscure of Jewish sources.

The Internet is perhaps the greatest tool of empowerment in relation to Jewish learning. Vast quantities of Jewish information can now be located on the Internet. Where it was once necessary for one to possess a basic Jewish education and research skills to write a *dvar Torah* (a short speech on a Torah theme often delivered at the Shabbat table or at other occasions), today they can just be lifted off the Internet. There is nothing that one cannot access, whether Jewish law, traditions, theology or even mysticism. While this empowers the individual it also weakens the need for one to consult a rabbi or scholar. In the long run this cannot be a positive thing, since so much Jewish learning depends on the bond between master and disciple. The Internet has its great faults, which are obvious but worth stating. Not every Jewish site puts out accurate or authentic information. While they may be a good supplement, one cannot substitute websites for serious Torah study.

The Internet has also revolutionized another aspect of Jewish life – dating. For busy young professionals, finding a suitable partner has become increasingly difficult, and finding a partner of one's own faith has become even more difficult. For many, the Internet is the answer. Various Jewish dating websites have developed over the years, bringing people together, often from different parts of the world. Until recently, finding a partner on the web was deemed pathetic, if not sleazy. Today that is most certainly not the case. Dozens of young happily married couples I know have found each other on Jewish dating websites.

Intermarriage is one of the most serious problems for the Jewish community. The rate of intermarriage in the United States stands at over 50 per cent while in the rest of the world it does not lag much behind. With a total world population of some thirteen million, the Jewish people can ill afford to lose half their children to intermarriage. However, attitudes towards intermarriage have changed over the years. Fifty years ago it was not unheard of for families to sit in mourning for the out-married child whom, for all intents and purposes, they considered dead. Even in the past decade I have personally witnessed a sea change in attitudes towards intermarriage. When I first took up my position as rabbi in 1996 intermarriage was taboo. A family whose son or daughter married out was very reticent to talk about it. While most parents today would prefer their child to marry in, they are no longer as ashamed as they once were if the child chooses to marry out. I believe this is largely due to the sheer numbers of intermarriages. There is hardly a family that does not have a relative, however distant, who has not married out. Another reason may be that whereas in the past intermarriage was usually to a Christian, today most young urban people have no religious affiliation. The idea of one's child choosing a partner from no faith is slightly more comforting than the idea of them choosing a partner from another faith.

How the Jewish community eventually deals with the

intermarriage issue will have a huge impact on the future of the Jewish people. Some Reform rabbis insist that it is better to gain an adherent than to lose one. They are very helpful and encourage the non-Jewish partner to convert to Judaism. Orthodox rabbis are far more reticent because their standards of conversion are higher. It may also be because the majority of the very Orthodox are for the most part insulated from this problem altogether.

Two of the big issues confronting Judaism today, and which will continue to do so for some time to come, is Israel and Islamist anti-Semitism.

The State of Israel, as mentioned above, has been in existence now for some sixty years. Yet despite numerous wars and peace initiatives, peace with all its neighbours remains little more than a dream. Moreover, Israeli society itself seems to be rupturing. On the one hand are the religious nationalists who believe that it is their sacred duty to hang on to every last shred of biblical Israel. Yet, on the other, are self-loathing Israeli academics who are ashamed of their country's history in taking land from the Palestinians and who have contributed to a growing genre of revisionist history. In between are many more fissures and cracks, secular vs. religious, Ashkenazi vs. Sefardi, and others, too numerous to mention. Diaspora Jews are, on the whole, supportive of Israel, although not all support a particular government's policies, and they can be quite critical.

Islamic anti-Semitism took many by surprise. Who would have thought that just decades after *nostra atate* and the laying to rest of close to 1,500 years of Christian anti-Semitism that a new threat would arise from modern Islam. Much of the anti-Israeli rhetoric is simply a smokescreen for what is really virulent anti-Semitism, which has taken root in, of all places, Europe, particularly in France and the United Kingdom. Despite ongoing efforts at dialogue with the Muslim community, it appears that the moderates are silenced or outmanoeuvred by the radicals, and the situation at present is far from positive.

I am a historian; I analyse and interpret the past. Predicting the future is a different story. Yet I will go out on a limb and make the following prediction: the Jewish people will still be around at the end of this century. We are a remarkably resilient people who have outlived numerous predictions of our demise. Yet what the Jewish people will look like in a hundred years' time is difficult to tell. My guess is that we will be numerically smaller than we are now. Intermarriage will continue and those at the outer periphery of Jewish commitment will for the most part fade out of Jewish life, while those who remain will be more committed and knowledgeable than their parents and grandparents.

At the moment it is difficult to see how, but Islamic anti-Semitism may pass. Yet even if it does, it is almost certain that another form of anti-Semitism will take its place. I am not being alarmist, just realistic. Anti-Semitism has existed as long as the Jewish people. It never really disappears, it simply mutates and re-emerges under new guises. It is unfortunate, but is something that we, as a people, have long ago learned to live with.

Israel's neighbours will eventually make peace with her. I do not think this is an unrealistic fantasy but a very real probability. It is just a question of how long it takes for Israel's enemies to realize that the Jewish people are there to stay and that the sooner peace is achieved the better off everyone will be. This sounds like such a simple formula, but it is often the simplest ideas that people have the most difficulty accepting.

Judaism will never become a dominant religion in terms of numbers, but it may very well begin to dominate the great debates in society over religio-ethical issues such as climate change, ethics in the global marketplace and human rights. For this to happen, Judaism needs courageous and articulate spokesmen who are able to look outwards and bring its rich tradition to bear on some of the world's great problems. Never before has there been such an opportunity to influence and communicate as widely as there is today. Jewish scholars and leaders must rise to this challenge by telling the world who we are and what we believe. Most importantly, it is our duty to demonstrate, through our own behaviour, how it is possible for man to create out of this lowly world a dwelling place for God.

GLOSSARY

Akeda
The biblical account in Genesis chapter 22 describing the binding of Isaac, in which Abraham's faith is tested by God, when he is asked to offer up his son Isaac as a sacrifice. God intervenes at the last moment sparing Isaac's life.

Ark of the Covenant
The chest containing the tablets of stone on which were inscribed the Ten Commandments.

Ashkenazi
Ashkenaz is the Hebrew word for Germany. The term Ashkenazi refers to Jews of European descent as opposed to the Sefardim of Spanish/North African descent.

Balfour Declaration
The Declaration authored by the British Foreign Secretary Arthur J. Balfour in 1917 stating that His Majesty's Government accepted in principle that Palestine should be reconstituted as the National Home of the Jewish People.

Bar Mitzvah
Literally 'the son of mitzvah', a term describing the coming of age for a Jewish male at thirteen when he becomes responsible for observing the Torah and for his actions.

Bat Mitzvah
Literally 'the daughter of mitzvah', describing the coming of age for a Jewish female at twelve when she becomes responsible for observing the Torah and for her actions.

BatSheva
One of King David's wives and the mother of his son and successor; King Solomon.

Chazzan
The cantor or prayer leader

Court of Priests, Women's Court, Men's Court
Different sections in the ancient Jewish Temple separating priests, men and women.

Diaspora
The Jewish presence in the lands to which they have been dispersed. A term used to describe the Jewish communities outside the Land of Israel.

Drash
The homiletical interpretation of the Torah

Gaon, Gaonim
A term derived from the Hebrew word for glory. It became an honorific title for the leading Babylonian rabbis during the period between the mid-seventh and eleventh centuries.

Gentile
A non-Jew

Halachic, Halachist
Halakhah is the term for Jewish law. A Halachist is an expert in Jewish law.

Hasid, Hasidic, Hasidut
Hasid, which literally means a 'pious one', is a term that describes a follower of the Jewish revivalist eighteenth-century movement which still flourishes today. Hasidut is the literature of the movement.

The Holocaust
Destruction by fire; a term used to describe the Nazi destruction of Europe's Jews

Holy of Holies
The innermost chamber of the ancient Jewish Temple in which stood the Ark of the Covenant

Hukkim
Statutes or laws of the Torah that transcend human understanding

Kabbalah
The esoteric or mystical dimension of the Torah

Kedoshim
Literally the sanctified ones; a term used to describe Jewish Martyrs

Kiddush Hashem
Sanctification of (the Divine) Name, describing any act that brings glory to God. A term used frequently in connection with martyrdom for the sake of the Jewish faith.

Kiddushin
The Jewish marriage ritual

Kippah
The skullcap worn by religious Jewish boys and men

Kosher
A term used to describe food that is permissible for Jewish consumption

Majdanek
A Nazi concentration camp on the outskirts of the Eastern Polish city Lublin

Maskilim
Followers of the Jewish Enlightenment movement with roots in eighteenth-century Germany

Marranos
Spanish for 'swine', a derogatory term used by the Spanish Inquisition to describe crypto-Jews who publicly converted to Catholicism but who secretly adhered to the Jewish faith.

Megilah
The Book of Esther; one of the books of the Bible

Menorah
The seven-branched candelabrum lit by the priests in the ancient Jewish Temple. Depending on the context it can also refer to the eight-branched candelabra that Jews kindle in their homes during the festival of Hanukkah.

Mezuzah
The scroll containing biblical passages that Jews affix to their doorposts

Mishnah
The earliest compendium of Jewish law completed in the second century.

Mishpatim
Jewish laws that can be supported by human logic

Mitnagdim
Opponents of Hasidim

Mitzvah, Mitzvot
A ritual obligation. Mitzvah is singular, mitzvot is plural.

Modern Orthodox
A term used to describe Orthodox Jews who while adhering to the strict interpretation of Jewish law are also open to secular culture. They are commonly contrasted with the Ultra Orthodox Jews.

Mussar
The nineteenth-century Jewish religious-ethical movement that strove to place ethics at the core of Jewish religious practice.

Oral Torah
All aspects of the Torah excluding the Bible

Passover Matzah
Unleavened wafer-like bread that Jews eat on the Passover festival, in commemoration of the Exodus

Pilpul
A pepper. A term used to describe a particularly sharp and complex form of Talmudic analysis developed in fifteenth-century Poland.

Promised Land
The Biblical land of Israel promised to the descendants of Abraham

Peshat
The literal meaning or contextual sense of any particular Torah passage

Rabbi
A Jewish spiritual leader

Rebbe
A Hasidic master

Remez
Allusions to ideas not explicitly expressed in the plain text of a Torah passage

Roshei Teivot
Acronyms made up of the first Hebrew letters of various words

Shema
One of the most central Jewish prayers in which one acknowledges the oneness of God

Sod
The esoteric dimension of the Torah

Shabbat
The Sabbath

Siddur
The Jewish prayer-book

Talmud
A vast body of Jewish legal and ethical literature based on the Mishnah and completed around the fifth century

Tanya
An early nineteenth-century Hasidic work

Tefillin
Black leather boxes that Jewish men and boys over the age of thirteen affix to their heads and arms each morning during prayer. The boxes contain parchment scrolls on which are inscribed biblical verses.

Temple
The house of Jewish worship, that stood on Mount Moriah in Jerusalem, representing God's dwelling place on earth.

Tzadik
A righteous man. A term that is often used to describe a Hasidic master or great mystic

Ultra Orthodox
Jews who observe the strictest interpretation of Jewish law and who eschew secular culture.

Written Torah
The Bible

Yeshiva
A religious school dedicated to Torah study. Yeshiva is singular, yeshivot is plural.

Yishuvim
The early settlements in the Land of Israel, many dating back to the eighteenth century

Zohar
The Book of Splendour; the seminal text of Jewish mysticism.

FURTHER READING

Torah and Jewish thought

Amsel, Nachum, *The Jewish Encyclopaedia of Moral and Ethical Issues* (Northvale, NJ: Jason Aronson, 1994).

Bleich, J. David, *With Perfect Faith: The Foundations of Jewish Belief* (Jersey City: Ktav Publishing, 1983).

Elon, Menachem, *Jewish Law: History, Sources, Principles*, 4 vols (Philadelphia: Jewish Publication Society, 1994).

Finkel, Avraham Yaakov, *The Great Torah Commentators* (Northvale, NJ: Jason Aronson, 1996).

Frank, Daniel H. (ed.), *History of Jewish Philosophy* (London: Routledge, 1997).

Hertz, J. H. (ed.), *The Pentateuch and Haftarahs* (London: Soncino Press, 1970).

Kaplan, Aryeh, *Hasidic Masters: History, Biography and Thought* (New York: Moznaim, 1989).

Lamm, Norman, *The Religious Thought of Hasidism: Text and Commentary* (New York: Yeshiva University Press, 1999).

Neusner, Jacob, *Invitation to Midrash: A Teaching Book* (New York: Harper & Row 1989).

Nosson, Scherman, *The Chumash*, Stone edn, ArtScroll series (New York: Mesorah Publications, 1993).

Peters, Simi, *Learning to Read Midrash* (Jerusalem: Urim Publications, 2004).

Rosner, Fred, *The Existence and Unity of God: Three Treatises Attributed to Moses Maimonides* (Northvale, NJ: Jason Aronson, 1990).

Scholem, Gershom, *Major Trends in Jewish Mysticism* (New York: Schocken Books, 1996).

— —, *Kabbalah* (Harmonsworth: Penguin, 1997).

Steinsaltz, Adin, *The Essential Talmud* (New York: Basic Books, 1976).

— —: *Biblical Images: Men and Women of the Book* (New York, Basic Books, 1984).

— —, *The Long Shorter Way: Discourses on Hasidic Thought* (Northvale, NJ: Jason Aronson: 1988).

— —, *The Sustaining Utterance: Discourses on Hasidic Thought* (Northvale, NJ: Jason Aronson, 1989).

— —, *The Talmud: A Reference Guide* (New York: Random House, 1989).

— —, *The Thirteen Petalled Rose* (Northvale, NJ: Jason Aronson, 1992).

TANAKH: A New Translation of The Holy Scriptures (Philadelphia: Jewish Publication Society, 1985).

To Touch the Divine: A Jewish Mysticism Primer (New York: Kehot Publication, 1989).

Twersky, Isadore, *A Maimonides Reader* (Springfield, NJ: Behrman Publishing, 1976).

Jewish history

Ben-Sasson, H. H., *A History of the Jewish People* (Cambridge, MA: Harvard University Press, 1976).

Cahill, Thomas, *The Gifts of the Jews: How a tribe of Desert Nomads Changed the Way Everyone Thinks and Feels* (New York: Anchor Books, 1999).

Cohn-Sherbok, Dan, *Atlas of Jewish History* (London: Routledge, 1996).

Gilbert, Martin, *The Holocaust* (London: HarperCollins, 1989).

— —, *Israel: A History* (London: Black Swan, 1999).

Johnson, Paul, *A History of the Jews* (New York: Harper Perennial, 1988).

Kantor, Mattis, *The Jewish Timeline Encyclopaedia* (Northvale, NJ: Jason Aronson, 1992).

Mendes-Flohr, Paul R. and Judah Reinharz (eds), *The Jew in the Modern World: A Documentary History* (New York: Oxford University Press, 1980).

Roth, Cecil, *A History of the Jews* (New York: Schocken Books, 1970).

Sachar, Howard M., *Diaspora: An Inquiry into the Contemporary Jewish World* (New York: Harper & Row, 1985).

Jewish practice

Agnon, S. Y., *The Days of Awe* (New York: Schocken Books, 1965).

Chavel, Charles B., *Maimonides: The Commandments*, 2 vols (London: Soncino Press, 1967).

Chill, Abraham, *The Mitzvot: The Commandments and their Rationale* (Jerusalem: Keter Books, 1974).

Donin, Hayyim Halevy, *To Pray as a Jew* (New York: Basic Books, 1980).

— —, *To Be a Jew: A Guide to Jewish Observance in Contemporary Life* (New York: Basic Books, 2001).

Greenberg, Blue, *How to Run a Traditional Jewish Household* (Northvale, NJ: Jason Aronson, 1989).

Kitov, A. E., *The Jew and his Home* (New York: Shengold, 1963).

Lau, Israel Meir, *Practical Judaism* (Jerusalem: Feldheim, 1997).

Steinsaltz, Adin, *Teshuvah: A Guide for the Newly Observant Jew* (London: Collier Macmillan Publishers, 1987).

Tales

Wiesel, Elie, *Souls on Fire: Portraits and Legends of Hasidic Masters* (London: Pocket Books, 1986).

— —, *Wise Men and their Tales: Portraits of Biblical, Talmudic and Hasidic Masters* (New York: Schocken Books, 2005).

Zevin, Shlomo Yosef, *A Treasury of Chassidic Tales*, Artscroll series (New York: Mesorah Publications, 1986).

Reference

Abramson, Glenda, (ed.), *The Blackwell Companion to Jewish Culture* (Oxford: Basil Blackwell, 1989).

Olitzky, Kerry M. and Ronald H. Isaacs, *A Glossary of Jewish Life* (Northvale, NJ: Jason Aronson, 1992).

Skolnik, Fred and Michael Berenbaum, *Encyclopaedia Judaica*, 2nd edn, 22 vols (New York and London: Thomson and Gale and Macmillan, 2006).

Solomon, Norman, *The Historical Dictionary of Judaism* (Lanham, MD: Scarecrow Press, 1998).

Telushkin, Joseph, *Jewish Wisdom: Ethical, Spiritual and Historical Lessons from the Great Works and Thinkers* (New York: William Morrow, 1994).

— —, *The Book of Jewish Values* (New York: Random House, 1999).

— —, *Jewish Literacy: The Most Important Things to Know about the Jewish Religion, its People and its History* (New York: HarperCollins, 2000).

Miscellaneous

Guggenheimer, Heinrich W. and Eva H. Guggenheimer, *Jewish Family Names and their Origins: An Etymological Dictionary* (Jersey City: Ktav Publishing, 1992).

Roden, Claudia, *The Book of Jewish Food: An Odyssey from Samarkand and Vilna to the Present Day* (London: Viking, 1997).

Telushkin, Joseph, *Jewish Humour* (New York: HarperCollins, 1998).

INDEX